institute of financial services

AF770547

Retailing of Financial Services

Christine Rose
Marketing and Promotions Manager,
Halifax Financial Services

Charley Watkins
Product Development Manager,
Norwich Union Direct

Apart from any fair dealing for the purpose of research or private study, or criticism or review, as permitted under the Copyright, Designs and Patents Act 1988, this publication may only be reproduced, stored or transmitted, in any form or by any means, with the prior permission in writing of the publisher, or in the case of reprographic reproduction in accordance with the terms and licenses issued by the Copyright Licensing Agency. Enquiries concerning reproduction outside those terms should be addressed to the publishers at the undermentioned address:

The Institute of Financial Services
C/o The Chartered Institute of Bankers
Emmanuel House
4-9 Burgate Lane
Canterbury
Kent
CT1 2XJ
United Kingdom

Institute of Financial Services Publications are published by The Chartered Institute of Bankers, a non-profit-making registered educational charity and are distributed exclusively by Bankers Books Limited which is a wholly owned subsidiary of The Chartered Institute of Bankers.

The Chartered Institute of Bankers believes that the sources of information upon which the book is based are reliable and has made every effort to ensure the complete accuracy of the text. However, neither CIB, the author nor any contributor can accept any legal responsibility whatsoever for consequences that may arise from any errors or omissions or any opinion or advice given.

Editorial and production services: Genesys Editorial Limited
Typesetting: Leech Design, Preston

Copyright © The Chartered Institute of Bankers 1997
ISBN 0-85297-426-4

Contents

		Page
The concept of the course		1
Study Guide		3
References		6
Unit 1	Background	7
Unit 2	The financial environment	12
Unit 3	The competitive environment for branches	29
Unit 4	Consumer buying behaviour and segmentation pricing	52
Unit 5	Marketing planning for branches I	65
Unit 6	Marketing planning for branches II	102
Unit 7	Distribution: branch location	112
Unit 8	Distribution: other channels	126
Unit 9	Product management	145
Unit 10	Pricing	170
Unit 11	The promotion	180
Unit 12	Service quality	195
Unit 13	Sales management	211
Unit 14	The changing environment	230
Index		248

Retailing of Financial Services

The Concept of the Course

This is a practical course written for students studying for banking and finance qualifications and also for practitioners in the financial services industry who are looking for a practical refresher. This study text is structured so that many will find it to be the most coherent way of learning the subject.

This book is the set text for the Retailing of Financial Services option of the ACIB-Degree link.

Each chapter or unit of the Study Text is divided into sections and contains

- learning objectives
- an introduction, indicating how this subject area relates to others to which the reader may have cause to refer
- clear, concise topic-by-topic coverage
- examples and exercises to reinforce learning, confirm understanding and stimulate thought.

Activities

Activities are provided throughout to enable you to check your progress as you work through the text. These come in a variety of forms; some test your ability to analyse material you have read, others see whether you have taken in the full significance of a piece of information. Some are meant to be discussed with colleagues, friends or fellow students.

Each of the main units consists of study notes designed to focus attention upon the key aspects of the subject matter. These notes are divided into convenient sections for study purposes.

At the end of each unit there are self-assessment questions. These comprise a number of short answer questions which you should be able to answer if you have studied the text carefully. If you cannot answer any of them, this will indicate that you need to review that unit. Students should remain aware of the fact that the examination itself will comprise questions drawn from across the whole Chartered Institute of Bankers syllabus; the key sections of which for this subject are as follows.

- Definition of Retailing.
- Marketing Planning for Retail Outlets.
- The Financial Environment.
- The Competitive Environment for Retail Distribution Channels.
- Consumer Buying Behaviour and Segmentation.
- Distribution: Outlet Location, Retail Outlet Environment and Other Channels.
- Product Management.

- Promotion.
- Pricing.
- Sales Management.
- Service Quality.

Although the workbook is designed to stand alone, as with most topics, certain aspects of this subject are constantly changing. Therefore it is of great importance that students should keep up-to-date with these key areas.

It is anticipated that the student will study this course for one academic year, reading through and studying approximately two units every three weeks. However, it should be noted that as topics vary in size and as knowledge tends not to fall into uniform chunks, some units in this workbook are unavoidably longer than others.

The masculine pronoun 'he' has been used in this Workbook to encompass both genders and to avoid the awkwardness of the constant repetition of 'he and/or she'.

Study Guide

In the next few pages, we offer some advice and ideas on studying, revising and approaching examinations.

Studying

As with any examination, there is no substitute for preparation based on an organised and disciplined study plan. You should devise an approach which will enable you to get right through this Study Text and still leave time for revision of this and any other subject you are taking at the same time. Many candidates find that about six weeks is the right period of time to leave for revision, enough time to get through the revision material, but not so long that it is no longer fresh in your mind by the time you reach the examination.

This means that you should plan how to get to the last chapter by, say, the end of March for a May sitting or the end of August for an October sitting. This includes not only reading the text, but making notes and attempting the bulk of the illustrative questions in the back of the text.

We offer the following as a starting point for approaching your study.

- Plan time each week to study a part of this Study Text. Make sure that it is 'quality' study time: let everyone know that you are studying and that you should not be disturbed. If you are at home, unplug your telephone or switch the answerphone on; if you are in the office, put your telephone on 'divert'.
- Set a clearly defined objective for each study period. You may simply wish to read through a chapter for the first time or perhaps you want to make some notes on a chapter you have already read a couple of times. Don't forget the illustrative questions.
- Review your study plan. Use the study checklist a couple of pages on to see how well you are keeping up. Don't panic if you fall behind, but do think how you will make up for lost time.
- Look for examples of what you have covered in the 'real' world. If you work for a financial organisation, this should be a good starting point. If you do not, then think about your experiences as an individual bank or building society customer or perhaps about your employer's position as a corporate customer of a bank. Keep an eye on the quality press for reports about banks and building societies and their activities.

Revising

- The period which you have earmarked for revision is a very important time. Now it is even more important that you plan time each week for study and that you set clear objectives for each revision session.
- Use time sensibly. How much revision time do you have? Remember that you still need to eat, sleep and fit in some leisure time.
- How will you split the available time between subjects? What are your weaker subjects? You will need to focus on some topics in more detail than others. You will also need to plan your revision around your learning style. By now, you

should know whether, for example, early morning, early evening or late evening is best.

- Take regular breaks. Most people find they can absorb more this way than if they attempt to revise for long uninterrupted periods of time. Award yourself a five minute break every hour. Go for a stroll or make a cup of coffee, but do not turn the television on.
- Believe in yourself. Are you cultivating the right attitude of mind? There is absolutely no reason why you should not pass this exam if you adopt the correct approach. Be confident, you have passed exams before so you can pass this one.

The day of the exam

- Passing professional examinations is half about having the knowledge, and half about doing yourself full justice in the examination. You must have the right technique.
- Set at least one alarm (or get an alarm call) for a morning exam.
- Have something to eat but beware of eating too much; you may feel sleepy if your system is digesting a large meal.
- Don't forget pens, pencils, rulers, erasers and anything else you will need.
- Avoid discussion about the exam with other candidates outside the exam hall.

Tackling the examination paper

First, make sure that you satisfy the examiner's requirements.

Read the instructions on the front of the exam paper carefully. Check that the exam format hasn't changed. It is surprising how often examiners' reports remark on the number of students who attempt too few – or too many – questions, or who attempt the wrong number of questions from different parts of the paper. Make sure that you are planning to answer the right number of questions.

Read all the questions on the exam paper before you start writing. Look at the weighting of marks to each part of the question. If part (a) offers only 4 marks and you can't answer the 12 marks part (b), then don't choose the question.

Don't produce irrelevant answers. Make sure you answer the question set, and not the question you would have preferred to have been set.

Produce an answer in the correct format. The examiner will state in the requirements the format in which the question should be answered, for example in a report or memorandum. If a question asks for a diagram or an example, give one. If a question does not specifically ask for a diagram or example, but it seems appropriate, give one.

Second, observe these simple rules to ensure that your script is pleasing to the examiner.

Present a tidy paper. You are a professional and it should always show in the presentation of your work. Candidates are penalised for poor presentation and so you should make sure that you write legibly, label diagrams clearly and lay out your work professionally. Markers of scripts each have dozens of papers to mark; a badly written scrawl is unlikely to receive the same attention as a neat and well laid out paper.

State the obvious. Many candidates look for complexity which is not required and consequently overlook the obvious. Make basic statements first. Plan your answer and ask yourself whether you have answered the main parts of the question.

Use examples. This will help to demonstrate to the examiner that you keep up-to-date with the subject. There are lots of useful examples scattered through this study text and you can read about others if you dip into the quality press or take notice of what is happening in your working environment.

Finally, make sure that you give yourself the opportunity to do yourself justice.

Select questions carefully. Read through the paper once, then quickly jot down any key points against each question in a second read through. Reject those questions against which you have jotted down very little. Select those where you can latch on to 'what the question is about' – but remember to check carefully that you have got the right end of the stick before putting pen to paper.

Plan your attack carefully. Consider the order in which you are going to tackle questions. It is a good idea to start with your best question to boost your morale and get some easy marks 'in the bag'.

Read the question carefully and plan your answer. Read through the question again very carefully when you come to answer it.

Gain the easy marks. Include the obvious if it answers the question and do not spend unnecessary time producing the perfect answer. As suggested above, there is nothing wrong with stating the obvious.

Avoid getting bogged down in small parts of questions. If you find a part of a question difficult, get on with the rest of the question. If you are having problems with something the chances are that everyone else is too.

Don't leave the exam early. Use your spare time checking and rechecking your script.

Don't worry if you feel you have performed badly in the exam. It is more likely that the other candidates will have found the exam difficult too. Don't forget that there is a competitive element in exams. As soon as you get up and leave the exam hall, forget the exam and think about the next – or , if it is the last one, celebrate!

Don't discuss an exam with other candidates. This is particularly the case if you still have other exams to sit. Put it out of your mind until the day of the results. Forget about the exam and relax.

References

The following publications are referred to in the text.

Ansoff, HI 1975, *Corporate Strategy*, Pelican Books

Betts and York 1994, See *Practitioners Guide to Direct Marketing*, Institute of Direct Marketing

Boston Consulting Group 1990, 'The Product Portfolio', *Perspectives*, August issue

Bowen and Schneider 1988, 'Services marketing and management' *Research in Organisational Behaviour* Vol 10

Christopher, Payne and Ballantyne 1991, *Relationship Marketing*, Butterworth Heinemann

Foxhall 1991, 'Consumer behaviour' *The Marketing Book* 2nd ed. Butterworth Heinemann

Frank Massy and Wind 1972, *Market Segmentation*, Prentice Hall

Gronroos 1981, 'Internal marketing – an integral part of marketing theory' *The Marketing of Services* ANA Proceedings, Chicago

Gronroos 1990, 'The marketing and organisational behaviour interface' *Journal of Business Research*

Kotler, P 1993, *Marketing Management: Analysis, Planning, Implementation and Control*, Prentice Hall

Lavidge RJ and Steiner GA 1961, 'A model for predictive measurement of advertising effectiveness' *Journal of Marketing*

Levitt, T 1960, 'Marketing myopia' *Harvard Business Review* July/August issue

Lewis 1982, 'Marketing Bank Services' *Services Industry Journal*

Lewis and Entwistle 1990, 'Managing the service encounter' *International Journal of Services Industry Management*

Lovelock 1981, 'Why marketing management needs to be different for services' *The Marketing of Services* ANA Proceedings, Chicago

McDonald and Payne (1996), *Marketing Planning for Services*

McKechnie 1992, 'Consumer buyer behaviour in financial services', *International Journal of Bank Marketing* vol. 10

Morgan 1994, *Managing and Marketing Services in the 1990s*, Cassell

Porter, Michael, *Competitive Advantage*

Robinson and Faris 1967, *Industrial Buying Creative Marketing*, Allyn & Bacon, Boston

Shostack 1977, 'Breaking free from product marketing' *Journal of Marketing*

Smith 1990, 'Quality aspects of service marketing' *Marketing Intelligence and Planning*, Vol 8

Teas, Dorsch and McAlexander 1988, 'Measuring commercial bank customers' attitudes towards equality of the financial services marketing relationship' *Journal of professional services marketing*

Thwaites and Lee 1994, See *Practitioners Guide to Direct Marketing*, Institute of Direct Marketing

Tuck, M 1976, *How do we choose?* Methuen

Turnbull 1982, 'The role of the branch manager in the marketing of bank services' *European Journal of Marketing*

Turnbull and Gibbs 1987, 'Marketing bank services to corporate customers – the importance of relationships' *The International Journal of Bank Marketing*

Webster, FE and Wind, Y 1972, *Organisational Buying Behaviour*, Prentice Hall

Yorke 1990, 'Interactive perceptions of suppliers and corporate clients in the marketing of services' *Journal of Marketing Management*

Zeithaml 1981, 'How consumer evaluation processes differ between goods and services' *The Marketing of Services* ANA *Proceedings*, Chicago

Zeithaml, Parasuraman and Berry 1990, *Delivering Quality Service: Balancing Customer Perceptions and Expectations*

Zeithaml, Parasuraman and Berry 1991, 'SERVQUAL – a multiple item scale for measuring consumer perceptions of service quality' *Journal of Retailing*

Unit 1

Background

Objectives

After studying this unit you should be able to do the following.

- **Explain the meaning of the term 'retailing' within the financial services industry.**
- **Describe the main characteristics of the industry and how these characteristics affect the way in which its products and services are offered for sale.**
- **State the elements of the retailing mix and explain their importance.**

1 What are financial services?

1.1 Financial Services can be defined as 'activities connected with money that offer the customer financial related value.'

1.2 Traditionally financial services providers have included the following types of organisations

- banks
- building societies
- insurance companies
- unit trust companies
- investment trusts
- credit card issuers
- stock exchange
- National Savings.

1.3 However, in recent years there have been many new entrants into the market; these have included companies not previously associated with the provision of financial services, for example, Virgin, Marks & Spencer and Tesco.

2 The changing environment

2.1 The environment within which the financial service providers operate has been changing rapidly over recent years. Three key elements of this change are diversification, customers and technology. We will consider each of these in turn.

Diversification

2.2 In the past each institution had a different role to play in the provision of financial services to the public. More recently, in addition to the new entrants, individual organisations have increased the services they offer.

- Banks now offer mortgage business on similar terms to building societies.
- Banks and building societies act as agents for insurance companies or offer their own insurance products.
- Many building societies now offer services that were previously seen as banking products (for example, current accounts). Some building societies are converting to bank status in order to extend the services they are able to provide.

These changes are generating extremely fierce competition for business.

Customers

2.3 Financial services customers are becoming more financially aware and sophisticated in how they choose to do business. Many are willing to shop around for the best deal when they buy financial products. They demand much more in the way of service and value for money. The industry has also experienced an increase in the number of women taking responsibility for their own finances. Providers must now, therefore, consider women as a serious segment of the market.

Technology

2.4 The number of people willing to purchase financial services and products with the use of technology is increasing. The use of automated teller machines is now common practice, as is the purchase of home and car insurance over the telephone. Another growth area is the Internet: many institutions operate web sites, and with the Internet attracting an estimated half a million new users a month, its use must be a consideration for any marketer.

3 Retailing

What is retailing?

3.1 In terms of financial services, the term retailing is widely accepted as meaning 'small quantity sales', ie sales to individuals rather than to the corporate market.

3.2 The techniques of retail marketing primarily associated with the sale of fast moving consumer goods (FMCGs) are now widely adopted by the financial services providers. There are, however, many characteristics that distinguish the financial services market from other retail markets.

Characteristics of the financial services industry

3.3 The following characteristics shape the way in which the products and services of the financial services industry are sold to the public.

Intangibility

3.4 Most of the services offered by a bank, for example, are intangible; they cannot appeal to a customer on the basis of the way they look or feel. They cannot be demonstrated or displayed. The only way to sell them is to explain how the product can be of benefit to the customer. The intangibility of such products limits the methods that the provider can use for marketing them.

Regulation

3.5 As well as the normal rules regarding such things as advertising, the financial services industry is governed by numerous regulators, all of whom issue rules as to how products can be sold. In many cases regulation restricts the marketing choices available.

Customer knowledge and perception

3.6 The public often find it difficult to distinguish one financial product from another. For example, very few people understand which products fall into the category of general insurance and which are categorised as life and pension products. Similarly, many people are unclear about the different services offered by bank and building societies. Because of this, many organisations suffer from a lack of name awareness, or have name awareness for one aspect of the services they offer rather than their whole range of products.

Lack of individuality in product offerings

3.7 The rules and regulations governing this industry mean that providers have very limited scope to be able to offer a product or service that is highly innovative or widely different from those offered by their competitors. This means that they must find other ways of making their products more appealing than those of other providers. This can be done by concentrating on the levels of service offered, for example.

Seasonal variations in demand

3.8 Demand for financial services products can vary enormously with the time of year and the economic climate. For example, the demand for Personal Equity Plans and Pensions is greatest at the end of a tax year. Similarly, the demand for mortgages is usually greater in the spring but can vary enormously from year to year depending on such things as the interest rate and the level of 'feel good factor' at the time.

Low consumer interest

3.9 It is fair to say that in general, the public has very little interest in financial services products such as banking, pensions and life assurance. People tend to buy such products when they *need* them, rather than because they *want* them. This lack of interest is why it is often said that such products are 'sold rather than bought'.

Single purchases

3.10 In the FMCG market, where the customer purchases items on a regular (ie weekly or monthly) basis, there is a high level of repeat business. In contrast, financial products such as mortgages and current accounts are generally only bought once by a customer. This means that a company marketing these products needs to attract a new customer for each sale.

The retailing mix

3.11 The retailing or 'marketing mix' used by retailers of financial services can be expressed as the 5P's: price, place, product, people and promotion. We will look at each of these in turn.

Price

3.12 Traditionally consumers had little knowledge of the costs of financial services and therefore cost played only a small part in the decision to buy. However, as customers become more financially astute, this is no longer the case.

Product

3.13 Because of the nature of the industry, the products offered by providers are all very similar. Any increase in business volumes brought about by the launch of a new and innovative product tends to be short-lived, as in a short space of time competitors start to offer very similar products.

Promotion

3.14 In recent years, many financial services companies have undertaken a great deal of promotional activity in order to increase the public's awareness of the products they offer and therefore to increase their sales volumes. They are using the full range of 'above-the-line' opportunities, with television advertising becoming increasingly popular. The use of special offers to attract consumers is also increasing. However, because of the nature of the products, the use of sales people for promotion is still widespread across the industry.

Place

3.15 As in many other sectors, the successful retailing of financial services requires outlets in carefully considered locations. This is particularly true for banks and building societies, where the customer desires regular contact and therefore demands accessibility. With advances in the use of technology, customers are now also looking for the ability to purchase financial services over the telephone and via the Internet.

People

3.16 As previously discussed, product differentiation is increasingly difficult to sustain. Companies therefore need to find other unique selling propositions (USPs). One of these can be people. The way in which the customer is treated by a member of staff, and the level of service provided by the staff of a company, are becoming increasingly important in a highly competitive environment.

Student Activity

1 State three characteristics of the financial services industry and explain the effects they may have on the way in which the products are sold.

2 List the five elements of the retailing mix and bricfly explain the role they play in the retailing of financial services.

Summary

Now that you have completed this unit, you should be able to do the following.

- ❑ **Explain the meaning of the term 'retailing' within the financial services industry.**
- ❑ **Describe the main characteristics of the industry and how these characteristics affect the way in which its products and services are offered for sale.**
- ❑ **State the elements of the retailing mix and explain their importance.**

Unit 2

The financial environment

Objectives

After studying this unit you should be able to do the following.

- **Explain how an individual's income influences their need for financial services products.**
- **Describe socio-economic, political and demographic trends and explain how such trends influence the retailing of financial services products.**
- **Explain the role played by compliance and regulation.**
- **Describe the use of information technology in retailing.**
- **Describe how internationalisation is affecting the sale of financial products.**
- **Explain how the market is structured, and describe how current trends affect both this structure and the market size.**

1 Introduction

1.1 The structure of the UK financial services sector has undergone great change during the past twenty years. Deregulation, advancing technology and a trend towards globalisation have increased the competitive pressure on organisations. This pressure has affected both the structures and the ways in which these organisations operate.

1.2 Building societies, for example, first merged to increase their size and position in the market place, and are now converting to bank status to enable them to compete in a wider range of activities.

1.3 It is now widely believed that the world of finance is 'over banked'. That is to say, there are too many organisations serving a relatively stable number of customers.

1.4 Macro environmental forces have a wide influence on organisations. This unit examines some of these forces — forces that can have an impact on the organisation but which fall outside its control.

2 Personal income and wealth

2.1 The general level of personal income has a great influence on the demand for the products and services that are offered by financial services. The earnings of an individual or, in the case of a family, the level of household income, dictates the amount they have available to spend on both necessities and luxury items.

2.2 People satisfy their basic needs first — their needs for shelter, food, clothing, etc. Individuals with low incomes have very little left once this has been done; they find it difficult to purchase financial services. People with higher income levels have a greater capacity to dedicate money to financial services products.

2.3 The amount of *disposable* income people have, that is the income that is left after they have satisfied commitments such as mortgage payments and bills, influences their capacity to save, to raise loans and to service credit arrangements.

2.4 It has also been shown that the level of savings and the amount of disposable income are likely to influence the level of risk a person is willing to take with their savings.

2.5 Between 1986 and 1996 the ratio of financial assets to personal income rose from just under 3 to 1 to over 4 to 1 (source ONS BOE). However, during this period, the portfolio of financial products held changed, probably because customers became better financially educated and had a greater awareness of the products on offer. There has been a fall in the level of liquid assets held (eg savings accounts), whilst the level of life assurance and pensions have remained relatively stable. There has, however, been a marked increase in the holding of company securities and unit trusts (source ONS BOE).

2.6 A continuing emphasis on individual home ownership has meant that the value of an individual's home is now a major consideration when looking at personal wealth figures. This is despite the fact that the number of house purchases has suffered a slight downturn in recent years.

2.7 The current generation is also likely to benefit from inherited wealth as property is bequeathed by the previous generation (the generation for whom purchasing property became the norm). Often such inherited wealth finds its way into financial services products, such as bank or building society accounts, and investment products such as PEPs or unit trusts.

2.8 Note also that there are marked differences in the levels of personal income and wealth across the country. Many also believe that there was a widening of the gap between the wealthy and the poor under the Conservative Government .

Student Activity

1 Describe the changes that have taken place in recent years regarding customers' personal income and wealth. Explain what effect these changes will have on the retailing of financial services.

2 How does an individual's income and wealth influence their purchase of financial services products? Give one example of how this has happened in recent years.

3 Socio-economic, demographic and political trends

Socio-economic trends

3.1 In recent years there has been an increase in the number of self-employed people and outworkers. These individuals have an increased need for financial planning, as they need to provide such things as sickness cover and pensions for themselves, rather than having them arranged by an employer.

3.2 There has also been an increase in the number of part-time workers, and again, many of these do not have the financial services products that are traditionally supplied by an employer.

3.3 There is an increasing trend for people to retire earlier. Gone are the days when everybody expected to have to work until they reached 65. Nowadays many people look forward to giving up work at any age from 50 upwards. This does, however, require serious planning and a high level of investment into some sort of financial services product in order to fund these extra years of leisure.

3.4 As discussed at the beginning of this module, the public are becoming much more financially astute and this in turn leads to much more demanding consumers as their inclination to shop around increases.

Demographic trends

3.5 The population is ageing. Between 1995 and 2020 it is expected that the number of young people aged between 15 and 29 will fall by almost 2%, whilst the number of people aged over 64 is expected to rise by 3.4% (source Advertising Association). These changing demographics will lead to a shift in the types of financial services products required; they will probably also cause a change in the way in which they are sold.

3.6 There has been an increase in the number of single-person and single-parent households. This has been caused by

- higher divorce rates
- longer life expectancy, particularly of women
- falling birth rates.

3.7 Each of these changes has an impact on the product requirements of a household. Table 2.1 illustrates just how much change there has been in the make up of households in Britain in the past 25 years. Of particular note is the large increase in single-person households.

Table 2.1 Households: by type of household and family
Source: Census and General Household Survey, Office for National Statistics: Department of the Environment

Great Britain				Percentages
	1971	1981	1991	1995-96
One person				
Under pensionable age	6	8	11	13
Over pensionable age	12	14	16	15
One family				
Married couple				
No children	27	26	28	29
1–2 dependent children	26	25	20	19
3 or more dependent children	9	6	5	4
Non-dependent children only	8	8	8	6
Lone parent				
Dependent children	3	5	6	7
Non-dependent children only	4	4	4	3

Political trends

3.8 Under the Conservative Government there was a move away from the state provision of such things as pension and illness cover. This burden has now fallen to either the employer or to individuals, who must now be prepared to support themselves in difficult times. This shift has led to many retailing opportunities, such as the sale of Critical Illness Cover and Permanent Health Insurance, to cover the shortfall where people had previously relied on the state to provide adequate sick pay.

3.9 The introduction of the new state retirement age for women, whereby females retiring after 2020 will not receive their state pension until they reach 65 rather than 60, is expected to lead to an increase in the level of private provision by women who do not want to have to work for an additional five years.

3.10 The introduction of the Personal Equity Plan (PEP) in 1987 allowed individuals an opportunity to invest, largely in UK equities, and to receive favourable tax treatment on their investments. This served to both increase the level of business for financial services retailers and to help to educate the general public as to the range of products on offer.

3.11 The continuing policy of lowering the basic rate of income tax (by 6% in the last ten years) and the reduction of tax on higher earners to a flat rate of 40% in 1988/89 have led to increases in the levels of disposable income, and therefore in the ability to purchase financial services products. Whilst initially it may be thought that the lowering of the tax rate might mean that tax free products lose some of their appeal, this has not been the case; a fact borne out by the level of sales of PEPs experienced by the industry.

Student Activity

1 Describe the demographic changes, likely to affect the retailing of financial services, that you expect to occur in the next few years

2 Give one example of how a political change has affected financial services product sales.

4 Regulation

4.1 The retailing of financial services has undergone dramatic changes over the past twenty years. Previously, banks and building societies had operated in separate marketplaces until the Financial Services Act in 1986 provided building societies with greater scope to operate in a marketplace previously dominated by the banks. This has increased the levels of competition, particularly in the area of personal lending.

4.2 The implementation of the Financial Services Act has meant a move from institution-based to market-based regulation in order to recognise the overlap of service provision between what had traditionally been separate institutions.

4.3 We will now look at the different regulations and regulators governing the retailing of financial services.

Financial Services Act 1986

4.4 This Act embraces all types of financial securities and collective investments and all types of investment activity, including the provision of advice for, management of, and arranging of, investments.

4.5 The purpose of the Act was twofold. First, to define and regulate investment business (affording protection to investors), and secondly, to promote competition in the savings market.

4.6 The FSA only applies to investment business and therefore excludes general insurance, short-term deposits, mortgages, loans, and deposit-based pensions, all of which are covered by other legislation.

Building Societies Acts

4.7 The Building Societies Act 1962 restricted the activities of building societies, and the interest rate cartel (which ensured that the interest rates offered moved closely in the same direction) limited competition between the societies. Although the interest rate cartél was ended in the early 1980s, building societies' ambition to compete with other financial services retailers was still restricted.

4.8 By the 1980s banks were increasingly moving into the mortgage market, traditionally an area dominated by building societies. They had also started to offer interest bearing cheque accounts, putting pressure on the societies' retail source of funds.

4.9 Changes in the Building Societies Act 1986 allowed societies to provide a much wider range of financial services. The main changes were the ability to offer the following

- unsecured lending (the maximum level was initially set at £5,000, but this has now been increased to £15,000)
- an integrated house-buying package including estate agency services
- insurance broking services
- full personal banking and money transmission.

4.10 To protect the societies' major function of providing finance for house purchase, they were permitted to create subsidiaries to carry out the riskier new activities. They were also permitted to provide some of the services through joint ventures, for example, the provision of regulated financial services products.

4.11 Societies were also permitted to raise funds from sources other than their members. The level for this was set at 20% of all funds.

4.12 Under the Building Society Act, three classes of society assets were created as follows.

Class 1 Advances secured on a mortgage of residential property. This was to remain the main activity of building societies, and 90% of advances must fall into this category.

Class 2 Other forms of secured lending, with a maximum of 10% being commercial loans.

Class 3 Unsecured lending, with a limit of 5% being commercial lending (this would be included in the 10% class 2 limit).

4.13 These limits imposed on building societies by the Act have an effect on how a society promotes its product; they therefore need to be considered when developing a retail strategy.

4.14 The changes in the legislation also allowed building societies to convert from mutual to PLC status. This would then mean that they would be governed by the Bank of England rather than being bound by the provisions of the Act. Many societies have decided that this option suits their long-term retailing plans, and have decided to convert.

4.15 Abbey National was the first to convert to PLC status, followed by the Alliance and Leicester, and the Halifax in 1997. There are a number of other societies proposing conversion at the present time. One of the rules that makes the conversion option more appealing to building societies is the protection from hostile takeover which the Act affords to converting societies.

4.16 The last few years have also seen a flux of mergers and takeovers in the retail financial services sector. For example, Cheltenham & Gloucester are now part of Lloyds, who have now merged with TSB bank. This spate of mergers and takeovers has been popular with the public, who have received windfalls in the form of cash or shares. Many members of the public have taken to spreading their investment between societies in an attempt to benefit from any future windfalls. This 'speculating' became so widespread that many societies imposed minimum initial deposit levels for new accounts in order to deter the activity. It has also led to some societies, the Bradford and Bingley being one example, publicly stating that they intend to maintain their mutual status. Whether this will be viable in the long-term remains to be seen.

4.17 A review of the Building Societies Act in late 1987 led to some further amendments. One major change allowed building societies to become more directly involved in the operation of life and general insurance companies. Although initially many societies preferred to form partnerships with existing companies to offer regulated products, as time passed many of the larger societies have seen the potential of offering their own products and have done just that. For example, the Halifax and the Alliance and Leicester both offer their own life and pension products to the public.

4.18 All of the changes contained within the Building Societies Act have opened new markets for the societies and have led to increased competition in the retailing of financial services.

Banking Act 1987

4.19 The introduction of this Act means that the Bank of England supervises the deposit taking functions of banks. If a bank then conducts other types of business, such as the sale of investments, there will be an overlap of supervision. Under the lead regulator approach the Bank of England co-ordinates the supervision which is conducted by itself and the other regulatory bodies. For example, the Bank of England monitors capital adequacy and the Securities and Investment Board and other relevant Self Regulatory Organisations monitor compliance and the conduct of business.

5 The Financial Services Authority (FSA)

5.1 In 1997 the government announced that there was to be a new structure of financial regulation in the United Kingdom. If the UK was to maintain a competitive advantage in the financial services industry, then the regulations should be seen to be effective and up to date. It also wanted a regulatory regime that would be viewed as fair, coherent, open and cost effective.

5.2 In October 1997 the new regulator was launched under the title of the Financial Services Authority (FSA).

5.3 The FSA will have three areas of operation, each managed by an appointed managing director. The three areas will be Operations; Financial supervision; and Authorisation, enforcement and consumer relations.

5.4 Much consultation has taken place within the industry, and it is hoped that this consultation process will help establish a regulator that meets the needs of both the industry and the consumer. The government intends to produce the draft legislation for the new regulator in the summer of 1998 by bringing together the best of the various approaches to regulation that currently exist. Prior to this, existing regulation will continue to be applied until this process is finalised.

5.5 Under the new regulation, banking supervision will reverse out of the Bank of England and into the new Financial Services Authority. However, the aim is that the legal framework for banking supervision should not be altered beyond the minimum necessary for the transfer, and the Board of Banking Supervision will continue in an advisory role.

5.6 There will also be a draft of the new Financial Services Bill, which should be published some time during the spring or summer of 1998. The aim of this piece of legislation is to replace rather than amend much of the existing law to create a single and coherent piece of legislation. The government feels that one of the problems with the existing Financial Services Act is that it does not have the flexibility to cope with the significant changes that are occurring in the financial services industry. They are keen to create a legal framework that will have the flexibility to take the industry into the future.

5.7 The new regulator will have a consistent set of powers across the financial sectors, and will build legal and practical frameworks which are comprehensive, easily understood and are seen to be sensible.

5.8 At the launch of the FSA the government announced some of the objectives for the new regulator. One of the purposes of these objectives will be to ensure that the regulator will be accountable to Ministers and through them to Parliament.

5.9 Some of the areas that the objectives are to cover will be as follows.

- The involvement of the regulator in the promotion and maintenance of confidence in the UK financial system and markets.
- The regulator having the powers to take prompt action, where necessary, to ensure that the UK is seen as a clean place to do business, and ensure that systematic risk is minimised.
- The involvement of the regulator in protecting customers and ensuring that organisations are competent and financially sound.
- The new regulator should take a role in educating the consumer in the benefits and risks associated with financial services products, although precisely what this role will be is yet to be defined.
- The involvement of the regulator in monitoring, detecting and preventing financial crime. Everyone involved in establishing the new body has agreed that the regulator has a key role to play here, ensuring that the supervisory effort and the systems of all organisations are directed towards protecting and preventing money laundering and other criminal activities.

5.10 The government also intends to set some internal objectives to guide the regulator going about its job. It is seen as essential that the new regulator is efficient and economic, ensuring that the costs and restrictions on the organisations it regulates are proportionate to the benefits of regulation.

5.11 The new regulator should also facilitate innovation within the financial services industry and not simply be cast in the role of policeman.

5.12 The FSA will be responsible for authorising members of the professions who carry out investment business. It is anticipated, however, that there will be a continuing role for the professional bodies and that they will co-operate with the new regulator.

5.13 The government is considering whether it would be sensible for the FSA to be able to refrain from making specified rules or categories of rules where it considers those of the established professions to be adequate. It is also looking at the feasibility of the regulator engaging professional bodies to carry out specified functions, for example monitoring, on its behalf.

5.14 The government has made it clear, however, that this does not mean that professionals will escape regulation by the FSA. The regulator will have the power to remove the authorisation of anyone who is carrying on investment business to inadequate standards. They have also stated that it is not a green light to form any new professional or quasi-professional bodies. The ultimate aim is to avoid dual regulation.

5.15 There will be a single compensation scheme, and the new regulator will appoint a single compensation board. There will be a common point of entry for consumers and common administrative arrangements. The government is to seek input on the practical aspects of such a scheme and final decisions will be included in the draft legislation in 1998.

5.16 It was felt that having a number of regulatory bodies in the past, SIB, IMRO and the PIA has led to overlap, confusion and gaps in the past. The creation of the FSA will mean one focused professional body.

5.17 The creation of the Financial Services Authority will provide both the industry and the consumer with one body to regulate the whole of the financial services industry. This will remove the confusion that sometimes occurred by having different bodies for different areas of regulation.

5.18 The government is seeking and encouraging input from the industry for the details of the Bill that will put the framework into place. This will then be translated into legislation, due to be published in draft format in 1998, on which further opinions will be sought prior to the Bill being finalised.

Student Activity

1 What was the purpose of the Financial Services Act 1986?

2 What were the main changes in the Building Societies Act 1986?

3 Who is regulated by the Financial Services Authority?

6 Compliance

6.1 Complying with the rules and regulations governing the financial services industry is always a major consideration in the retailing of financial services products. The Securities and Investment Board has a three tier structure of rules designed to ensure high standards of integrity and fair dealing by all who conduct investment business.

First tier rules: the Statements of Principle

6.2 The first tier is the SIB's ten principles of investment business. These underpin all the rules and must be included in the rule books of all the SROs. These statements of principle cover integrity, skill, care and diligence, market practice, information about customers, information to customers, conflicts of interest, customers' assets, financial resources, internal organisation and relations with regulators.

6.3 These principles, as well as stating the standards expected of the industry highlight the importance of both the spirit and the law of the regulations.

Second tier rules: the core conduct of business rules

6.4 The FSA seeks to protect the customer from unscrupulous and fraudulent operators in the financial services industry in all circumstances. The second tier of rules is intended to set out the detailed industry-wide requirements, and to define acceptable behaviour. The seven most important points included cover independence, advertising and marketing, customer relations, dealing for customers, market integrity, administration and general provisions.

The third tier rules: SRO/RPB rules

6.5 The third tier rules provide a statement of good practice which indicates the ethics expected when acting in the interest of customers. These rules vary between the individual SROs and RPBs because of their different membership and sales contexts, but all are expected to provide adequate investor protection.

6.6 Although this is only a very brief overview of the legislation governing the retailing of financial services, it is apparent that complying with these rules and regulations is extremely important and can place constraints on the way in which products and services are sold.

Student Activity

What is the purpose of the SIB's ten statements of principle?

7 Information technology

7.1 There have been major developments in the technology used in the retailing of financial services over the last few years. Technology is a fast moving environment and companies have invested millions trying to keep pace with the changes and to ensure that their systems are customer oriented.

7.2 Developments in the use of technology have changed the ways in which organisations interact with their customers and promote their products. This technology is not only key when dealing with customers, but is also crucial internally as it allows for the development of Marketing Information Systems (MKISs). In a highly competitive environment it is vital for companies to be able to develop and maintain customer databases. Such databases make it possible to develop and maintain a relationship with what may otherwise be a single purchase customer.

7.3 It is now apparent that technology is no longer a support mechanism; instead it is a key to the development of new services and products.

Technology is often used by companies to enable them to offer a Unique Selling Proposition (USP). The following are some examples of the technology currently being used in the retailing of financial services.

Automatic Teller Machines (ATMs)

7.4 First launched by Barclays in 1967, there are now over 22,000 machines in the UK. Many financial retailers have reciprocal agreements for their customers to allow them access to services through other providers' technology. These ATMs have advanced from being simple cash dispensers to machines that can provide a whole range of services, such as producing statements, checking balances and accepting deposits.

Electronic Funds Transfer at Point Of Sales (EFTPOS)

7.5 EFTPOS is a means of purchasing items without using cash or cheques. A debit card such as Delta or Switch is supplied to the customer, who is allocated a Personal Identification Number (PIN). Suppliers' sales terminals are connected to the financial institution. When the customer wants to purchase goods the card is 'swiped' through the terminal. The customers' and retailers' accounts are then debited and credited, respectively, at the point of sale.

The smart card

7.6 This is a card with a conventional magnetic strip, but which also contains a programmable micro chip. The concept was recently piloted in Swindon under the name 'Mondex' in a joint initiative between NatWest and Midland. Funds are transferred to the card and then the card is used to purchase items from any retailing outlet with a Mondex terminal. The initial trials of this cashless system were not as successful as was first anticipated and the system is now under review.

Home and office banking

7.7 The customer, either corporate or personal, can use a terminal, a visual display unit and a telecommunications link to access a service offered by the financial services institution. For example, a customer could transfer money from one account to another using this system.

Global cash management

7.8 This allows customers to transmit instructions regarding their accounts and to electronically transfer funds. It also allows reporting facilities for global accounts as well as transactions and foreign exchange deals.

Internet

7.9 Customers who have personal computers and who are linked to the Internet can check financial information such as mortgage and interest rates. It is also possible to purchase some financial services products via the Internet. In addition, certain financial services institutions will allow customers to complete the fact-finding part of a regulated sales process themselves and then transmit this over the Internet. The company then makes recommendations in a personal report and sends this to the customer for them to read prior to an appointment. This approach greatly reduces the amount of time that the customer and the salesperson need to spend together to complete a sale.

Interactive television

7.10 This is one of the latest introductions and is currently being trialed by a number of retailers. Customers 'enter' the outlet via their television screens, scanning the products available before placing their order. Although not currently widely available, this is most certainly a valuable opportunity for the future of financial services retailing.

7.11 Over the next few years electronic commerce will continue and there will be further developments. It is possible that one day the 'cashless' society will exist.

Student Activity

1 What is EFTPOS and how is it currently used by customers?

2 How is the Internet currently helping the retailing of financial services products?

8 Internationalisation

8.1 As institutions continue to seek organic growth they must increase their market share. One way of doing this is to look beyond the domestic market. However, the regulatory constraints of some foreign markets may make this difficult. Because of this there have been a number of directives issued in an attempt to harmonise the provision of financial services in the European Union. The creation of the free flow of capital and the free trade in financial services firms, is an attempt to establish a single market. Unfortunately, in spite of the directives, governments may still erect barriers to entry in an attempt to protect their own markets. These barriers can take the form of bureaucratic procedures which companies have to follow if they wish to trade in that particular country. Companies may also face initial rejection from the marketplace: customers may be reluctant to use a foreign provider for their financial needs.

8.2 A further barrier to entry to a foreign market can be the cost of acquiring a distribution network in a new country. To overcome this, many organisations have preferred to form alliances with foreign companies or to make acquisitions in the country they wish to do business in.

8.3 Foreign companies wishing to trade or increase their business in the UK face a similar situation. For example, the Hong Kong and Shanghai Banking Corporation have acquired the Midland Bank, and the National Bank of Australia has acquired the Yorkshire Bank. More recently, a number of American Financial institutions have established credit card operations in the UK — MBNA and Associated Capital Corporation are just two of them. In comparison UK organisations have been slow to move into the international market; this is due to the existence of barriers to entry rather than because of any lack of desire to increase their business.

9 Market structure and trends

Market structures

9.1 Most retail financial markets are oligopolistic in structure. Broadly, this means that they contain a significant number of suppliers of varying size. A key point of oligopoly theory is that individual organisations are cautious of provoking rival firms, as this can create uncertainty and risk. Organisations therefore try to avoid aggressive price competition, which can lead to a spiral effect of price cutting and ultimately to a full blown price war. Many markets, therefore, are arranged around some term of co-ordinated pricing arrangement, such as the interest rate cartel discussed earlier in this unit.

9.2 Throughout the 1980s and 1990s the position of retailers of financial services has moved. Where clear boundaries once existed, it is now the case that each organisation is attempting to be a full range provider. For example, banks were known as current account providers, building societies as mortgage providers and insurance companies sold life policies. Today, financial organisations move between product markets much more readily and co-ordinated pricing arrangements are a thing of the past.

9.3 The opening up of the financial markets heightened consumer awareness of the wider range of products and services available; this process was further aided by the Government led innovation of products which were market rather than supplier specific, namely PEPs and TESSAs.

9.4 More recently, organisations outside the traditional retail financial services (for example, Marks & Spencer, Tesco and Sainsbury's) have taken the opportunity to join the market place, using to their advantage, the increase in consumer awareness and the more open competitive environment.

9.5 In widening the range of suppliers operating within the financial markets, deregulation also enabled industry groupings with different cost structures to compete directly with each other. For example, building societies maintain a cost-to-income ratio of around 50%, but in contrast to this, banks have a higher ratio of 65%. The cost advantage afforded to building societies can provide them with some competitive advantages. The aim of an organisation is to reduce the cost-to-income ratio year on year.

9.6 A further issue to consider in this area is that, as some of the building societies take the decision to convert to bank status, they are entering the arena with a cost-to-income ratio that may be significantly lower than some of their competitors. However, banks have long been aware of their cost uncompetitiveness and have undertaken measures to reduce their operating expenses. In the early part of the 1990s all the large clearing banks substantially reduced their numbers in both personnel and service outlets. In 1990 Midland announced a programme to axe 4,000 jobs followed by plans in 1992 to close 500 branches. In 1991 Barclays announced a 5,000 personnel reduction, plus plans to contract by a further 15% over the following five years. Also in 1991 NatWest made proposals for a 15,000 job reduction programme, saving the organisation an estimated £400m by 1993.

9.7 In the current competitive environment, particularly in the banking arena where there are currently an ever increasing number of new entrants further cost cutting is inevitable and the streamlining of businesses through the use of IT, especially at point of sale, can only increase.

9.8 Deregulation and the shift in the traditional market divisions also posed some interesting problems for insurance companies. Prior to the Financial Services and Building Societies Acts, insurance companies, in the main, distributed their products through a direct sales force or independent brokers; the high street retailing of insurance products alone was not an economically viable proposition.

9.9 With deregulation, however, the insurance companies were able to reach distribution agreements with banks and building societies, and so were in a position to retail their products on the high street. These associations proved valuable for the insurance companies as volumes of business substantially increased. However, the prime weakness in this type of arrangement is the lack of direct control over distribution. Some insurance companies have attempted to minimise this by tying to a range of distributors, which can be a costly solution because of the costs involved in setting up the necessary administration units.

9.10 A further problem evolved for the insurance companies when the banks and building societies with whom they had made distribution arrangements recognised regulated products (life and pensions etc.) as a growth area. An increasing number of the major financial retailing organisations set up their own companies and terminated the distribution arrangements, leading to a significant drop in business volumes for some insurance companies. Many insurance companies are now in the position of having to either find new distribution agreements or alternative distribution methods.

9.11 The evolution of market structure in the financial services sector has had many consequences, but three warrant particular attention.

1 The intensification of competition has increased the need to eliminate unproductive costs, compete on price and operate efficiently.

2 Mergers and takeovers have created a concentration within certain industry groups.

3 It has created the emergence of retail financial service conglomerates.

9.12 The basis of the financial conglomerates is that the organisation combines a number of institutions under a single company umbrella, for example Halifax plc and Halifax Life. This occurrence is known as 'bancassurance'. The foundation of the bancassurance model is that it combines the sales skills of an insurance operation with the stronger consumer orientation and loyalty of the banks and building societies. When linked together there is great potential for cost effective and profitable cross-selling of insurance and investment products.

9.13 As a bancassurer, an organisation has the ability to improve profitability by retaining all commissions within the group and to reduce some of the administration costs that are involved when distributing through a third party. It also allows an organisation the opportunity to co-ordinate the ways in which it approaches customers and to establish multi product relationships with them.

9.14 Although financial services retailing is a competitive environment the bancassurers regularly meet with each other to discuss current issues. Many of them also take part in benchmarking exercises which take place regularly. Benchmarking is research which is carried out, usually via mystery shopper exercises, to ascertain if an organisation is attaining a certain level of service. Individual results are compared against competitor results to provide an organisation with an overview of their position, as percieved by the consumer in the market-place.

Market trends/developments

9.15 Two major innovations have taken place in financial service retailing in the UK. The first is the introduction of 'telephone banking' and the second is the introduction of point of sale debit cards.

Telephone banking

9.16 The first launch of a telephone banking system was in a joint initiative between the Bank of Scotland and Nottingham Building Society in 1986. TSB followed with their Speedlink service in 1987 and then First Direct was launched in 1989.

9.17 First Direct, a division of HSBC, is widely acknowledged as a leader in the field of direct banking, and its success has quickly been recognised by competitors who have set up their own direct operations. At the start of 1991, First Direct had 100,000 accounts. Of these accounts only 25% had been converted from Midland, which meant that the bank had acquired 75,000 new customers in what is considered a mature market. Even in the early stage of customer acquisition First Direct claimed to be acquiring 2,500 new customers per week. According to the chief executive, this is equivalent to the number of new accounts a new branch would open in a one year period. Fifty two branches would therefore have been required for this rate of customer acquisition, which would have required large capital expenditure. In the main, telephone banking has been geared to younger more affluent customers, who are technologically literate and who do not need the comfort factor of face-to-face dealing.

9.18 The advantages of 'telephone banking' are not only a reduction in overheads but the freeing up of the main distribution channel (i.e. branches). This has enabled organisations to develop other products and services for customer segments which require face-to-face contact.

Point of sale debit cards

9.19 The launch of the debit card allowed customers to pay for goods and services in a cashless transaction at the point of sale. The payment is debited from their accounts and the funds electronically transferred to the retailer's bank.

9.20 The first debit card in the UK was launched by Barclays Bank in 1987 and was branded 'Connect'. There were some initial problems with resistance from retailers who felt that the transaction charges were too high. In 1988

Midland, Royal Bank of Scotland and NatWest launched 'Switch' as a consortium. This debit card offered retailers a flat transaction fee as opposed to the percentage fee charged by Connect, and Switch quickly established itself as a market leader.

9.21 It is now projected by APACS (Automated Payments and Clearing Systems) that by the year 2000 the total number of debit card transactions will exceed 3 billion, which is more than ATM withdrawals and credit card payments combined.

Summary

Financial Services retailing has changed significantly in the last ten years and, with the growing trend for takeovers and mergers, will continue to do so in the foreseeable future. As the single European market becomes stronger the integration of financial services could see an increase in the number of UK organisations owned by foreign companies, as well as UK organisations forming alliances on the continent.

The current mortgage, savings and retail banking markets are reaching mature levels. Competition for market share becomes more intense as organisations become more reliant on the turnover of existing business as opposed to the addition of completely new business. For the regulated markets, and for some areas of insurance, there is still the potential for growth, particularly as the Government seeks to remove reliance on state provisions. Currently, penetration levels for pensions, private health care insurance, critical illness and long-term care cover are low.

The regulatory bodies are exerting greater pressure on organisations to ensure consumers' interests are protected. The cost of setting up the systems and administration levels required will undoubtedly force some organisations to look for partners in order to share the costs involved. As we enter the millennium the trend is definitely towards financial retailer conglomerates.

Now that you have completed this unit you should be able to do the following.

- [ ] **Explain how an individual's income influences their need for financial services products.**
- [ ] **Describe socio-economic, political and demographic trends and explain how such trends influence the retailing of financial services products.**
- [ ] **Explain the role played by compliance and regulation.**
- [ ] **Describe the use of information technology in retailing.**

- **Describe how internationalisation is affecting the sale of financial products.**
- **Explain how the market is structured, and describe how current trends affect both this structure and the market size.**

Most of the remaining units of this text will conclude with self-assessment questions to help you reinforce your learning and prepare for the examination.

Unit 3

The competitive environment for branches

Objectives

After studying this unit you should be able to do the following.

- **Identify key competitors.**
- **Identify competitors' strategies and objectives.**
- **Assess a competitor's strengths and weaknesses.**

1 Identifying competitors

1.1 Competitive analysis is a part of external analysis; its aim is to provide an insight into what will influence a product to market decision, or what will maintain a sustainable differential advantage.

1.2 Competitive analysis concentrates on identifying the threats, opportunities and strategic questions that are created by emerging or potential competitors' actions, weaknesses or strengths.

1.3 The first step in a competitor analysis is to identify both current and potential competitors. The following factors should be considered.

- Who are the competitors and how strong are they?
- What are the characteristics of the market they compete in?
- What will be the likely response of competitors to your organisation's strategies?

1.4 In financial services a number of competitors compete in each market segment, so it is important to understand not only who the competition is, but how strong they are.

2 Current competitors

2.1 Initial analysis should focus on *current* competitors, as these, in the short term, will affect any strategic and tactical decisions your organisation makes. There are two ways in which this can be done.

- Look at the competition from the customers' perspective. You can then group competitors by the degree to which they compete for a buyer's custom.
- Position the competition into strategic groups on the basis of their competitive strategy.

2.2 Most main competitors are easily identifiable. However, it is important to look beyond the immediately obvious. For example, the competition for a financial retailer who uses branches as a distribution method could be described as being

- all financial retailers using a branch network.

2.3 However, other competitors should include

- direct financial service providers (for example, Virgin)
- financial service providers using alternative distribution methods (for example, supermarkets such as Tesco and Sainsbury's).

2.4 Remember that competition can also appear in the form of substitute products (sometimes known as *indirect competition*). In financial services, a substitute product can be classed as 'any other item on which a customer can spend their money'. For example, a customer may prefer to buy a new car rather than invest in a Bond, or they may wish to spend an extra £25 per week on clothing rather than a Pension Plan.

2.5 A further complication arises from the fact that in financial services some products compete against each other. For example, a customer wishing to save money has a wide range of choice of savings accounts: Peps, Unit Trusts and Pensions, to name but a few. The competition for an investment house would therefore be providers of any alternative savings vehicles.

2.6 For simplicity, this unit will not look at substitute products, but will concentrate on the competition in the form of other providers of financial services.

Customer perspective

2.7 Much of the work involved in examining the customer's perspective is normally carried out by a market research department. However, it is helpful to have an understanding of the methodology they apply and how the results can be used.

2.8 Customer perspectives can be approached in two ways: (a) by exploring consideration decisions for alternative suppliers ('customer selection'), and (b) by examining how customers associate products with use applications ('appropriateness of use').

2.9 These approaches are described in the following sections. Both approaches use a conceptual basis for identifying competitors, and can be used by managers even when market research is not available. The concepts of customer selection and appropriateness of use can also be useful tools in helping to understand the competitive environment.

Customer selection

2.10 Customers are asked questions relating to the brand or service they purchase. These questions are then followed by questions about consideration decisions for alternative suppliers if their usual purchase were unavailable. For example, a customer purchasing a Pep from his bank could be asked where else he would have bought it if the bank was unable to offer this product. His answer might indicate a direct supplier in preference to alternative retail outlets. If so, then the competition should not be classed as 'other banks'.

Appropriateness of use

2.11 It is possible to seek to gain insight into how customers associate products with specific use applications. Here a group of customers for a certain product are asked to identify a list of 'use situations' relevant to that product. This is then reversed, and customers are asked to name all the appropriate products for a single use situation. A further group of customers are then asked to make judgments on how appropriate each product would be for each use situation. The products are then clustered based on their similarity in the use applications.

2.12 For example, a group of instant-access savings account customers asked to identify use applications for the product might give the following answers.

- a holiday
- a new car
- a house
- a 'rainy day'
- retirement.

2.13 This list of use applications is then presented to another group who are asked to name appropriate products for the use application. Typical answers could be as follows.

A holiday – savings account
– personal loan
– credit card

Retirement – pension plan
– Pep/Unit Trusts, etc.

2.14 Although this is quite a simple example, it illustrates the fact that an instant-access account is viewed as a means to purchase mainly luxury items; this is substantiated when the use application is matched to products, which are savings and credit accounts.

Strategic grouping

2.15 The strategic grouping approach differs greatly from customer perception and is directed towards creating an understanding of the competitive structure of an industry – in this case financial services.

2.16 A strategic group is described as a group of companies who

- over a period of time pursue similar competitive strategies (for example, use the same distribution channels)
- have similar characteristics (for example, size and positioning)
- have similar assets and skills (for example, brand values).

2.17 In financial services, one strategic group is the banking organisations, such as NatWest, Barclays, Lloyds, TSB and Halifax. All distribute through high street retail outlets, have strong established brands, use advertising and promotions effectively and have similar cost-to-income ratios.

2.18 A second strategic group is consumer banks: organisations who do not offer corporate lending and banking services. The Halifax also competes in this market.

2.19 A third strategic group is direct banking operations. Once again the Halifax competes in this market.

2.20 A strategic group set should include characteristics that are 'mobility barriers'. Mobility barriers are factors that will inhibit, or even prevent, an organisation from moving from one strategic group to another. Financial services organisations have large amounts of funds available and are unlikely ever to be prevented from entering a strategic group. However, in some instances entry will require high levels of funding and resources (for example, when entering into direct banking) and this may inhibit entry for a period of time.

2.21 Barriers to entry can come under many headings, including: brand values, reputation and customer perception. Organisations attempting to compete across numerous strategic groups can be disadvantaged by becoming good at many things but excellent at nothing.

2.22 Some strategic groups also have barriers to exit, for example assets such as specialised labour skills and technology investment.

2.23 The mobility barrier is an important concept and is supported by both economic theory and empirical study. One of the ways to develop a sustainable differential advantage is to determine and follow a strategy that is protected from competitors by the service, assets and skills that would allow entry to the market.

2.24 The definition of strategic groups can vary, and will depend on their use application, but the grouping can take into consideration any of the strategies that are discussed in Unit 5. Strategic groups could therefore be defined using the following criteria.

- which distribution channels they use
- positioning
- use of technology
- pricing – skimming or penetration.

2.25 Different groups have different bases on which they compete, and therefore different competitive advantages. Characteristics such as size, diversification and global presence can also be of strategic importance.

Student Activity

1 Name two approaches used in the identification of competitors.

2 Describe how they differ.

Using and projecting strategic groups

2.26 Understanding strategic grouping can make the task of competitor analysis more manageable. Most industries, and certainly financial services, contain so many competitors that it would become an overwhelming task to analyse each one. It is not feasible to consider twenty competitors, let alone hundreds.

2.27 By reducing competitors to smaller strategic groupings, the analysis becomes compact, feasible and, more importantly, usable. Placing the organisation into a strategic group also has the benefit of ensuring that insight into competitor activity is not lost: if the grouping has been carried out correctly then economic or legislative developments will affect everyone within the group in a similar way. This, in turn, helps in projecting future strategies of competitors.

2.28 Strategic grouping can also focus any strategic investment decision. Rather than basing investment decisions on an industry, a decision can be based on the attractiveness of a particular strategic group within the industry. To do this it is necessary to determine the profitability, both current and potential, of each strategic group. The selection of a strategy and the skills and resources required to support it will mean selecting, or indeed creating, a strategic group in which the organisation will compete.

2.29 The concept of strategic grouping can also assist in projecting competitive strategies of the future. A study in America carried out by McKinsey Consulting Group looked at the effects of deregulation on five deregulated industries and was able to forecast that successful firms would move towards one of three strategic groups, as shown in Table 3.1.

Table 3.1 McKinsey Consulting Group study: Strategic groups emerging from deregulation

Group	*Industry*	*Examples*
1 National distribution company with full line differentiated products and emphasis on attractive service/price positioning	Brokerage Airlines Transport	Merrill Lynch Delta Consolidated Freightways
2 Low cost producer – often new entrant following deregulation	Brokerage Airlines Transport	Charles Schwab Midway Air Overnite
3 Speciality firm with strong customer loyalty and specialised service targeted towards an attractive market segment	Brokerage Airlines Transport	Goldman Sachs Air Wisconsin Ryder System

2.30 The evolution of group 1 involves three phases.

- In the first phase the medium and small organisations attempt to gain market share, by merging, to compete with the large organisations.

- In the second phase, the strong organisations make acquisitions to fill gaps in their product lines or market segments. Also during this phase, which usually occurs in a period of around three to five years following deregulation, the main players in the industry try to develop broad product lines and distribution coverage.
- In the third phase, mergers within the industry take place with dominant players emerging.

2.31 The second group is made up of low cost producers who enter the industry post deregulation and provide simple products with minimal service aimed at price sensitive customers.

2.32 The third group consists of those organisations who have decided to pursue a focus strategy, with a specialised service targeted at a chosen market segment.

2.33 Although this study was carried out in America and involved a number of industries, it is significant that the financial services industry within the UK has followed a very similar pattern, although after increased regulation rather than deregulation. In this case, group 1 consists of the large clearing banks, group 2 is companies such as Virgin, and group 3 is where you would place organisations such as M&S Financial Services.

3 Potential competitors

3.1 The competitors of today may not always be the competitors of tomorrow. It is therefore important to understand who are the *potential competitors*.

3.2 This understanding can be gained from observing a competitor's activities and realising when it may pose a competitive threat. Possible activities could be as follows.

Market expansion

3.3 One of the most obvious sources of potential competitors are organisations who operate in other geographic regions or in other countries. UK financial services companies need to be aware of foreign banks wishing to expand through acquisition outside their own country.

Product expansion

3.4 Organisations can take advantage of their technology and distribution capabilities to begin selling a larger product range.

Backward integration

3.5 Many of the major banks and building societies have established their own life companies, enabling them to sell their own branded products and not those of an unrelated life company.

Forward integration

3.6 Suppliers can become potential competitors if they believe they have the critical ingredients to succeed in the market. They may be attracted by profit margins and the control that forward integration brings.

Export of assets or skills

3.7 A small organisation that has strategic weaknesses can become a major entrant if it is purchased by another organisation that is capable of eliminating these weaknesses.

3.8 The prediction of such occurrences is difficult, but an analysis of competitor strengths and weaknesses can sometimes reveal possible synergistic mergers to look out for. A competitor who is operating in an above average growth industry but who does not have the management or financial resources to sustain its operation is an attractive candidate for merger.

Retaliatory or defensive strategies

3.9 Organisations that are threatened by a potential or an actual move into the market in which they operate may well retaliate.

3.10 A move by a competitor needs to be assessed in the context of a specific strategy, but the general response is an external factor to the organisation and should therefore be considered as an opportunity or threat when undertaking the SWOT analysis.

Student Activity

1 State the benefits of using strategic grouping.

2 What are the six possible activities that may indicate a possible competitive threat?

4 Understanding competitors

4.1 There are four key benefits derived from understanding the activities of competitors.

1 An understanding of current strengths and weaknesses of a competitor can suggest opportunities and threats that require a response.

2 Insights into future competitor strategies may allow forecasting of emerging threats and opportunities.

3 Decisions regarding strategic alternatives may be easier if the organisation has the ability to forecast the likely reactions of competitors.

4 Competitor analysis may highlight strategic questions that require monitoring, such as: 'will competitor A decide to move into direct sales?'

4.2 Competitor actions can be said to be influenced by eight elements, as illustrated in Figure 3.1.

Figure 3.1 Competitor analysis: the eight elements

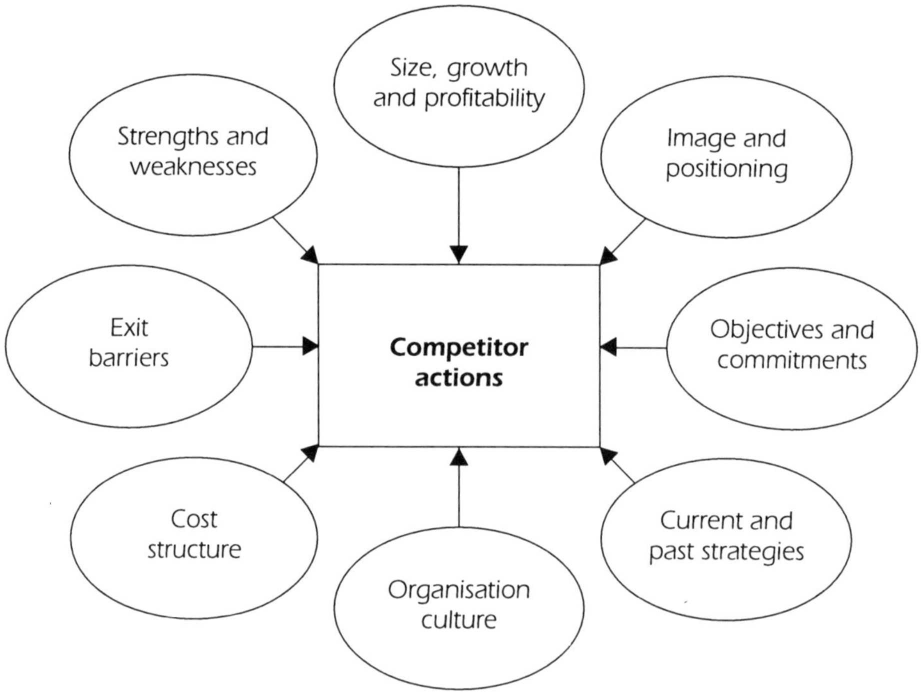

Size, growth and profitability

4.3 Levels of growth and market share provide an indication of the strength of a business strategy. An organisation maintaining a strong market position or achieving rapid growth is usually a strong competitor operating in a strong strategic group and following a successful strategy. In contrast, an organisation that is experiencing a declining market position may be experiencing financial problems that are affecting the ability of the company to follow certain strategies.

4.4 Profitability is also a consideration, as a profitable organisation normally has access to capital for investment (unless it has a parent company who has decided to 'milk' it). An organisation that is losing money or that is experiencing a steep decline in profitability may be unable to gain access to capital from either internal and external sources.

Image and positioning

4.5 Many organisations attempt to succeed in image and positioning through tangibles; that is, by being seen to produce the best car or the most advanced hi-fi equipment. Stronger positioning can be attained by moving beyond this to include intangibles, such as quality, innovation, personality and relationships.

4.6 The intangible nature of the products they sell means that many financial services companies have no choice but to build their position and image in the market place on intangible attributes. For example, Midland use the strapline 'the listening bank' to convey personality and customer relationships.

4.6 When developing positioning alternatives it helps if there is an understanding of the image and brand personality of the major competitors. Any weaknesses identified in competitors' relevant attributes and personality traits can signify an opportunity to differentiate and to develop competitive advantages. Any strengths that are identified relating to important factors represent a challenge to exceed or out do them.

4.7 Competitor image and positioning information can be gained simply by studying an organisation's products, advertising, branding and actions, but ideally this should be reinforced with market research to ensure that an accurate portrayal is made. The standard approach to this is to use qualitative customer research to establish what an organisation and its brands mean to a customer.

Objectives and commitment

4.8 Understanding a competitor's objectives gives the potential to assess whether that competitor's current performance is satisfactory and to forecast whether strategic changes are likely.

4.9 The financial objectives of the competitor can indicate the willingness to invest in the business, even if the pay back is long term. It is useful to consider what the competitor's objectives are with regard to market share, profitability and sales growth.

4.10 Non-financial objectives are also important. Does the competitor wish to expand distribution, develop new services or become a leader in technology? The answers to these types of questions can provide a good idea of what the future strategy of a competitor may be.

4.11 If the competitor has a parent company, then their objectives are also relevant, as these will ultimately affect the business unit that is a direct competitor.

4.12 Much of this type of information can be obtained by reading report and account documents, mission statements (which usually clearly state long-term objectives) and trade press articles about the competitors.

Current and past strategies

4.13 It is necessary to review a competitor's current and past strategies, paying particular attention to any strategies that have failed – as any failure will inhibit the competitor from pursuing this type of strategy again.

4.14 Also helpful is a knowledge of a competitor's pattern regarding new products or new market moves, as this can assist in anticipating future growth directions. For example, if a differentiation strategy is detected, how much does it rely on the product line, service, distribution method or brand identification? If a low-cost strategy is identified, is it based on economies of scale or the experience curve? If a focus strategy emerges then identify the business scope. (These three strategies are discussed in greater depth at the end of this unit.)

Organisation and culture

4.15 An understanding and knowledge of the background and experience of a competitor's top management can provide insight into possible future actions. For example, are the managers drawn from a marketing, manufacturing or fast moving consumer goods background? Are they from another industry or were they brought in from another company? If a Chief Executive has arrived from another successful company, he or she will often implement similar management styles and strategies to those operated at the previous organisation.

4.16 The culture of an organisation is supported by structure, people and systems and will be reflected in the strategy. Cost-oriented, highly structured organisations rely on tight control to achieve their objectives and motivate employees and may therefore experience difficulty if they attempt to switch to an innovative marketing oriented strategy. Similarly, an organisation with a flat structure that acts on innovation and risk taking will probably encounter difficulties if it attempts to pursue disciplined product refinement and cost-reduction programmes.

4.17 Generally, organisational elements, such as culture, structure, people and systems, have an impact on the range of strategies that can be considered.

Cost structure

4.18 Knowledge of the cost structure, particularly if a competitor is relying on a low cost strategy, can help you to understand what possible pricing strategies may be used in the future and whether they are likely to be sustainable. The goal is to obtain a feel for both fixed and direct costs, and thereby to determine break even levels.

4.19 The following information can normally be obtained.

- The number of employees and a rough estimate of direct labour and overheads.
- Investment in equipment and outlets.
- Sales levels.
- Relative costs of supplies and materials.

Exit barriers

4.20 Michael Porter identified, in his competitive strategies, barriers that are crucial to an organisation's ability to exercise an exit alternative, and therefore that become indicators of commitment. These include

- specialised assets
- fixed costs – leases and personal contracts
- relationships with other business units within the organisation
- government and social barriers
- managerial pride or emotional attachments to a business/employees, which will affect economic decisions.

Student Activity

1 Describe how an understanding of competitors might assist in the strategic planning process.

2 Name eight elements of competitor activity that should be considered in a competitor analysis.

5 Assessing strengths and weaknesses

5.1 The final element in understanding competitors and their possible actions revolves around assessing their strengths and weaknesses. This provides insight into an organisation's ability actually to pursue certain strategies. It also allows input into the planning process by identifying and selecting strategic alternatives.

5.2 An organisation can choose to exploit a competitor's weakness if it has an existing or developing strength that enables this. The end result is to pit its strength against the competitor's weakness.

5.3 At the opposite end of the scale, a knowledge of a competitor's strength provides the foresight to bypass or neutralise it.

5.4 The assessment of a competitor's strengths and weaknesses begins with the identification of skills and assets relevant to the industry. A competitor can then be evaluated against those skills and assets.

Relevant skills and assets

5.5 Competitor strengths and weakness are based on the existence, or lack of, skills and assets. For example, a skill could be the ability to provide financial advice to customers, and an asset could be a prime retail site or well known brand name; all these would be identified as strengths. On the other hand, the absence of skills or assets would be identified as weaknesses.

5.6 To analyse competitor strengths and weaknesses it is necessary first to identify the skills and assets relevant to the industry. Listed below are five questions that can help in this task.

1 Why are successful businesses successful? Why are unsuccessful businesses unsuccessful?

2 What are the key customer motivations?

3 What are the large cost components?

4 What are the mobility barriers in the industry?

5 What components of the value chain can create competitive advantage?

5.7 We will look at each of these questions individually and at an organisation level. However, each question can be as easily applied to a Regional Area or Branch Office to gain an understanding of the competitor strengths and weaknesses that affect these operational levels.

Success/lack of success

5.8 Which organisations have been successful over time? What skills and assets contribute to this? Which organisations have continuing poor performance? Why? Which skills and assets do they lack?

5.9 Skills and assets that provide sustainable competitive advantage should affect performance over time, and therefore organisations whose performances differ over time should also differ in their skills and assets. Analysis of the causes of good or poor performance usually relates to sets of relevant skills and assets. Characteristically, stronger performers have developed and maintained key skills and assets that have sustained their performance.

5.10 Conversely, weakness in the skills and asset base required for the industry should contribute, over time, to the weak performance of a competitor.

Key customer motivations

5.11 What are the key customer motivations? What is really important to the customer?

5.12 Customer motivations drive buying decisions (Unit 4 explains this in greater detail), and so can dictate which skills and assets can create meaningful advantages.

5.13 Sometimes needs exist that are unmet by current offerings. An unmet need can represent an opportunity. For example, Direct Line Insurance was established to realise the potential of offering a service that excluded brokers and therefore cut costs. An unmet need can also represent a threat: for example, for the brokers and the insurance suppliers who lost business to Direct Line.

5.14 An analysis of customer motivations can identify skills and assets that an organisation must deliver if it is to pursue a certain strategy. For example, if a prime buying criteria for a personal loan is an 'instant decision', then the organisation must develop the skills and assets to deliver this attribute.

5.15 Organisations who lack competence in areas that are perceived to be important by the customer segment they are servicing can experience problems, even if they have other significant sustainable competitive advantages.

Large cost components

5.16 What are the large value added parts of the service? What are the large cost components?

5.17 Analysing the cost structure of an industry can show which value added stage represents the highest percentage of total costs. If a cost advantage can be gained in a key value added stage then it could represent a significant sustainable competitive advantage, which could support a low price of differentiation strategy. Cost advantages in the lower value added stages have less leverage.

Mobility barriers

5.18 What are the mobility barriers in the industry?

5.19 Mobility barriers result from the costs involved and the difficulty of creating the skills and assets required to support a sustainable competitive advantage. These barriers include both entry barriers and barriers to movement from one strategic group or competitive area to another.

5.20 For example, in financial services, barriers prevent organisations from simply moving from a regional operation to a UK operation to a global operation. Global operations require specialised skills and assets in establishing offices, dealing with foreign governments and laws, and operating in different countries.

The value chain

5.21 Consider the components of the value chain. Do any provide the potential to generate competitive advantage?

5.22 Michael Porter (in *Competitive Advantage*) set out the various activities of an organisation in a 'value chain', as shown in Figure 3.2. This model represents the value activities (which procure inputs, process them and add value to them in some way, to generate outputs for customers) and the relationships between them.

Figure 3.2 Michael Porter *(Competitive Advantage)* The Value Chain

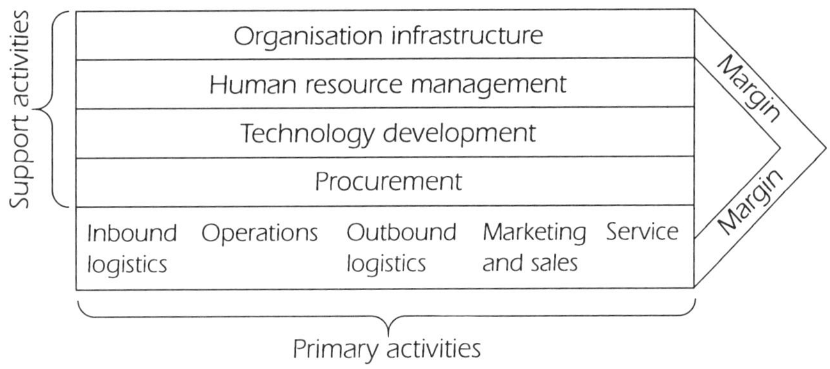

5.23 An organisation's value chain consists of two types of value creating activity: primary activities, and support activities.

Primary activities

5.24 Primary activities are those directly related to production, sales, marketing, delivery and services. These activities are summarised as

- inbound logistics – receiving, handling and storing inputs to the production system
- operations – converting inputs into final products; in a service organisation, operations include activities that make up the basic service, for example, the issuing of statements by a bank to its customers is part of its operations
- outbound logistics – order processing and distribution
- marketing and sales – communication, pricing and channel management
- service – providing the products, upgrading them as necessary.

Support activities

5.25 Support activities are those that provide purchased inputs, human resources, technology and infrastructure to support the primary activities. These activities are summarised as

- procurement – procedures and information systems
- technology development – improving the service and processes and systems
- human resource management – recruiting, training, developing and rewarding people
- management planning – management, planning, finance, quality control.

5.26 Each activity in the value chain is a potential source of competitive advantage and should be considered when assessing competitors.

Student Activity

Discuss with colleagues how you would analyse a competitor's strengths and weaknesses.

A checklist of strengths and weaknesses

5.27 We have discussed what steps can be taken to analyse the competition, and the fact that assessing their strengths and weaknesses will assist in identifying your own opportunities and threats. Table 3.2 provides a checklist of the areas in which the competitors' strengths and weaknesses may lie. This list is equally applicable to service or manufacturing industries.

Table 3.2 Analysis of strengths and weaknesses

Innovation	**Management**
Technical or service superiority	Quality of top and middle management
New product/service capability	Knowledge of business
Research and development	Culture
Technologies	Strategic goals and plans
Patents	Planning/operation systems
	Loyalty – turnover
	Quality of strategic decision making
Operations (manufacturing)	**Marketing**
Cost structure	Service/producer reputation
Flexible operations	Service characteristics/differentiation
Equipment	Brand name recognition
Vertical integration	Breadth of product line – system's capability
Staff attitudes and motivation	Customer orientation
Capacity	Segmentation
	Distribution
	Advertising/promotion skills
	Sales force
	Customer service and support

Finance – access to capital
From operations
From net short-term assets
Ability to use debt and equity financing
Parent's willingness to finance

Customer base
Size and loyalty
Market share
Growth of segments serviced

5.28 By analysing the skills and assets for each of the categories it becomes possible to make judgments regarding a competitor's strategy and its ability to react to any strategic decisions the organisation makes.

Competitive strength grid

5.29 When all the relevant skills and assets have been identified, the next step is to scale the organisation you work for against the major competitor, or the strategic groups of competitors, on the relevant skills and assets. The result is known as a 'competitive strength grid', which summarises the position of the competitors with respect to skills and assets.

5.30 This exercise can be carried out on any level, and is as applicable to branch planning as it is to head office planning. A sustainable competitive advantage is nearly always based upon having a superior position in one or more skills and asset areas that are relevant, not only to the industry, but also to the strategy employed. Information about a competitor's position on skills and assets is therefore an integral part of strategy development and evaluation. If a superior position is not found to exist then it will need to be created, or the strategy should be modified or abandoned.

5.31 At times there may be no differences between the competitive offerings, as a skill that everyone possesses cannot be a basis for a sustainable competitive advantage. For example, the ability to cash a cheque is important to bank customers, but if all banks are perceived to offer exactly the same service then there is no sustainable competitive advantage.

5.32 Figure 3.3 illustrates what a competitor strength grid could look like for competitors in mortgage lending. Skills and assets are listed on the left and are grouped according to primary or secondary importance levels. The main competitors are then shown as column headings. Each cell is coded to show whether the brand is strong, above average, average, less than average or weak in the required skills or assets category. This particular grid uses a five-point scale, but it could be amended to a three-point scale of strong, average and weak, if appropriate.

Figure 3.3 Example of a competitive grid for the top six mortgage lenders

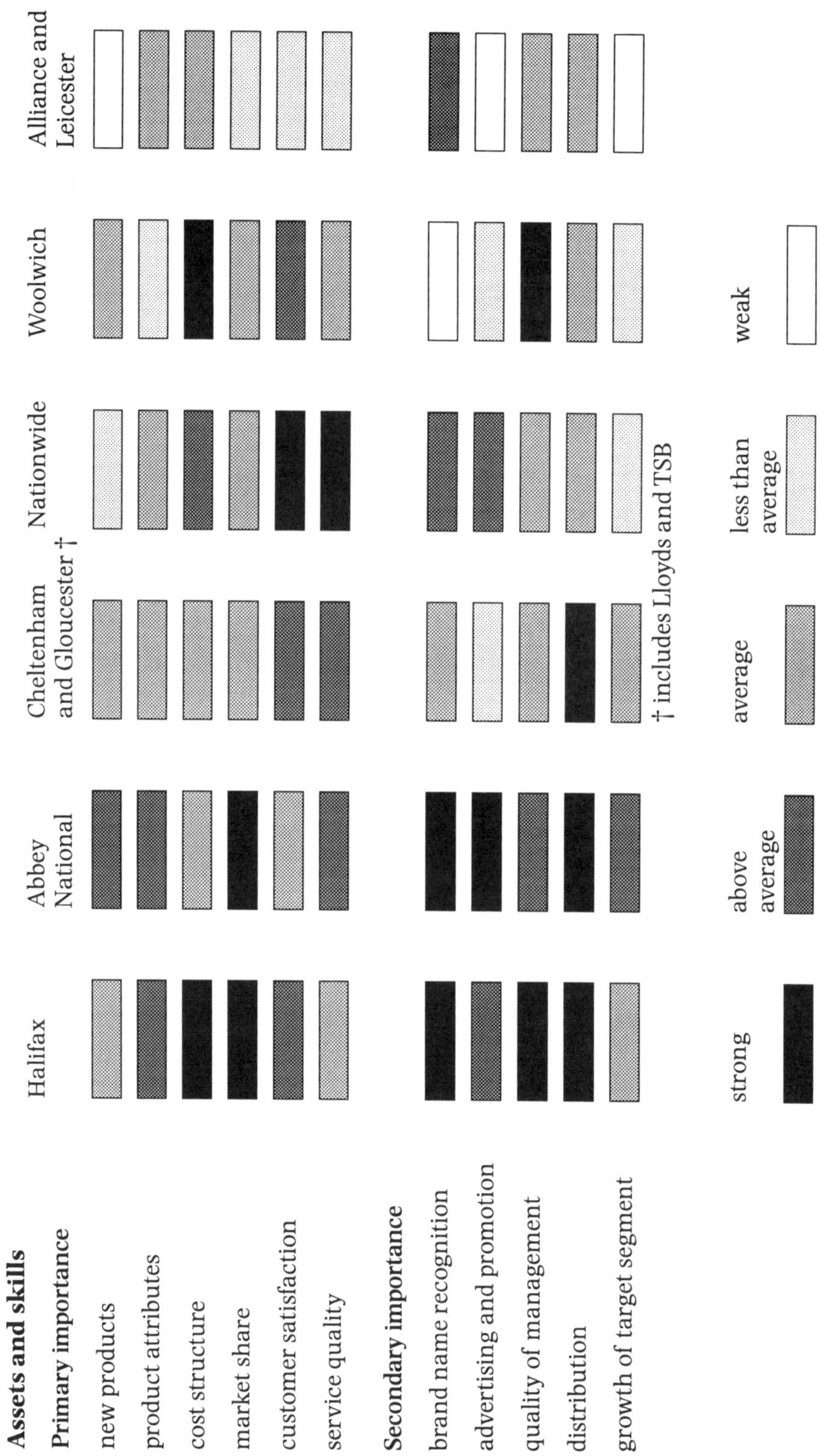

Source: Council of Mortgage Lenders (Figures based on institutions' financial years between 1.2.95 and 31.1.96.)

5.33 It may be helpful to analyse submarkets or strategic groups, or even products, as an organisation may not compete with all other organisations in the industry but only with those involved in similar strategies and markets.

5.34 The process of developing the competitive strength grid is useful and informative. One method is to have a number of managers create their own grids independently: the differences between them can highlight different assumptions and information bases. A reconciliation stage can then disseminate relevant information and identify strategic questions. For example, different opinions on the service quality of competitors may stimulate a strategic question that justifies market research.

5.35 A second method for building a grid is to use a group that is supported by preliminary desk research. This information can then be used when any disagreements arise regarding where a competitor should be scaled on a particular dimension.

Competitor information

5.36 Information about competitors is available from a number of sources. Competitors regularly communicate with customers and suppliers, city analysts and stockholders, as well as with the financial services regulators and government bodies. Contact with any of these can provide information. Monitoring trade magazines and the financial press, as well as attending seminars and trade shows, can also provide information.

5.37 If detailed information on customer perception is required, market research may need to be commissioned. Alternatively, the research function at head office will usually have research findings on these types of questions.

Student Activity

With your colleagues, develop a competitor strength grid for a financial services supplier and its main competitors.

6 Competitive strategies

6.1 Once the competitors have been established and analysed it is important to determine their strategic direction. This will enable the organisation to do a number of things.

- To benchmark its success against its competitors.
- To forecast possible competitor activity.
- To anticipate and counteract competitor tactics.

6.2 Michael Porter suggests that any strategy that is adopted by the organisation should be done so on the basis that its ultimate goal is to achieve a sustainable competitive advantage. You may think that a competitive strategy is only required for organisations that face competition (that is, commercial organisations), but even government departments may need to plan competitively. For example, the National Health Service needs to be aware of competition from private medical care.

6.3 Organisations that operate in a monopoly must also compete to retain their monopoly position, and some monopolies compete with each other.

6.4 Competitive strategy is largely based on product marketing strategies, which Porter places under three broad headings

- overall cost leadership
- differentiation
- focus (that is, segmentation).

6.5 The strategy an organisation chooses to adopt depends upon the competitive strategies adopted by the competitors. It has implications for product design, quality, pricing and marketing.

6.6 The most appropriate strategy is also influenced by the structure of the organisation and the type of service or product that it offers. There are three categories of product

- search products
- experience products
- credence products.

These are discussed in more detail in Unit 5.

Cost leadership strategy

6.7 Cost leadership strategy aims to achieve the position of lowest cost producer in the industry. By producing at the lowest cost, an organisation can compete on price with all its competitors in the industry, and so earn the highest unit profits.

6.8 There are a number of contributing factors to achieving overall cost leadership, as follows.

- Setting up production facilities for mass production, so obtaining economies of scale.
- Using the latest technology.
- In the high-technology industries, and industries that depend on labour skills for product design, there will be a learning curve effect (also known as the cost experience curve). In producing a greater number of items than any of the competitors, an organisation can benefit from the learning curve and achieve lower than average costs.
- Concentrating on productivity objectives, seeking productivity improvements and cost reductions (that is, zero based budgeting).
- Cost minimisation in areas of overhead costs – sales force, advertising.
- Favourable access to sources of raw materials may also contribute to overall cost leadership.

6.9 Some industries may have a low critical mass of production output where maximum economies of scale are achievable. In this case cost leadership is difficult to achieve because competitors are able to achieve similar low costs. This is the case for the high street banks now that they all possess similar numbers of staff and retail outlets.

6.10 Only when the critical mass of production is high is a cost leadership strategy likely to be effective.

6.11 You may find it difficult to relate the contributing factors for cost leadership to financial services. Consider the industry as divided into specific service or product areas: for example, the mass production factor can be seen in some of the financial services companies who have set up direct mortgage operation centres.

6.12 As overall cost leadership relies on large scale production, economies of scale and learning scales, etc., it is necessary that the strategy for the organisation should aim for market leadership or another competitive advantage such as distribution advantages.

6.13 The strategy carries implications for product quality, pricing and marketing.

Product quality

6.14 This type of strategy is particularly suited to search products, where the customer is easily able to compare competing products. With these products an organisation must be able to match the quality of its competitors' products, or it will lose customers. Equally, an organisation should not commit large amounts of resources to improving products with attributes that ultimately have little or no relevance to the customers' purchasing decisions.

Pricing

6.15 Prices may need to be kept low if the price elasticity of demand for the product is high (meaning that the demand for a product is sensitive to its price). The organisation may also need to use promotional pricing.

Marketing

6.16 Advertising can be used to boost sales volumes, particularly when it focuses on discounting or special offers.

Resources

6.17 To implement an overall cost leader ship strategy the organisation will require

- a large amount of 'up front' capital expenditure on leading edge technology and equipment
- aggressive pricing and a willingness to bear initial losses while building market share.

Risks

6.18 The strategy carries risks, as indeed do all strategic decisions, and ultimately these must be balanced against the benefits. In the case of the overall cost leadership the risks could be identified as follows.

- Technological changes may occur at such a rate that the capital investment required to keep pace may nullify all the cost advantages achieved on the experience and learning curve.

- There may be a threat of competition from overseas competitors in countries where certain costs are lower. An organisation that sells on price is always vulnerable to price cutting.
- There is the threat of competition fragmenting the market or building a high price, high quality image. This would result in an overall low cost product being forced into competing in each market segment and trying to pit cheaper prices against a brand image. This is difficult in markets where customers perceive quality in terms of price.
- Cost inflation is also always in the background, particularly when foreign competitors do not have the same problems.

Differentiation strategy

6.19 Differentiation strategy is almost the complete opposite to cost leadership in that it attempts to raise the quality of a product and, by doing so, to raise the product's cost and sales price. The improvements in quality need to be of more value to the customer than the price increase, so that the customer is willing to pay more for superior quality: there must be perceived added value.

6.20 This type of strategy aims to achieve an optimal balance for the customer between quality and price. ('Quality' as used here refers to desirable attributes, such as customer service.)

6.21 Organisations who adopt this strategy must seek to offer customers greater quality relative to price than do their competitors. There is, however, a limit to what customers will pay for a product, and so the trade-off, by the customer, between quality and price should be anticipated by the organisation and incorporated into the differentiation strategy.

6.22 The strategy bases itself on the assumption that competitive advantage can be achieved through certain characteristics of the organisation's products, which can be categorised as follows.

- Advanced products that can offer (a) a vast performance advantage over competitor offerings, (b) a much lower price, or (c) (in an ideal situation) both.
- Improved products that do not usually differ from the competitors' products but that have better performance at a competitive price. Quite often this is achieved through the incorporation of technological advances applied to particular products.
- Competitive products that appear to have no obvious advantages over other product offerings but that derive appeal from a particular compromise of cost and performance.

6.23 When a differentiation strategy is successfully applied it allows the organisation to build customer loyalty. The products can then be sold at a higher price than the least cost product. Quite often an organisation that operates on a differentiation strategy will not be the market leader in terms of market share.

Risks

6.24 A risk of the differentiation strategy is that customers will not pay the higher price for the product because, although differentiation exists, they do not perceive the product to be of greater value than a cheaper competitor product. This is particularly likely in times of recession, when customers become more price sensitive. The marketing strategy can then become a critical success factor. For example, the big mortgage lenders competed on rates to gain market share when, during the recent property recession, customers became decreasingly interested in added benefits such as free surveys and legal fees.

Key points

6.25 If an organisation takes the decision to implement a differentiation strategy it should always remember the following.

- The organisation must provide superior quality and service, relative to price, in the opinion of the customer.
- The organisation must continually seek to innovate in order to stay ahead of competitors in quality. If a competitor innovates then they should quickly be equalled or excelled. A differentiating organisation will usually therefore have a large research and development or promotional budget.

Focus strategy

6.26 Focus strategy is the third strategy identified by Porter. It involves an organisation concentrating on one or more particular market segments rather than attempting to service the whole market with a single product.

6.27 The strategy segments the market and then focuses on particular segments. The organisation does not attempt to sell its products industry wide. as in a differentiation strategy, but concentrates on a particular type of buyer or geographical area.

6.28 To be successful in this strategy an organisation must be able to serve its narrow strategic target more effectively and efficiently than competitors who are competing on a broader basis. As a result of this Porter states that the organisation then achieves either differentiation, due to better meeting the needs of the segment, or lower costs in serving the segment, or both.

6.29 Focus strategy can further be divided into the following.

- Cost focus – choosing a market segment and then specialising in a product (or products) for that segment. Through this specialisation, the organisation can keep costs to a minimum within that market segment.
- Differentiation focus – choosing a market segment and then competing on the basis of product differentiation for that segment.

6.30 Focus strategies are particularly relevant to organisations attempting to enter a market for the first time. The implications for product, quality, price and advertising are similar for cost focus and cost leadership strategies and differentiation focus and differentiation strategies.

Risks

6.31 The risk of a focus strategy is that the market segment that is targeted may not be large enough to sustain the organisation with a profitable basis for operation.

Selecting a strategy

6.32 Porter states that, although each of the competitor strategies he identifies carries risks, an organisation must select and pursue one of them. Not to do this would result in the organisation having a 'stuck in the middle' strategy, which, Porter argues, would almost certainly result in only low profits.

6.33 Most financial services organisations attempt to operate a differentiation strategy. This has much to do with the fact that many of the products are unable to carry sustainable price differences, and most competitors have very similar core product offerings. Differentiation is usually gained through advanced and improved products and services. The 'Tax Free Home Plan' launched by the Halifax is an example of an advanced product.

6.34 Some organisations attempt to operate on a cost leadership strategy by providing 'direct' services. However, as we have discussed, this is a very difficult position to sustain – more so perhaps in financial services where so many competitors have the financial ability to compete when their market is threatened.

Student Activity

1 Identify and summarise the three competitive strategy options.

2 What are the risks associated with each strategy?

Summary

Here are the key points from this unit.

- ❑ **The first step in competitor analysis is to identify who the competitors are. One method is customer based and uses customer choice and perception as a reference point. Another method uses product-use associations.**
- ❑ **In nearly all industries, competitors can be illustrated in terms of how intensely they compete with a reference business. Alternatively, competitors can be identified by strategic group (groups of competitor organisations that follow similar strategies and that have similar skills, assets and other characteristics).**
- ❑ **Mobility barriers between the strategic groups are important because they can protect a profitable strategy, and it is therefore also important to identify potential competitors – organisations with not only the motivation but also the ability to enter an industry.**

- **Understanding the competitor is key and can be achieved through analysis using several criteria. A competitor's size, growth and profitability will provide a gross measure of its importance. Image and positioning strategy provide strategic insights, and an analysis of objectives and current and past strategies provides insight into commitment and intentions. Organisational issues such as culture and exit barriers may highlight strategic constraints, and cost structures can provide clues to possible pricing strategy.**
- **To identify competitor strengths and weaknesses it is necessary to identify the skills and assets relevant to an industry. The factors for consideration should be characteristics of successful and unsuccessful organisations, customer motivations, cost components, mobility barriers and the value chain. The competitive strength grid is a useful tool for summarising this key strategic information.**
- **The three options available to organisations are: cost leadership strategy, differentiation strategy and focus strategy. Each has advantages and disadvantages, but these must be weighed against the ultimate risk of not adopting any one strategy and therefore lacking direction and focus.**

Through much of this unit 'the product' has been discussed, and you should remember that this title not only applies to products such as personal loans, bank accounts and credit cards, but also to the service that is provided to the customer. The 'product' for financial services is the service: financial advice, mortgage advisers, ATM facilities, etc.

Competitor analysis can be implemented at any level: it can be applied to competing organisations (for example, Barclays and NatWest) but can also be applied to competing branches in a high street.

Now that you have completed this unit you should be able to

- **identify key competitors**
- **identify competitors' strategies and objectives**
- **assess a competitor's strengths and weaknesses.**

Self-assessment exercise

1 Describe how you would identify an organisation's key competitors.

2 Identify the strategy and objectives of a company of your choice.

3 Assess the strengths and weaknesses of a company of your choice.

Unit 4

Consumer buying behaviour and segmentation pricing

Objectives

After studying this unit you should be able to do the following.

- **Describe the way in which customers behave when buying a service, in particular, a financial service.**
- **Describe customers' attitudes towards credit and debt, and explain the effect that these attitudes have on the retailing of credit and debt.**
- **Describe customers' attitudes towards savings and investments.**
- **Describe the segmentation of the financial services retailing industry at both a national and a local level.**

1 Buyer behaviour for services

1.1 Most of the literature to date has been concerned with either the extent to which the marketing of services requires a different approach from that adopted for the marketing of goods, or with identifying specific marketing strategies to deal with the problems posed by the differing characteristics of services.

1.2 Although goods and services do not have completely opposite characteristics, services are usually distinguished from goods on the grounds of intangibility, inseparability, heterogeneity and perishability. These characteristics do seem to dominate in services and can cause problems for their marketing.

1.3 To understand the purchase decision process, a marketer should recognise the ways in which buyer behaviour can be affected by these characteristics.

Intangibility

1.4 Intangibility is the main distinguishing feature of services. Services are experiences or processes; they are not physical objects and therefore cannot be possessed (Shostack, 1977; Lovelock, 1981 and Bowen and Schneider, 1988).

1.5 Intangibility can be double edged as, in addition to the above, it can also mean that services are not easily understood by the consumer.

1.6 At pre-purchase stage, consumers find services difficult to evaluate, as any evaluation is low in *'search qualities'* (tangible attributes that can be considered in advance).

Inseparability

1.7 Conversely, services have high *'experience qualities'* (attributes that can only be assessed after purchase and consumption). Additionally, many professional or specialist services are high in *'credence qualities'* (attributes that cannot even be assessed after purchase and consumption) (Zeithaml, 1981).

Heterogeneity

1.8 Inseparability can therefore lead to some services being subject to variations in quality, which can further aggravate the consumer's uncertainty of the outcome. If production and consumption are an interactive process, then quality depends not only on a consumer's ability to relate to what is required, but also on the uneven temperaments of customer-facing staff and on computer technology. Some financial services have a greater possibility for variation than others. In addition, technology can be employed to 'industrialise' the service (Levitt, 1960) and to improve consistency. However, in an area such as financial advice, the standards are vulnerable to the shortcomings of human nature.

Perishability

1.9 Service providers are not the only ones to be inconvenienced by the fact that services cannot be stored. A consumer is only in a position to pay a bill when (a) it arrives and (b) they have the time. Consumers require cash when they run out, whether their bank or building society is open or closed, and whether or not the ATM machine is empty. When buying stocks and shares the availability of service is needed to 'make a killing'.

1.10 Suppliers therefore have a need to synchronise supply and demand. This does not mean simply ensuring that adequate numbers of cashiers are available. Rather, it means offering convenient trading hours and locations – that is to say, convenience for the consumer. Until fairly recently, the banks' and building societies' interpretation of 'convenience' – 3.30pm closing and high street locations – was frustrating to the consumer.

1.11 In 1992, McKechnie supplemented these four goods/services distinctions with a further two distinguishing features relevant to buying behaviour in financial services. These were

- financial responsibility, and
- two-way information.

Financial responsibility

1.12 Ultimately the financial consumer purchases a promise that the supplier will take responsibility for looking after the buyer's funds and welfare. However, there are rarely sufficient dependable search qualities to enable these promises to be validated. A consumer must therefore have trust and confidence in the organisation and its staff. Consumers often rely on what they see as tangibles, such as the size, image and history of the company, to help them to decide whether the promises made are likely to be kept. The development of trust can bring about a level of inertia in a customer–supplier relationship, as buyers do not wish to repeat the strenuous task of searching for, and evaluating, alternative suppliers.

Two-way information

1.13 Financial services often involve a number of regular two-way transactions, usually over a period of time. (As a result of the inertia mentioned above, this period may be the lifetime of the customer.) Companies can use the wealth of information captured during these transactions to influence behaviour through the development of customer retention and acquisition programmes.

1.14 When discussing the implications for buyer behaviours you should note that the existing literature is full of unsubstantiated principles regarding service excellence, service quality and related topics. Too little evidence exists to demonstrate whether or not these principles result in outcomes such as long-term customer satisfaction and profitability.

2 Buyer behaviour for financial services

2.1 Although a lot of material exists explaining how buyers make a purchase decision, much of it is based on studies of the purchases of physical goods rather than services. The material on financial services buyer behaviour is not so well developed.

2.2 There may be a number of reasons for this paucity of information. First, there may be problems with the actual models used, in that they do not lend themselves to empirical testing (see Tuck, 1976; Foxhall, 1991). Secondly, it is still not clear whether these models are the most appropriate conceptual frameworks to use. Thirdly, there has been a lack of appropriate measures of salient dimensions for testing concepts in services marketing situations (Teas, Dorsch and McAlexander, 1988).

2.3 An example of a model that has been used specifically for financial services is an adaptation of 'AIDA' (Awareness, Interest, Desire, Action) (by Guirdham, 1988) for complex financial products such as PEPs, shares and unit trusts. Figure 4.1 on the next page illustrates this model.

- A lack of knowledge, for example, can hamper the penetration of PEPs. So with complex financial products, knowledge becomes 'know how' (or know how to buy), and must be accompanied by adequate self confidence to buy. Both know how and confidence are critical factors for first time buyers (Guirdham, 1987).

Figure 4.1 'AIDA': An adaptation for complex financial products Guirdham, M. (1987)

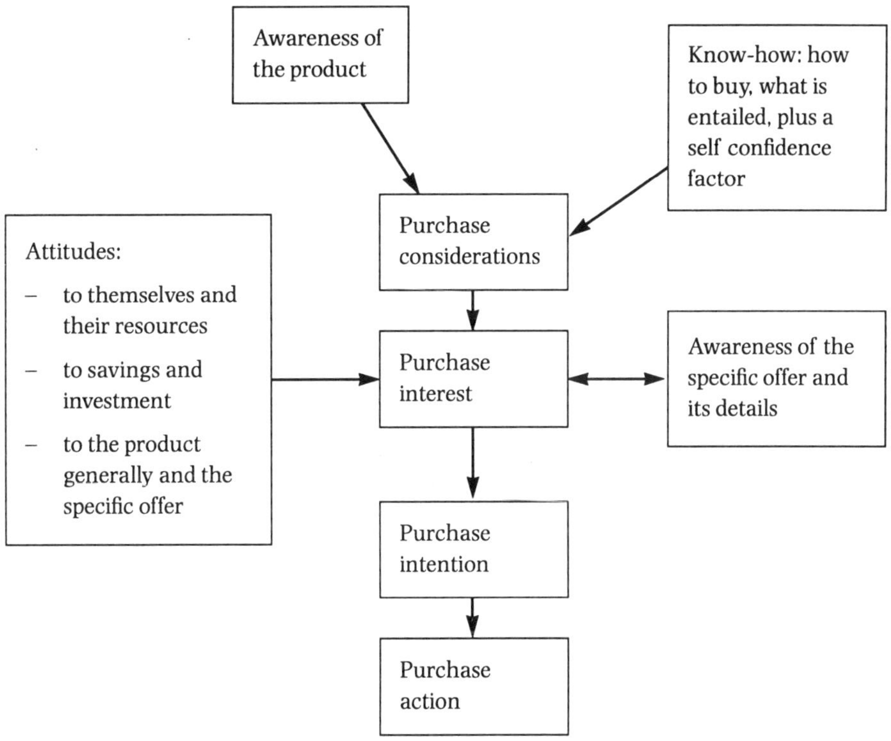

- 'Awareness' is a two-stage process and covers both the product category (for example, unit trusts, shares) and, in the later stages, the specific offer or brand details.
- 'Interest' still reflects the affective or emotional part of attitudes.
- Here 'intention' replaces 'desire', which may be a result of the fact that a typical financial product cannot stir the emotion implied. It also reflects the fact that consumers rarely evaluate financial products unless they intend to act upon their findings. In contrast, goods such as cars, stereos and luxury items may be investigated simply as a matter of interest.

2.4 The focus on buyer behaviour in financial services has tended to be on specific issues: the factors that affect the choice of bank and usage of financial services, customer loyalty, customer expectations and perceptions and service quality.

2.5 Most studies on buyer behaviour have highlighted the importance of factors such as confidence, trust and customer loyalty. Some common choice criteria in bank selection are

- size of the organisation
- dependability
- location
- convenience and ease of transactions
- professionalism of the personnel
- availability of loans.

2.6 It would seem that the personal consumer is more interested in functional quality dimensions (how the service is delivered) as opposed to technical quality dimensions (what is received as the outcome of the production process) (see Gronroos, 1990). Given the difficulties that consumers have in evaluating services, this is not surprising.

2.7 So far we have considered consumer behaviour, but studies also cover organisational buying behaviour. Turnbull (1982) attempted to apply some of the organisational buying behaviour models to the purchase of international financial services. He concluded that no single model adequately explains all the complexities of these purchases. However, he did find that certain aspects of three theories do offer some understanding of the purchase process.

2.8 The Interaction Model by the IMP group addressed the importance and nature of relationships between companies and banks. This model examines factors that influence the search and decision process, and looks especially at the 'atmosphere' in which the relationships are conducted.

2.9 Two further models, Robinson and Faris (1967), and Webster and Wind (1972), which looked at the purchasing process sequence, are also appropriate.

2.10 The importance of company–bank relationships was further highlighted by Turnbull and Gibbs (1987) in a discussion of the concept of 'financially responsive relationship management' and the interactive process this involves, as well as the valuable benefits to be gained by both parties. In more recent research it was claimed that, to be successful, commercial banks would have to develop a system for financial responsiveness and to ensure that their customer-facing staff and senior management have a good understanding of corporate customer buying behaviour.

2.11 Yorke (1990) fully supported the adaptation of the Interaction Model for the purchase of services, particularly in the case of corporate rather than personal services. He stressed the important implications this model has for professional supplier firms.

2.12 Teas *et al.* (1988) acknowledge the importance of establishing long-term working relationships in services marketing. Their empirical research concludes that, when a bank behaves in a certain way, commercial customers are well disposed towards them. Their research showed that customers required the bank to

- be responsive to their requests
- initiate the interaction
- be knowledgeable about their business and business needs
- develop close informal working relationships with them.

2.13 The relationship aspect has also become more important in the personal sector and this highlights the importance of the role of customer-facing staff. This type of interaction is now categorised as 'relationship marketing', something that has become a key issue for any company that values the marketing ethos.

2.14 To summarise, in services marketing, where there is a complex interface between a buyer and the seller, the relationship between a customer and the service provider is important, as is the job of managing the total customer – organisation personnel interaction process. The relationship built between a buyer and the seller needs to be based on mutual trust and commitment if it is to be developed and maintained in the long-term.

2.15 The nature of financial services is such that they tend to be one-off purchases that require regular reviewing or servicing. There is therefore a clear need for financial services suppliers to establish initial relationships with their potential customers. However, at the same time they must strive to maintain and develop long-term relationships with existing customers. In addition to this, financial services are based on high levels of customer trust and confidence. This trust and confidence must reside in both the organisation supplying the services and, perhaps more importantly, in the customer-facing staff themselves (Christopher, Payne and Ballantyne, 1991). The existence of confidence and trust, and the good management of the relationship aspect involved in service supply, are very significant indicators of the successful retention of customers and the recruitment of prospects.

Student Activity

1 Describe how the concept of financial responsibility affects the behaviour of the buyer of financial services.

2 List the four stages a buyer must go through according to Guirdhams AIDA concept.

3 Attitudes

3.1 Attitudes are an expression of inner beliefs and emotions and reflect an individual's disposition (favourable or unfavourable) to something (a service, an organisation or an object).

3.2 According to Louden and Delia Bitta (1988) all attitudes share four common properties.

- Attitudes have objects; the objects can be abstract, such as consumerism, or material, such as an ATM.
- Attitudes have direction, intensity and degree; they express how an individual feels towards an object.

  a) Direction – either favourable or unfavourable. For example, older people tend to dislike ATMs.

  b) Degree – how favourable or unfavourable the individual feels.

  c) Intensity – the level of confidence or conviction the individual has in their belief. Although they are related, intensity is not the same as degree. For example, an individual may think that unit trusts offer a very attractive investment opportunity, but they may not have great strength in this conviction.

- Attitudes have structure; they have a core, comprising the individual's most important values and self-concept and, as all other peripheral attitudes are related to those in some way, they must display a reasonable level of consistency. Attitudes are also generalisable, so that a person's opinion of a particular service may be generalised to include all of an organisation's services.
- Attitudes are learned; they may be learned from personal experience, from family or other peer groups, from the media, as well as from many other influential sources. Because they are learned, attitudes tend to become stronger, or at least more resistant to change, the longer they are held; hence the 'set in their ways' adage that could be applied, for example, to the reluctance of the over 60s age group to accept more relaxed social attitudes towards credit and borrowing (Henley Centre, 1993).

Attitudes towards credit and debt

3.3 The deregulation of the financial markets put consumers in a position to be able to borrow greater amounts of money than ever before. However, the subsequent rises in personal debt could only take place if consumers had a favourable attitude towards debt. (Although the phrase 'debt' became transformed into 'credit' – a more socially acceptable term.)

3.4 Conspicuous consumption increased. It became the norm to hold store cards and credit cards, to shop for designer labels and to own the latest technology.

> **'Borrowing is no longer seen to be shameful, an admission of weakness, and evidence of a lack of restraint, most people do not believe that it is wrong to want goods before one has the money to pay for them. With present inflation, more people are content to borrow in order to buy at today's prices and pay back in tomorrow's devalued money. Also, the fear of not being able to repay loans has decreased due to greater personal security made available by state intervention in unemployment pay, sickness benefits and allowances, and by pensions and life assurance.' (Lewis, 1982).**

3.5 However, attitudes towards buying on credit are affected by the consumer's belief in the economy, and spending patterns are often seen as an indicator of how confident consumers are in the country's economy. Three key factors can affect these attitudes: the housing market, recession/unemployment, and inflation.

The housing market

3.6 The feeling of personal wealth increases with escalating house prices. When house prices were rising in the UK, consumers not only felt affluent, but lending organisations actively encouraged people to spend their paper gains. As house prices crashed, the practice of borrowing on the back of housing assets dropped dramatically. In addition, more cautious lending policies were reintroduced by the banks and building societies.

3.7 Attitudinally, consumers no longer felt wealthy and their enthusiasm for further borrowing became muted.

Recession and associated unemployment levels

3.8 Consumer confidence was severely restricted when, a few years ago, unemployment passed the three million mark. A fear of unemployment prevents many people from making major purchases. This applies especially to the lower socio-economic groups who may be less likely to have adequate reserves, or who, being less skilled, may be less confident of their ability to secure new employment should they need to.

3.9 The Henley Centre suggests that high unemployment is a major motivation to strengthen personal balance sheets, which would in turn subdue credit growth.

Inflation

3.10 When inflation levels are low the consumer appeal of repaying the debt with 'tomorrow's devalued money' is lessened. But although this attitude towards the idea of credit may be less favourable, the dislike is restrained by the fact that the cost of servicing the debt is lowered as a result of falling interest rates.

3.11 It is worth mentioning here the attitude towards mortgage debt. Property purchases have for a long time been viewed as an investment, not as a debt. Despite the property crash in the late 1980s/early 1990s, this attitude is still prevalent. Home ownership in the UK is still highly regarded and very much part of the British consumer psyche.

Student Activity

1 Describe the common properties that all attitudes have.

2 List the factors that may affect the customer's attitude to borrowing.

Attitudes towards savings and investment

3.12 There has been little change in social attitudes towards wealth, either earned or unearned, since the 1980s. The words 'profit' and 'money' are now perfectly acceptable in most social circles.

3.13 The savings ratio increased over the course of the recession in the late 1980s and early 1990s, but this was principally to reduce debt, rather than because of the emergence of a new savings mentality. The Government's determination to make consumers accept greater responsibility for their own financial security (namely, the inducements for contracting out of SERPS and the reduction in sickness benefits) had the effect of raising awareness of financial schemes.

3.14 In 1993 the falling rates of interest paid on savings accounts prompted people to search for options with higher yields, and there was a rise in the interest shown in investment plans. Figure 4.2 illustrates this fall in personal-sector liquid assets against the rise in other areas, such as pensions and trusts. Consumers have also become increasingly financially aware as a result of the increase in media coverage of financial matters.

3.15 1996 and 1997 saw a large increase in the number of consumers becoming shareholders, and it is estimated that approximately £20 billion will be paid out in conversion/takeover 'windfalls'. This sudden increase in the personal wealth of the average consumer is expected to trigger an increase in savings and investments, as opposed to spending, and can only serve to further increase financial awareness amongst consumers.

Figure 4.2 Breakdown of financial assets for 1979 to 1996

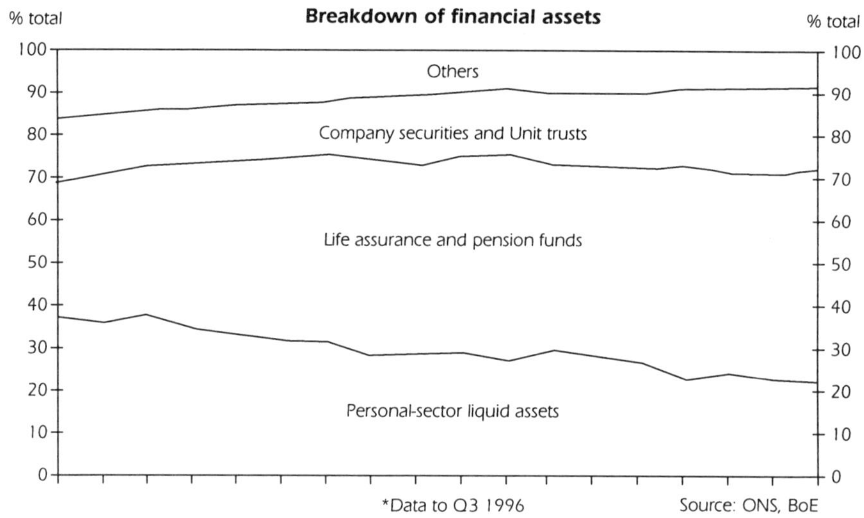

Student Activity

1 Describe the possible causes of the fall in personal-sector liquid assets that took place around 1993.

2 Many customers have received 'windfall' shares during 1996–97. What effect is this likely to have on their attitude to savings?

4 Market segmentation

4.1 There is no single way to segment a market, but according to Kotler (1991) segmentation should be

- measurable – there must be some way of measuring the size and purchasing power of the segment(s)
- accessible – the firm should be able to reach the segment(s)
- substantial – the segment(s) should be of a sufficient size and value to be profitable.

4.2 The traditional bases for segmentation have been classified as geographic, demographic, psychographic and behavioural. It is widely accepted that segmentation is the core to modern strategic marketing. The process comprises a number of stages, beginning with the identification and profiling of different market segments. This is followed by the selection of certain target markets and, finally, the positioning of the offering in the mind of the customer.

4.3 Segmentation bases then fall into two groups: 'general bases' (which are independent of a product or service and a specific circumstance faced by the customer), and 'situation specific bases' (related to both the customer and the product) (Frank, Massy and Wind, 1972). Additionally, the bases can be classified as 'observable' (able to be measured objectively) or 'unobservable' (they must be inferred). Frank *et al.*'s classification is shown in Figure 4.3.

Figure 4.3 Segmentation. Adapted from Frank *et al.* (1972).

	General	Product specific
Observable	Cultural, geographic, demographic and society economic variables	User status, usage frequency, brand loyalty, store loyalty and patronage, usage situation
Unobservable	Psychographics: personality and lifestyle	Psychographics, benefits, perceptions, attitudes, preferences and intentions.

4.4 This large number of bases does not necessarily mean that they apply to all markets, and organisations must decide the most appropriate basis on which to divide a particular market. However, there are a number of preferred bases that seem to offer better segmentation results for a number of marketing decisions; these are: benefits sought, needs and product usage patterns.

Possible segmentation

4.5 Financial services organisations have a great advantage over many other companies in that the very nature of their business entails holding large amounts of data about a customer. The data may also follow a customer through his life stages, if the customer maintains a relationship with the organisation.

4.6 Examples of data that can be gathered at the point at which the customer joins a financial organisation are

- age
- income level
- type of job
- home ownership
- family situation
- life/pension/unit trust holdings
- level of assets
- relationships with other suppliers.

4.7 Once a relationship with a customer is established it should be possible to track that customer's behaviour in dealing with the organisation (for example credit card spending, current account usage, deposits and withdrawals). It should also be possible to identify opportunities to promote and cross sell a targeted range of products and services to the customer.

4.8 This relationship, once established, is a key issue. Not only does it provide the ability to track behaviour, but it becomes possible to identify milestones in a customer's life stages for the promotion and selling of products such as mortgages, savings accounts, life cover and pension plans as the customer buys their first home, marries, raises a family and plans their retirement.

4.9 Possible segmented life stages are

- children
- younger singles
- independent adults
- young families
- better off established families
- high net worth older couples
- pensioners.

Depending upon the customer's personal circumstances at a particular time, each of these segments will require different financial products during one of these life stages.

4.10 A further possible segmentation is by attitude. Here a customer (or potential customer) is classified according to their attitude or behaviour when faced with a particular situation. Classifying customers into groups based on psychographic segmentation can help an organisation to develop a better understanding of a customer's desires, needs, anxieties and possible behaviour and therefore to enable the presentation of tailored offers to address these issues.

Student Activity

1 Describe the traditional bases for segmenting.

2 Why may retailers of financial services find themselves with an advantage when looking at market segmentation?

3 Describe the possible segmented life stages.

5 Possible targeting

5.1 Once market segmentation is decided, it is necessary to select the most appropriate method of targeting: how and where to find the segment and then, if it is a potential customer, how to recruit them.

5.2 Two possible methods are micro-targeting and global targeting.

Micro-targeting

5.3 Micro-targetting involves analysing and modelling the customer database and then allocating each customer a score, based on life stage, life style or behavioural modelling. These segmented customers are then sold to, using direct selling methods (telephone, mail or face-to-face sales people), and are offered carefully selected branded products. This method means that the organisation requires dedicated products delivered through a dedicated distribution system focused on a targeted customer. To support this, micro-targeting requires a support team who will deliver appropriate product messages to the customer on a one-to-one basis. This approach should engender a high level of credibility at the point of sale.

Global targeting

5.4 Global targeting involves building long-term customer relationships based on the complete brand image of the organisation, and from this, offering a wide range of unbranded products that are simple to understand and are delivered through multi-channel distribution. For successful delivery using this method, a high level of customer awareness must be achieved, which should be supported by either strong national or regional branch coverage.

5.5 When using global targeting it is less necessary to identify and segment customers, as the reliance is on the customer including the organisation in their list of providers to visit or contact when they are seeking a product or service. Using global targeting means that the organisation requires less investment in target marketing techniques, but more investment in overall brand image.

5.6 Because this method relies more heavily on the customer making the final decision, an organisation needs to ensure that the image it portrays is credible, and that the organisation is capable of delivering its promises.

5.7 The Halifax (formerly Halifax Building Society) has long used the global targeting approach. The marketing of the organisation has promoted its size, its professionalism, its approachability and accessibility (as demonstrated by advertisements featuring large numbers of people). The underlying intention of this type of marketing is to convince customers that the Halifax can be all things to all people over their lifetime. In fact the Halifax financial services division uses the strapline 'Partnership for Life' on its marketing literature in an effort to reinforce the message of the Halifax being a 'cradle to grave' provider.

5.8 Once an organisation has undertaken micro-targeting or global targeting, further work can be carried out to enable specific segmentation and targeting at local or branch level. Market information can be acquired on a branch-by-branch basis by looking at: geographical location, the customer base specific to the branch, and competitor positioning. An analysis of this information can then lead to more specific targeting at this level. For example, a branch may be based in a small town, with the customer base consisting of a large proportion of high net worth older couples with little competition. This would indicate that the potential exists for selling investments and pensions, and so lead an organisation to offer a financial planning service at that location.

5.9 With increasing competition within financial services retailing, many organisations who undertake global targeting, such as the Halifax, are now moving towards combining this with micro-targeting. This is because, with so many players in the market place, organisations can no longer rely on the customer to identify them as a particular product or service provider.

Student Activity

1 Explain what you understand by the terms: (a) micro-targeting, and (b) global targeting.

Summary

Underpinning all of the information discussed in this unit is the fact that financial services providers are still in the position of being unable to identify the 'trigger point' at which a customer is motivated to shop for and purchase a financial service product. Greater research is required to understand the customer behaviour and the factors that contribute to a customer's level of awareness, their decision to include a particular supplier on their list, the comparative shopping process involved and the actual buying decision.

Now that you have completed this unit, you should be able to do the following.

- ❑ **Describe the way in which customers behave when buying a service, in particular, a financial service.**
- ❑ **Describe customers' attitudes towards credit and debt, and explain the effect that these attitudes have on the retailing of credit and debt.**
- ❑ **Describe customers' attitudes towards savings and investments.**
- ❑ **Describe the segmentation of the financial services retailing industry at both a national and a local level.**

Self-assessment questions

1 Describe customers' behaviour when buying a financial service. Include the following in your description: the six features that distinguish services from goods and reference to a theoretical model that helps in the analysis of customer behaviour.

2 (a) Draw up a table showing the factors that influence customers to look favourably or unfavourably on credit/debit and savings and investment.

(b) How do customers' attitudes to credit/debit affect the retailing of it?

3 (a) Name the three criteria that any market segmentation should satisfy.

(b) Describe the segmentation of the financial services retailing industry at both a national and a local level.

Unit 5

Marketing planning for branches I

Objectives

After studying this unit, you should be able to:

- **understand the marketing planning process**
- **identify the steps in the planning process**
- **develop a branch marketing strategy.**

1 Marketing planning – the process

1.1 Marketing planning can be described as a sequence of activities which, when completed, will lead to the setting of marketing objectives and decisions about how they can be achieved. The marketing plan is therefore the blueprint for the allocation of marketing resources, identifying when and where they should be utilised and how they should be integrated to obtain maximum impact. The output of this process is known as the strategic marketing plan and is shown in Figure 5.1.

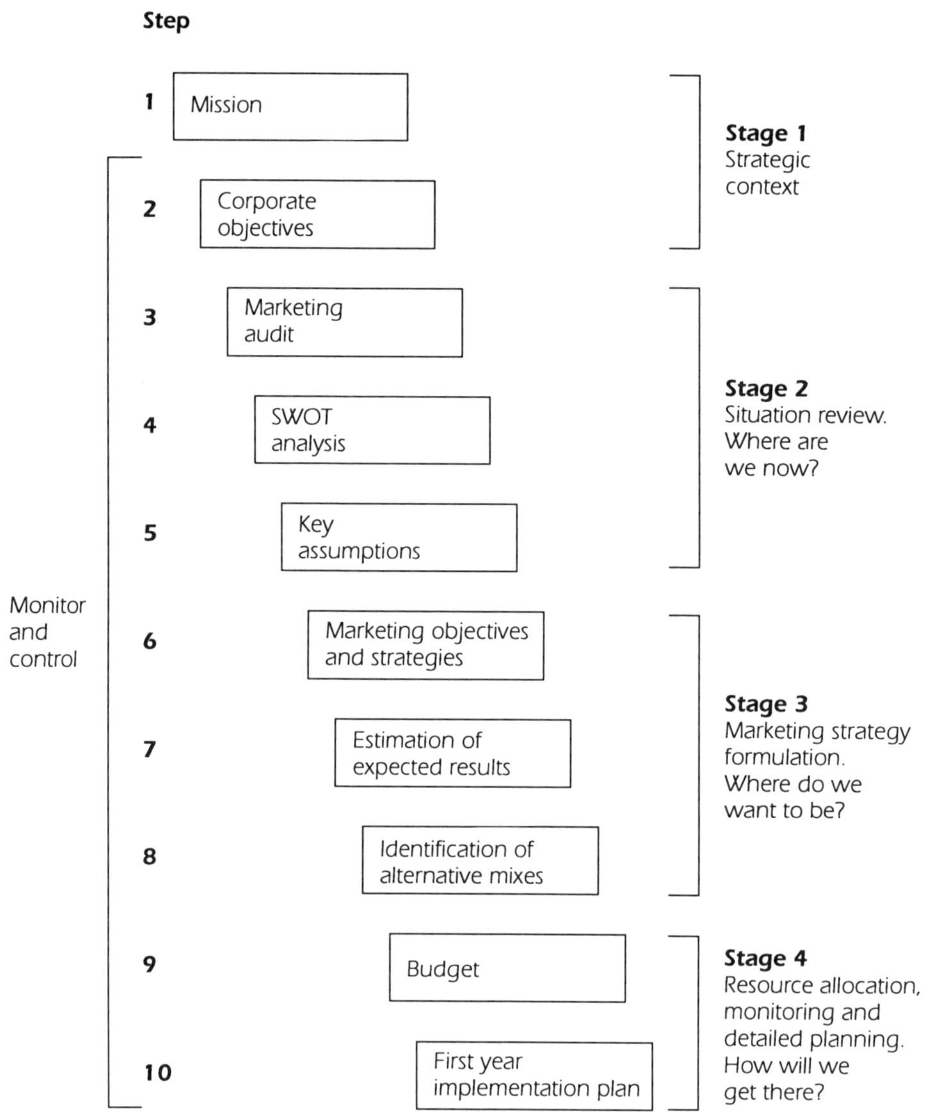

Figure 5.1 The strategic marketing planning process.

1.2 Marketing plans are an essential part of business in today's competitive environment. In the past the competitive environment was less volatile and complex than it is now and organisations prospered without paying detailed attention to the marketing planning process.

1.3 However, in periods of recession and high levels of competition, undertaking the marketing planning process can give an organisation focus and aid in dealing with external environmental factors. Research has shown that a marketing plan will ensure better coordination between activities and individuals whose actions are interrelated over time. Further, it instils a discipline within an organisation that results in:

- preparing an organisation to meet change
- improving communications between head office and branches
- reducing the conflicts that can arise when the direction of the organisation is unclear

- forcing management to think systematically and make forward plans
- the provision of a framework to continually review operations
- the balancing of corporate resources more effectively
- minimising non-rational responses to unexpected events
- increasing the opportunities to identify external developments.

1.4 Many smaller companies have failed due to their objectives being short-term and financially dominated. The marketing planning process should be considered over a reasonable time frame and should work within a strategic context. Many service organisations have a three-year or five-year planning period which is judged to be a balance between short-termism and planning so far into the future as to make plans meaningless. However, this will not be applicable for all services. For example, technology-based services will require shorter planning periods in order to keep pace with change, whereas energy utilities will probably use a longer planning period.

1.5 Setting a time frame in the first instance means that the emphasis is on a three-year or five-year marketing strategy and not on tactical plans, which are usually produced annually. It is important to recognise that both strategy and tactics are ways of achieving objectives. The difference between them is simply one of detail and depends upon the level from which you are looking. However, if there is no strategic plan, an organisation cannot function successfully on a one-year tactical plan. This is because tactics ('to do things right') originate from strategies ('doing the right things'), which involve the objectives an organisation must set for itself.

1.6 The ten steps indicated in Figure 5.1 will not all be followed at a branch level when the marketing plan is being formulated. This is because the mission statement and the corporate objectives will have been set by head office. However, without an understanding of what is contained in these two elements the planning at branch level cannot be carried out, as there would be no understanding of the strategic context of the organisation.

1.7 Before considering the four stages of the process we will look at each individual step and briefly explain what is involved with each one.

Step 1 – Mission

1.8 The mission statement is usually a general statement outlining the strategy of a business. It may include information on the scope of the business and the markets and products it does and does not wish to compete in. The growth direction of the business depends on the key assets and skills on which the business is based.

The mission statement should be relevant and realistic. Part of its role is also to provide employees, customers and stakeholders with a business definition which establishes the identity, corporate values and ethos of the organisation.

Step 2 – Corporate objectives

1.9 An objective is a statement of what the organisation intends to achieve and the corporate objectives are those which form the focus of the business as a whole. An objective should be specific, achievable and quantifiable. A corporate objective should outline the expectations of the organisation, and it is the goal of the strategic planning process to determine the method by which the objectives will be achieved. Typically, the corporate objectives will relate to financial factors which are key to business success, that is:

- profitability (return on investment)
- market share
- growth
- cash flow.

It is also sometimes stated that there can be a hierarchy of objectives and these are divided into primary objectives (restricted by certain constraints on corporate activity) and secondary objectives (strategic objectives which combine to achieve the overall corporate objective).

Step 3 – The marketing audit

1.10 The aim of the marketing audit is to gather together all the relevant information which can determine how well equipped the organisation is to compete in its chosen market place – at the present time as well as the future. Most of the information is gathered from external sources and looks at the economic and business environment as well as at competitors and market trend analysis. The current situation is analysed and the future trends are considered for their significance to the organisation. Internal sources will provide additional information to aid in the analysis process.

1.11 Care should be taken when carrying out marketing audits, as it is all too easy to become overwhelmed with the amounts of data available and the audit process should therefore be practical in its approach.

Step 4 – SWOT analysis

1.12 The SWOT (strengths, weaknesses, opportunities and threats) analysis is designed to identify key elements of marketing information which result from the marketing audit. The information is grouped under the four headings and this allows an organisation to understand the external environment factors (opportunities and threats) and balance them against internal factors (strengths and weaknesses). Once the information is set out like this a clearer picture of the way forward may be identified.

Step 5 – Key assumptions

1.13 In order for the marketing audit and the SWOT analysis to have any benefit an organisation must make some assumptions regarding the future. The assumptions (or, if you prefer, educated guesses) should be kept to a minimum and should be relevant to the planning period. Examples of assumptions to be made include:

- political climate
- legislation
- economic wellbeing of relevant markets
- competitors.

These should be put into black and white so that everyone understands how things may change over time and they should also identify areas which may need to be supported by contingency plans.

Step 6 – Marketing objectives and strategies

1.14 Once the SWOT analysis is completed and the key assumptions have been made, the output of these exercises should allow an organisation to set its marketing objectives and strategies. The marketing objectives should focus on the provision of services and products for the specified market and the strategies should focus on how this will be achieved.

		Service/Products	
		Existing	New
Markets	Existing	Market Penetration	Product/service Development
	New	Market Development	Diversification

Figure 5.2 The Ansoff matrix.

1.15 The Ansoff matrix shown in Figure 5.2 is a model which is commonly used to assist in making strategic decisions. The market penetration quadrant is the area with least risk and this is an area in which the company already operates. At the opposite end of the scale is the diversification quadrant. This represents operating in new markets with new services/products and would therefore carry a greater degree of risk.

1.16 The marketing objectives are then determined by these strategic decisions and provide the basis from which the organisation will operate.

Step 7 – Estimation of expected results

1.17 The direction and objectives set in the marketing strategies and objectives exercise can only be considered as being valid if, in pursuing them, they contribute to corporate objectives. This means that the financial outcome of undertaking the exercise must be weighed carefully. If, in doing this, it is calculated that the results would greatly exceed the corporate objectives, it may be that the corporate objectives require reviewing and should be set at a higher level. However, if the results would fall short of the corporate objectives, then the objectives and strategies may need to be re-appraised. As an alternative, Step 8 considers whether a different marketing strategy may assist in meeting the required objectives.

Step 8 – Identification of alternative mixes

1.18 At this stage the SWOT analysis and the key assumptions are re-assessed in order to identify whether there are any alternative models of the marketing objectives and strategies available. This is a useful exercise as it may yield alternatives which did not appear when the exercise was first undertaken, and you should always remember that the first solution is not necessarily the best one. This step also helps if the original mix is found to be incapable of achieving the corporate objectives. However, the level at which the corporate objectives have been set should only be reconsidered if a shortfall still exists after many permutations have been tried.

Step 9 – Budgets

1.19 No organisation has a limitless supply of funds and, therefore, once the marketing strategies and objectives have been achieved the budgets that will be required to meet the various programmes must be identified.

Step 10 – First-year detailed implementation plan

1.20 With a three-year or five-year strategic plan in place, the tactical plans (which are normally annual) can be developed. The aim of the tactical plan is to move the organisation towards achieving its strategic goals.

Monitoring and control

1.21 The ten-step plan is a system which can be used by any organisation in its planning process. One element that is not included, however, is the monitoring and control procedure for the whole plan. This is a task that should be undertaken on a continuous basis, thereby ensuring that things happen when they should and that any corrective action required can be implemented sooner rather than later.

Student Activity

Discuss with colleagues why it is important for companies to employ a strategic marketing plan.

2 Marketing planning – relationships and issues

2.1 Before we look at the ten steps in relation to producing a branch marketing plan it would be useful to discuss some of the issues which affect the marketing planning process and the relationship between marketing and corporate planning and the business functions of an organisation.

Relationships

2.2 By now it should be clear that planning and control will essentially be management tasks and that they are required at all levels of management. However, these tasks cannot be undertaken in a vacuum and although marketing planning is a relatively simple exercise to carry out on paper there must be an acceptance at all levels of an organisation before it can become a working system.

2.3 Initially, the planning process must be driven and supported by senior management if it is to be used as a process in an organisation. A system must be established so that all functions of an organisation – from branch level to head office – can provide data which can be input into the plan. All levels must also be aware of what it is they are expected to contribute. For example, senior management will input at the 'macro' level, but a contribution from a branch manager would be expected to be at a 'micro' level. This ensures not only that everyone is working together but that everyone is supplying data about their own field of knowledge.

2.4 Managers at regional area offices and branches have the responsibility of delivering the organisation's services on a daily basis. Therefore they have, even if they do not realise it, valuable and meaningful marketing information regarding customers and market trends. When seeking this input and knowledge it is important that the people responsible for coordinating the marketing planning process do not simply send out batches of questionnaires and forms for completion, the results of which are never seen. Managers should be trained not only in the concept of planning but also in the process used to achieve the final results. In doing this, managers will understand that marketing planning is an integral and important part of their role which will assist them in developing their own business strategies and plans.

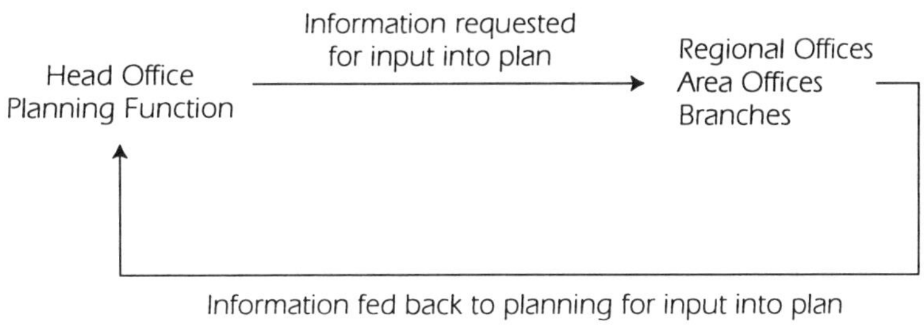

Figure 5.3 The relationship between head office and branches.

2.5 This method of gathering information from all levels of the distribution chain is sometimes known as 'bottom-up' planning. Once an understanding of what the process requires is achieved it can be very motivational to managers, since they feel they are contributing to the success and direction of their organisation. However, it should be remembered that this only applies if the information they have provided is valued and is seen to be used and that the completed strategic plan is seen by everyone.

Issues

2.6 If an organisation has not previously had a formalised planning process, implementing one will mean managing the behavioural and procedural issues that accompany such a move. Indeed, the first problem encountered may be a lack of acceptance, particularly at a senior management level. Employees quickly perceive which plans are fully supported by senior management and which issues are destined to be swallowed into corporate politics, never to reach a conclusion. Senior management will also be responsible for approving the allocation of resources and if this – which could be viewed as the basic sticking point – is initially restricted it is unlikely that any real progress will be made.

2.7 All the above will reflect the organisation's commitment, or lack of it, and will be instrumental in either implementing marketing planning successfully or sabotaging it before it reaches the starting gate.

2.8 Once the agreement and support is there, the next major task is to implement marketing planning. There will, in all probability, be a number of issues which need to be taken into account for this to happen.

- The concept must be communicated to all employees to give them an understanding of why it is taking place.
- Training must be provided to all the relevant people to provide them with an understanding of what is required of them.
- Adequate resources must be put in place to ensure the planning process can actually take place once it is implemented.
- The systems must be established to ensure that the ideas and information required can be fed into the planning function.
- It is probably wise to 'test run' the systems to ensure that any problems are ironed out prior to launch.
- Finally, the marketing planning process should be tailored to the organisation's needs.

2.9 All the above will take time to implement. However, by carefully preparing the introduction of marketing planning, an organisation is much more likely to have a successful implementation, and it should be accepted that the whole process may take some two to three years.

2.10 We have seen the importance of acceptance by senior management of marketing planning, but the support of line management is equally important. These are the people who will provide the planners with a great deal of the information that is required for input into the plan. Whether their 'buy in' to the process is achieved through training or by direct involvement in setting up the systems, allowing them to become advocates of the programme, failure to achieve their acceptance will severely hamper the success of any marketing planning function.

2.11 When starting any marketing planning programme it must be remembered that although the people involved in producing a plan will be well qualified in this area, the people from whom they require the information will probably not be. This means ensuring that all communications use terminology that is understood and accepted by everyone, avoiding terms such as 'models', 'matrices', 'positioning' and 'brand development' and using terms such as 'strategies', 'objectives' and 'key points'.

2.12 Leading on from terminology is the problem of asking managers to move away from quantitative information and into qualitative information. Managers in financial services are by the very nature of their roles highly numerate and percentages, return on investments, capital growth and expenditure are all part of everyday life, with much of their performance being judged against numerical targets. Marketing planning, however, is not driven by numbers only and any move towards this may encourage short-term thinking. A balance must be sought between quantity and quality and managers should be trained to make analyses based on key issues and assumptions regarding their business environment.

2.13 If a manager lacks the necessary skills to perform the qualitative analysis that would lead to the identification of key marketing issues, he may overreact and either identify problems that are not as severe as he perceives them to be or opportunities which are so numerous that an organisation would never be able to tackle them all. Multiply this problem by hundreds of managers and any key information will disappear under a mountain of paper, or the plan may become so complicated that it directs the organisation into trying to do many things and achieving nothing.

2.14 Each level of management must have a clear understanding of the depth of analysis it is expected to undertake. The information should then be fed upwards, with the planning function passing only key decision information to each level. In simple terms, this means that each level of management undertakes its own audit – SWOT analysis, assumptions, objectives, strategies and plans – with the information being relevant to its own operating environment and level of influence within the organisation. Undertaking these tasks, which are accepted as being time-consuming, should not be seen as a yearly ritual. A planning calendar should operate on a rolling basis and become an integral part of any manager's role.

Summary

2.15 You should now have an understanding of the benefits of marketing planning, the issues which may surround its production and the steps which need to be undertaken to produce a strategic marketing plan.

2.16 As shown in Figure 5.1, the ten steps are further divided into four stages. Stage 1 sets the strategic context and will usually be produced by head office not the business units. However, as illustrated in Figure 4.3, information is two-way and input should therefore have been sought by the planning department to enable the setting of realistic corporate objectives. When producing a marketing plan at branch level, stage 3, which involves the formulation of marketing objectives and strategies, should refer back to the corporate objectives and should support them, otherwise it is unlikely to gain approval.

Student Activity

Write about how the issues and relationships described above apply to your own organisation.

3 The branch marketing plan – the marketing audit

3.1 The corporate mission and corporate objectives (Stage 1 of the marketing planning process) having been decided by head office, each branch manager now conducts a situation review (Stage 2) to answer the question 'Where are we now?' The marketing audit provides the branch with an understanding of the environment within which it operates. The audit should be systematic and unbiased as it will provide the information which enables a manager to position his branch in a particular environment. It should provide the answer to the question 'Where are we now?' The marketing audit is not a plan in itself, however. Some of the information contained within it should appear in one final plan.

3.2 The audit should be carried out on a regular basis so that managers are able to recognise trends and identify problems which are fundamental to the branch. This will enable a manager to address problems, as opposed to merely responding to them.

3.3 The areas which should be covered in an audit are divided into internal and external ones. These are further sub-divided into five elements, as illustrated in Figure 4.4.

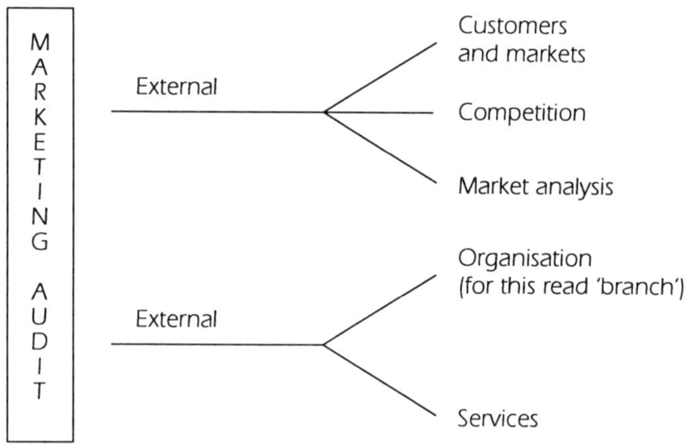

Figure 5.4 The elements of a marketing audit.

Customers and markets

3.4 As we have stated, the purpose of marketing planning is to help an organisation understand and exploit market opportunities, and the customer and market audit should focus on analysing trends, both positive and negative, in this area. The understanding gained from this will assist the organisation in selecting opportunities that will offer long-term success.

3.5 The audit should be based on factual information, not assumptions. One of the tools which can be used in this part of the audit is that of market segmentation. Although there are many ways of segmenting a market (some of which are discussed in more details in Unit 4), for the purposes of the audit we will segment under two broad headings: customer characteristics and customer responses. Simply put, this means finding out who our customers are and why they behave as they do. It is unlikely that, when developing a branch marketing plan, this information will be held on a database at branch level – it is more likely to be held on a central database at head office – but a manager should have an understanding of what customer characteristics and responses involve so that he is in a position to request this information to use in his audit, thereby ensuring an effective marketing planning process.

Customer characteristics

Geography

3.6 Segmentation based on geography is relatively simple and is often the first approach to be considered. In dividing customers by where they live or work it is possible to identify local or regional trends. This can also provide an indicator of population density, which in turn can be an indication for the possible use of communications media, e.g. local newspaper or radio advertisement opportunities. Geographical segmentation may also reveal supplementary information such as groupings of ethnic minorities or sites of industrialisation.

Demographics and socio-economics

3.7 Demographics refers to details such as gender, age, family size and occupation; socio-economic factors are details such as income, social class, religion and education. The purpose of producing customer groups in this way is to make judgements regarding the types of services and products that would appeal to the specific groups as well as their propensity to spend. It should also help a branch to understand trends and predict future demand. This exercise can also be carried out for businesses and here demographics refers to company size and structure and their SIC (Standard Industrial Classification type) code.

Psychographics

3.8 This is a more detailed and developed method of segmenting and is concerned with understanding customers' lifestyles and behaviour. Its purpose is to develop more meaningful segmentation bases than demographics or socio-economics by understanding more about the customers' attitudes, motivations and aspirations.

Customer responses

3.9 Here we are looking at what a customer may purchase and why. At least one of these categories should be combined with one or more of the customer characteristics to enable a complete profile to be built up. There are a number of customer responses to be considered as follows.

Usage

3.10 Customers can be divided into non-users, low, medium and heavy users of a product or service. By studying the pattern of, for example, branch visits to make transactions, a manager can devise strategies to encourage low users to visit branches more frequently, thereby providing opportunities for the staff to make cross sales, as well as to reinforce relationships with heavy users.

Benefit

3.11 This is the reason why a customer buys a product. Benefits can be divided into a number of basic needs, of which the following are a few:

- the realisation of ambitions and dreams (personal loans)

- protection and security (life assurance, pensions)
- an easier life (credit cards)
- saving for the future (savings accounts).

By identifying the segments that have a common benefit, offers can be tailored to meet those needs.

Service

3.12 This looks at the services surrounding a product and measures the importance that different customer groups attach to the individual elements. For example, one group may prefer to deal with sales staff but another group may prefer to use ATMs. By gaining a detailed understanding of the value customers place on the service elements, a branch can ensure its service provision matches customer needs.

Loyalty

3.13 It is possible to segment customers by their degree of loyalty:

- hard core loyals (who purchase from the company all the time)
- fence-sitters (who shift between two companies)
- switchers (who demonstrate little loyalty to any company).

3.14 If this type of segmentation is to be used, the organisation must understand the underlying reasons for customers' behaviour and should never make the assumption that loyalty equals satisfaction. Quite often, the fact that a customer purchases from one organisation continuously is due to apathy on his part. This is particularly relevant in financial services where approximately 70 percent of customers remain with the same bank throughout their lives.

The segmentation process

3.15 The next step in the customers and markets audit is to gather together the information and establish the segmentation to be used. In market segmentation, the market is sub-divided into distinct groups of customers; each such group constitutes a target market and may require its own specific marketing mix. The end result of this should provide both a qualitative and quantitative idea of the branch's position in relation to each of the following: size, future prospects, competitive environment and current position. This should then identify the branch's competitive position and what steps it may need to take to adapt to any market changes. The segmentation process suggested is as follows.

Define the market

3.16 This means specifying the customer groups to which a branch would wish to market its products. The mission statement should give some indication of where the organisation sees itself.

Identify alternative bases for segmentation

3.17 If a number of markets are being addressed then these will be accompanied by differing segmentation. Much of this information will probably come from head office.

Select the method of segmentation which will give the branch a distinctive advantage

3.18 This involves evaluating and then prioritising the various segmentation bases to identify the best approach.

Identify individual market segments and assess their attractiveness

3.19 This takes an individual segment (as identified above) and matches a specific offering to it. The segments should be clearly separate from each other and be profitable enough to justify any investment the organisation will make to market to them. A branch should not attempt to take too many segments at once as this can have the effect of trying to be all things to all people and not achieving a distinctive competency in any segment.

Competition

3.20 The first step in competitor analysis is to identify the competitors. It is a good idea to group them, as this allows identification by strengths and weaknesses and enables a manager to better assess direct competition and may highlight competitors not previously considered. SWOT analysis may usefully be applied to our competitors as well as ourselves.

3.21 There are a number of approaches that can be used in this analysis. The first is customer-based and considers customer choice, i.e. the set of competitors from which customers make their selection when purchasing a product. The second approach involves product-use associations. This relates to competitors whose products can be used in the same use situation, e.g. mortgage providers. Alternatively the competition could be identified by strategic groups. Here a manager would look at competitors who pursue similar strategies and have similar assets and propositions.

3.22 To understand competitors it is useful to be able to analyse them on the basis of several factors. Their size (in terms of branches and staff), growth and profitability will all provide a measure of their importance. Their image, positioning and communication strategy will provide strategic insights.

3.23 To further support this, an analysis of objectives and of previous and current strategies can provide insight into a competitor's intentions and ambitions. The type of information being sought is usually available from a number of sources. Competitors will regularly communicate with suppliers, customers, shareholders and government bodies and even with competitor companies, so contact with any of these can provide information. A further source can be trade journals and shows, annual reports, seminars, speeches and advertising.

3.24 If more detailed information is required regarding customers' perceptions of competitors then market research can always be commissioned. Questions can then be asked regarding choice, service quality, accessibility, etc.

However, this route of information-gathering is more likely to be commissioned at head office and not by a branch. In carrying out the competitor audit thoroughly the branch can be proactive in future plans rather than being reactive to the competition.

Market and environmental analysis

3.25 Initially it seems a daunting task to scan the external environment for relevant information. However, if the audit is carried out in a pragmatic way and looks at the dimensions which directly affect the business it is a relatively simple task, though time-consuming.

Actual and potential market size

3.26 The potential market size includes any gaps which can be penetrated through increases in user frequency (more visits to the branch), a greater variety of uses (a visa card and cheque book account), new users (student accounts) and new uses (purchasing travel money and insurance).

Market growth

3.27 Forecasting growth patterns can help in understanding the outside forces which drive sales, highlight indicators which may put pressure on prices and show the existence of substitute products.

Market profitability

3.28 It is stated that the competitive intensity of any market will depend on five factors. These are:

- existing competitors
- supplier power
- customer power
- substitute products
- new entrants.

This is based on Porter's model (Figure 5.5) and a detailed analysis of these five forces can provide an understanding of the prospect of future profitability.

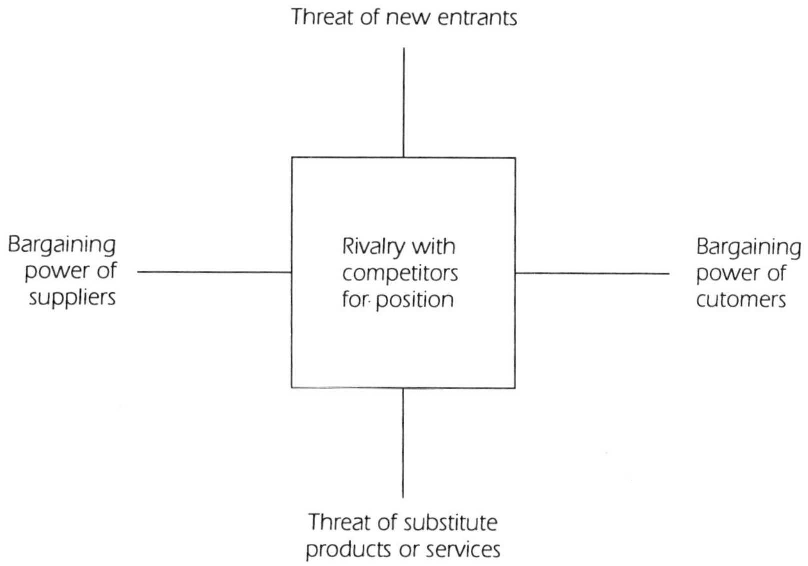

Figure 5.5 Five forces (from M. E. Porter, *Competitive Strategy*)

3.29 Barriers to market entry should also be considered and these may include: capital investment, access to distribution channels, product differentiation and economies of scale.

Distribution systems

3.30 New trends in distribution channels should be identified and their relative importance analysed.

Market trends

3.31 Trends in the marketplace will affect the future profitability of the branch.

Key success factors

3.32 Skills and assets are required to compete with the identified strategic group, not only at the present time but also in the future.

PEST

3.33 This part of the audit should also look at some of the PEST (political, economic, social, legal) factors which may affect the business. It should take into account possible changes in government fiscal policy and legislation, consider implications from tax changes, etc. It should never be assumed that changes will affect all competitors equally, as this will not be the case and to assume this can only lead to the competitors becoming market leaders.

Service audit

3.34 A company possesses a great deal of knowledge about the services and products it is offering. Sometimes this means that an objective view is not always taken, but to carry out the audit successfully a manager must be as critical about the internal environment as he was about the external environment.

3.35 For the purposes of the branch marketing planning we will focus this part of the audit on service provision and not on the products. The reasoning behind this is that while the theory is the same for both, the branch manager is unlikely to be in a position to influence product strategy, other than feeding back information in the corporate planning round.

3.36 Many organisations offer more than one service. For example, a bank may offer a counter service, a mortgage advice service and share dealing. Each service is open to competition and as services become easier to duplicate, particularly financial services, many former service monopolies, e.g. telephone banking, are now subject to competition from either new entrants or from the diversification of existing competitors.

3.37 It is recognised that if an organisation can identify and offer a differential advantage (DA) then it will have an edge on its competitors. One of the major purposes of the service audit is to analyse the relative strengths and weaknesses of the organisation's range of services in comparison with its competitors.

3.38 One method of analysis is to benchmark the features of the service being offered against the competition. It then becomes clear if the performance is better or worse than the competitors. This can also be carried out at a market segment level, as not all features will be relevant to all markets.

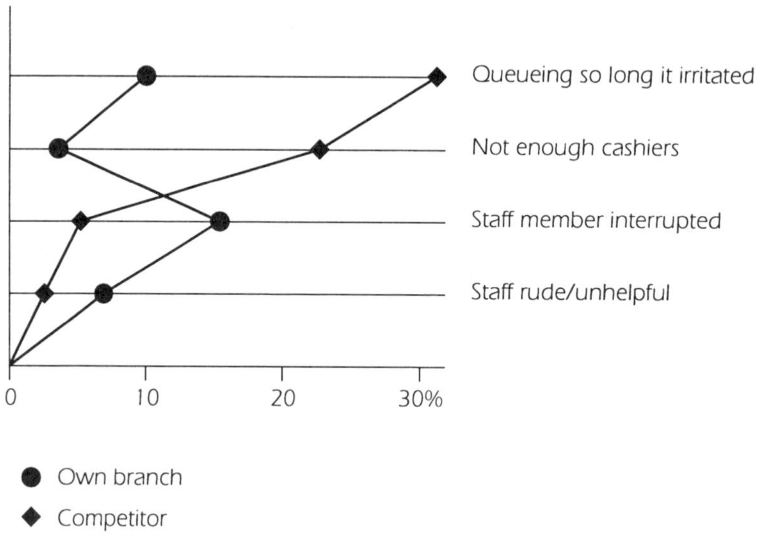

Figure 5.6 Comparative analysis.

3.39 The example in Figure 5.6 gives a clear indication that the competitor has a much slower service but that customers felt the staff were much more helpful. The aim should therefore be to improve the staff performance to at least that of the competitor.

Positioning

3.40 There are two further analyses that should be carried out in the marketing audit: positioning and life cycles. Once again, these are areas that a manager should be aware of when producing a branch marketing plan, although they will probably be determined by head office. However, there is value in being able to understand and make use of the models associated with these analyses.

3.41 Positioning should be considered at a number of levels:

- industry positioning – customer perception of the industry as a whole
- organisational positioning – positioning of an organisation as a whole
- product sector positioning – positioning of a range of services and products offered
- individual service of product positioning – positioning of a specific service.

3.42 Most organisations will require positioning at more than one level, so there needs to be some integration. A watch should be kept on what competitors are doing in terms of positioning, as any changes in their positioning strategy may require a response. Figure 5.7 shows how a bank may position itself. The problem for banks is that one bank is very much like another and trying to find a differentiated positioning is a complex problem. In recent years many of the major financial services companies have committed expenditure to corporate advertising campaigns in an effort to position the organisation in the mind of the customer.

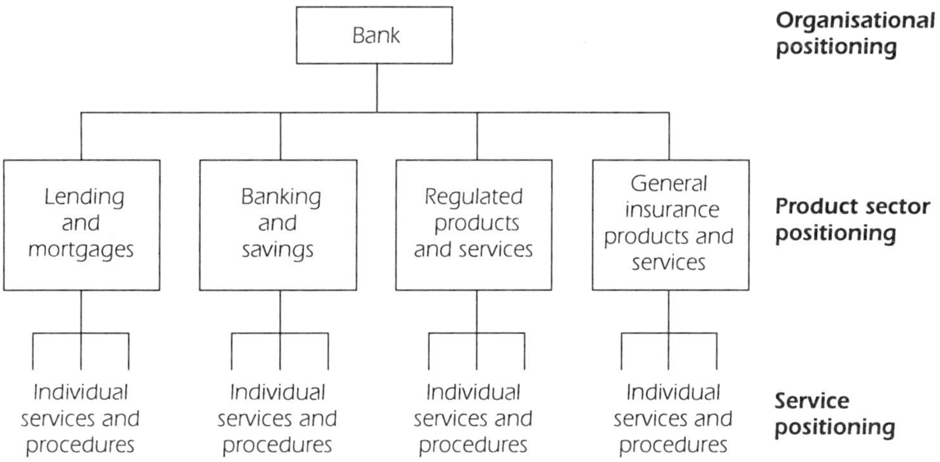

Figure 5.7 Possible positioning of a banking organisation.

3.43 The actual process of positioning can be divided into five phases.

Phase 1 – Ascertaining level(s) of positioning

3.44 This should be consistent with the organisation's strategy within each market segment.

Phase 2 – Identifying the key attributes which impact on the selected segments

3.45 The key underlying this step is how the purchasing decision is made. This would normally be identified through research, to establish what customers perceive to be the difference between competitors. This is an important factor, as a customer's perception of the most important attribute may not be the same as the organisation's. For example, the decision to buy a pension may have more to do with the behaviour of the sales person than how the pension fund performs.

3.46 There are a number of specialised techniques available to market research to identify key attributes. Most of these are computer-based and include: multiple correlation and regression analysis, factor analysis, discriminate function analysis and perceptual mapping.

Phase 3 – Locating attributes on a positioning map

3.47 A positioning map has two dimensions in which each axis represents an attribute. On to this map an organisation's own services are plotted alongside those of competitors. For accurate plotting the axis must have suitable graduated scales and the maps can be based on either subjective or objective attributes, or a combination of the two. Several maps may be required to consider the positioning accurately if a complex service or product is being considered, but the variables which are recognised as having the greatest influence on the purchase decision are those upon which the focus should lie.

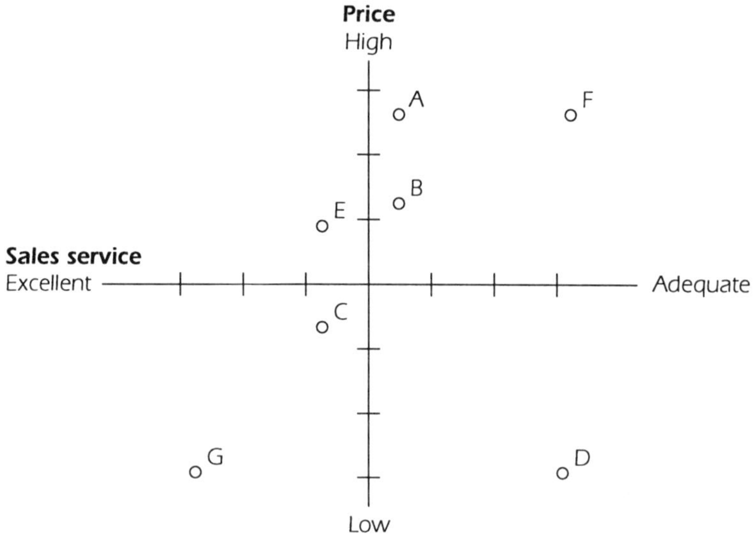

Figure 5.8 An example of a positioning map.

Phase 4 – Evaluating alternative positioning options

3.48 There are three broad options which can be considered. First, an organisation can strengthen its current position. This avoids direct confrontation with competitors and relies on consolidating the core strengths of the organisation. Alternatively, an organisation could identify an unoccupied position on the map and then look to fill it. The last option is to reposition the competition. This involves checking the customers' perception of competitors. However, this is not without risk, as care needs to be taken not to 'run down' the competitors. Whichever positioning statement is finally selected the following guidelines are worth considering: the positioning should be meaningful, believable and unique.

Phase 5 – Implementing the positioning strategy

3.49 Positioning strategies may have a limited life span and should be evaluated periodically to ensure that they still adhere to the criteria discussed above. Once the strategy has been decided it should be put into effect in relation to the target customers. Then the organisation and its staff have the responsibility of ensuring that all their actions – customer-staff interaction, image, policies etc. – reflect the positioning strategy chosen.

Life cycles

3.50 Life cycles are a further tool which can be used in the audit process. As with all other models and tools they are designed to assist the decision-making process and are not stand-alone decision-makers. The life cycle can be used to determine the position of both services and products and its use in product management is detailed in Unit 9. The basis of the life cycle is that it acts as a tracker to position a service or product during its lifetime in the marketplace, working on the theory that exponential growth will occur until a natural limiting factor is reached which will then cause growth to slow down and eventually decline (see Figure 5.9).

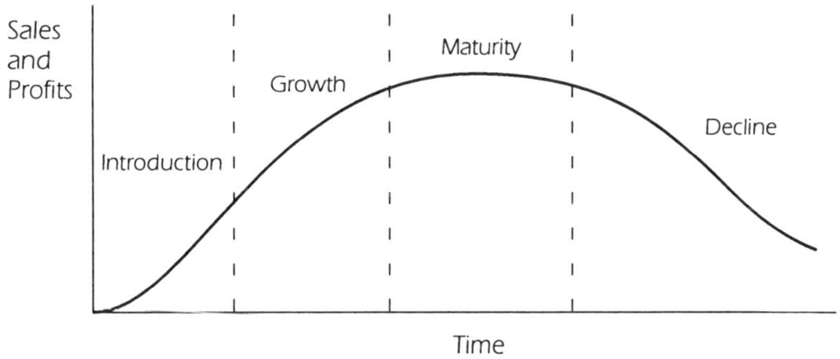

Figure 5.9 A life cycle curve.

Introduction	The growth is upward but slow as the service is positioned and accepted in the market.
Growth	If the service is successful it will now begin its growth period as more customers buy and early customers make repeat purchases. Successful growth will also attract the competition, which may enter the market at this stage.
Maturity	The rapid growth begins to slow down as the market reaches capacity. Sales level out and there are now too many firms competing for too little business.
Decline	The market falls into decline. Price wars may occur and competitors may make tactical withdrawals from the market.

3.51 This traditional curve will not always occur in a life cycle. Some services may not reach a maturity stage and go straight from growth to decline, while others go into decline only to experience a second growth period. Other services appear to stay in the maturity stage. Financial markets provide a good example of competitors quickly entering the market with 'me too' products, which usually results in competition being built up well in advance of demand – simply consider the number of pension providers in the marketplace. The life cycle should probably be treated as a descriptive tool rather than a predictive tool.

Organisation (or branch) audit

3.52 The purpose of this audit is to focus on aspects of branch performance which have a positive or negative effect on business performance. It relies upon asking a series of questions about skills, resources, systems and procedures. Listed below are some of the questions which can be asked, although this list is by no means exhaustive and the aim should be to ensure that all relevant issues are evaluated.

- What skills does the branch have?
- What essential skills are lacking or under-represented?
- At what level is there an essential skills shortage?
- What will happen if the skills shortage is not addressed?
- How does the branch compare with competitors?
- Do we have the right type of working environment?
- Are we under-resourced?
- Are any areas over-resourced?
- Can we switch resources between roles?
- How is one service delivered?
- How are complaints and queries handled?
- How are sales leads generated?
- Do we follow up sales leads?
- How are referrals across the services managed?

Conclusions of the marketing audit

3.53 The areas outlined above are the basis of a marketing audit and should answer the question 'Where are we now?' To answer some of the questions external researchers may be required and in some cases the unbiased view they bring will be of a high quality and pertinent to the exercise. If the audit is to be undertaken internally then guidelines should be issued, not only to ensure a consistent approach but also to help managers through what can appear to be a daunting task. Each organisation will need to develop its own guidelines and checklists which will be appropriate to their own market.

Student Activity

Plan how you would begin to tackle a marketing audit at your branch.

4 The branch marketing plan – the SWOT analysis

4.1 Having completed the audit the information is now available to enable the SWOT analysis to go ahead and this is what will appear in the strategic marketing plan. It is worth mentioning at this point that some people believe that this should actually be a TOWS analysis – i.e. threats, opportunities, strengths and weaknesses – as this initially focuses on external elements and then matches internal capabilities that are available to address them. This route also quickly shows if there are any gaps within the organisation, leaving it unable to react to external events (both threats and opportunities).

4.2 The analysis should be as concise as possible and focus only on key factors. It is also worthwhile including a summary of the reasons for both good and poor performance. The traditional way of presenting a SWOT analysis is shown in Figure 5.10. However, many variations and improvements have been made on this basic model and Table 5.1 illustrates a SWOT analysis which highlights the implications of each element plus possible actions to be taken.

4.3 SWOT analyses should be undertaken at various levels and managers should complete them in a manncr relevant to the scope of their own role and responsibilities. To get the most from a SWOT analysis the elements identified should be ranked in order of significance and quantified against a criterion which is based on a broader knowledge of the business and the markcts it operates in.

Strengths	**Weaknesses**
• ______	• ______
• ______	• ______
• ______	• ______
• ______	• ______
Opportunities	**Threats**
• ______	• ______
• ______	• ______
• ______	• ______
• ______	• ______

Figure 5.10 Traditional SWOT analysis.

Element	*Implications*	*Possible Actions*
Strength		
• Highly qualified staff	• Professionalism and customer reassurance	• Recognise and reward top achievers • Career programme • Ongoing training programmes
Weakness		
• Poor branch coverage by financial advisers	• Lack of service to customers • Staff demotivation	• Increase number of advisers • Plan diaries more efficiently
Opportunities		
• Move away from state provisions	• Increased sales opportunities	• Increase staff awareness for lead generation • Increase presence of maketing literature in banking hall
Threats		
• Entry of direct services (e.g. Virgin)	• Loss of sales	• Sell face-to-face service • Position, qualifications and professionalism of sales staff

Table 5.1 Extension of the traditional SWOT analysis.

5 The branch marketing plan – key assumptions

5.1 In all plans some assumptions will need to be made, as these will help establish a basis for the setting of objectives and strategy. It is important to state assumptions explicitly so that they are not ignored and to emphasise that they are assumptions and not facts. This also makes it possible to monitor them and check that they are still valid, as contingency plans should be developed to deal with them if they become invalid.

5.2 The purpose of the assumptions is to identify factors that will be critical to the success or failure of the strategic marketing plan. They should be considered in terms of how they will impact upon the branch or on each market segment. Key assumptions may include:

- growth of the economy
- interest rates
- inflation rates
- changes in legislation
- changes in taxation.

5.3 Once the assumptions are identified it is important to consider implications for and impact on the marketing plan. Key assumptions should be few in number. A good measure of the usefulness of an assumption is that if the marketing plan is achievable regardless of the assumption, then it is unnecessary.

5.4 Stage 2 is now complete. It has provided an up-to-date situation review and should have focused the mind. The audit stage is the most time-consuming and although consultants can be retained to carry this out it is wise to involve managers in order to generate understanding and commitment. At branch level the manager, given the right guidance, is best placed, with the help of his management team, to carry out this task himself. The information from the audit is focused at the SWOT stage and the key factors identified are put into context by considering them with the key assumptions. The next stage is to take the information from Stage 2 and begin the formulation process.

Student Activity

Discuss the importance of Stage 2 ('Where are we now?') in the marketing planning process.

6 The branch marketing plan – marketing objectives and strategies

6.1 We are now ready to begin formulation of a marketing strategy (Stage 3) and must answer the question 'Where do we want to be?' The first thing to be clear on is the difference between objectives and strategies. Marketing objectives are precise statements which outline what will be achieved by the marketing activities. Marketing strategies are the means by which objectives are achieved. The purpose of setting marketing objectives is to target the return on investment, market share, growth and cash flow which is set out in the corporate objectives. This in turn provides guidance for the strategies and allows a marketing mix to be formulated to meet the objectives set for each segment.

Marketing objectives

6.2 In the branch marketing plan we are concerned with setting unit objectives, which are also sometimes known as operational objectives, and are specific to the branch environment. A logical approach to setting the objectives would be to:

- set broad marketing objectives – these would be in relation to longer-term profitability and would support corporate objectives
- set objectives for key result areas – these objectives are more precisely defined
- set sub-objectives – objectives which are set at the basic level and are concerned with sales volumes, service extension, etc.

6.3 It is best to limit objectives to two or three, as this ensures that the plan does not try to achieve everything all at once. Objectives can also be long-term and short-term. When setting a marketing objective it should meet the following SMART criteria:

- Specific
- Measurable
- Achievable
- Relevant
- Timely.

6.4 If objectives are set in the way we have discussed it is clear that there are actually only four courses of action:

- to sell existing services to existing markets (market penetration)
- to extend existing services into new markets (market development)
- to develop new services for existing markets (product/service development)
- to develop new services for new markets (diversification).

The easiest way to illustrate this is by using the Ansoff matrix in Figure 5.2.

6.5 The marketing audit and SWOT analysis will have provided the information regarding buyer behaviour, competition, which market segments are attractive, etc., and the interpretation of this information should make it possible to set objectives for all the service/market combinations. The end result should provide the total sales revenue to meet corporate objectives.

Gap analysis

6.6 Another more analytical tool that can be used is the Gap analysis. This is an assessment of the difference between:

- the organisation's targets for achievement over the given planning period
- what the organisation would expect to achieve if it did nothing and proceeded with 'business as usual'.

If there is a difference between the targets and the expected achievements, this is known as the Gap. New strategies will need to be developed if an organisation wants to meet its targets in the planning period.

This method of analysis can be applied to many areas: profit forecasting, human resources, sales, performance risk or whatever Gap is being measured between the current position and targets for a planning period. The analysis we will use as an illustration is based on sales revenue (see Figure 5.11).

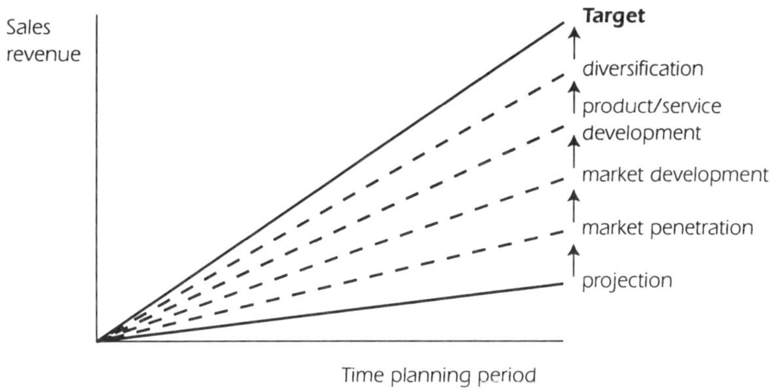

Figure 5.11 Sales revenue Gap analysis.

6.7 Each of the options available to close the GAP must be carefully considered to identify its potential in achieving this. The first option to consider should be market penetration as this draws upon the current strengths of the organisation and carries the least risk. For example, the manager could look at:

- generating higher sales through a more effective sales force
- reducing costs
- improving customer service to achieve higher levels of customer satisfaction
- changing branch advertising to promote a wider range of products.

In using the Gap analysis and the Ansoff matrix the manager can focus on the marketing objectives and calculate if they will achieve the corporate objectives.

6.8 A manager may find it difficult to distinguish between the corporate strategy and the marketing strategy. Two guidelines to assist in separating them are as follows.

- Corporate strategy involves decisions and direction for all the functions of an organisation.
- Marketing strategy incorporates decisions relating to the positioning of the marketing mix to exploit and develop service/market opportunities.

6.9 In establishing the Gap which needs to be filled the next step is to consider the alternative strategies available to fill that Gap. It is an important part of the planning process that the alternatives are carefully evaluated.

Choice of competitive strategy

6.10 Michael Porter states that an organisation should adopt a competitive strategy which aims to achieve some form of competitive advantage. This type of strategy is defined as 'taking offensive or defensive actions to create a defensible position in an industry, to cope successfully with ... competitive forces and thereby yield a superior return on investment for the organisation. Organisations have discovered many different approaches to this and the best strategy for a given organisation is ultimately a unique construction reflecting its particular circumstances' (Porter, *Competitive Strategy*).

6.11 Competitive strategies are mainly based on product-market strategies and fall into three broad categories:

- overall cost leadership
- differentiation
- focus, e.g. segmentation.

6.12 The type of strategy adopted will usually depend on competitor strategies and will have implications for product design, pricing, quality and marketing. It will also depend on the types of products or services an organisation produces and these can be identified under three categories.

- Search products

Products which can be easily evaluated and compared by the customer and are easily assessed in the purchase decision, e.g. cars, clothing, household goods.

- Experience products

Products whose attributes cannot be evaluated until the consumer has had some experience of them, e.g. counter service in a branch, ATMs.

- Credence products

Products whose attributes cannot easily be evaluated by the consumer, even if they have been purchased previously, e.g. financial advice, life assurance, PEPs. The consumer must therefore show faith or credence in the product.

6.13 The primary strategy of interest in the branch marketing plan is that of differentiation but it is useful to note the definition of the two alternative strategies first.

Cost leadership

6.14 A cost leadership strategy seeks to achieve the lowest-cost products in the industry. In producing at the lowest cost the manufacturer can compete on price with every other producer in the industry and earn the highest unit profits. A good example of a company using this strategy is Virgin, who attempt to apply it in whatever they sell, from airline tickets to PEPs and pension sales.

Focus strategy

6.15 Focus strategy is where an organisation concentrates its attention on one or more particular segments or niches of the market and does not seek to serve an entire market with a single product. This strategy is based on segmenting the market and can be further divided into cost-focus strategy and differentiation strategy.

Differentiation strategy

6.16 The aim of the differentiation strategy is to raise the quality of the product and also the product's cost and sales price. These improvements in quality should be of more value to the customer than the price increase, the end result being that the customer is willing to pay more for superior quality; therefore there is perceived added value.

6.17 There is a balance to achieve between quality (quality here refers to desirable attributes, including customer service) and price as there will be a trade-off by the customer between the two, and an organisation will need to build this concept into its differentiation strategy.

6.18 The differentiation strategy is based upon the assumption that competitive advantage can be achieved through certain characteristics of the organisation's products, which can be categorised as:

- breakthrough products, which offer radical performance advantages over competitors, much lower prices or ideally both
- improved products, which are not usually very different to competitors but are superior in performance at a competitive price.
- competitive products which demonstrate no obvious advantage but derive appeal from a particular compromise of cost and performance.

6.19 If a successful differentiation strategy is achieved, loyalty to an organisation will soon develop and because the customer will not always be price sensitive the organisation can sell its products at a price which is higher than the least-cost competitors. The major risk with this strategy is that customers will not pay higher prices for the different products and this is particularly true in times of recession when price sensitivity will probably increase.

6.20 The organisation must continually innovate to stay ahead of rivals and consequently differentiation strategies will probably carry large development or promotional budgets. As customers become more financially aware they are more likely to shop around for products based on price, e.g. lower mortgage rates, better interest rates on savings accounts. However, financial organisations also operate in a 'me too' environment where it is very difficult to have any sustainable advantage from a product range. Therefore differentiation of the services provided to customers is possibly one of the few ways left for an organisation to both recruit and retain customers.

Student Activity

Discuss how you might put Step 6 of the strategic marketing planning process into practice in your own branch.

7 The branch marketing plan – estimation of expected results

7.1 Having determined a possible strategy, it is important to know if it will achieve the required objectives and this forms the next part of Stage 3 (see Figure 5.1). The financial implications must therefore be evaluated and this requires a review of:

- the projected sales revenue
- the cost of marketing
- the cost of sales
- operating expenses
- overhead expenses.

7.2 If the anticipated financial results are not achieved once the analysis is complete, the strategies must be re-examined with a view to developing or redefining them, in order to achieve the required targets. In most cases it is best to undertake three analyses: a worst-case scenario, a best-case scenario and a conservative estimate. This enables the identification of a possible range of results and indicates the margin of error that would be acceptable. Forecasting is never an easy task, but there are a number of techniques that can be used to assist in this, such as extrapolation, regression analysis, test marketing and consumer surveys, and the results will contribute to identifying demand patterns. These methods should be supported by qualitative information which can quite often be found internally from the knowledge and experience of managers in the business.

8 The branch marketing plan – identification of alternative mixes

8.1 The marketing mix decisions are an important part of the strategic plans and each element of the mix will become a plan at a tactical level. The end result of each plan for each element is that it should support the stated objectives and be consistent with the strategic direction identified. The marketing mix may well evolve as it will be affected by environmental changes. However, it should always be customer-focused and the allocation of resources to the mix should ensure that there is a maximum return on outlay.

8.2 Many managers find it simplest to categorise the marketing mix under the seven Ps.

- **Product:** the success of a product will be improved if it has distinguishing characteristics and features.
- **Price:** this requires consideration in line with demand.
- **Place:** an organisation must ensure that its services are available in a place where customers would want to have access to them.
- **Promotion:** this relates to the total communication by an organisation to its customers, both existing and potential.
- **People:** this reflects the importance of the perceived service quality provided by an organisation's staff.
- **Process:** this should establish that the process a customer undertakes when purchasing a product is efficient and friendly.
- **Physical evidence:** this refers to the branding and the service outlets used by the customers.

8.3 The branch marketing plan is made up of decisions relating to each of the elements of the mix, and its content will be decided using judgment based on the audit and the analysis steps undertaken. The ideal marketing mix should have a balance between each of these elements and too much emphasis should not be placed on one individual element, as this will usually result in the allocation of resources being disproportionate to the results. Each product or service sold will have its own optimum balance of the seven Ps so the identification of alternative mixes will require analysis of each of the seven in relation to the product/service concerned.

Product

8.4 The product, in the case of the branch marketing plan, consists of the services delivered to the customer through the branch outlet and for simplicity we will now substitute the word 'service' for 'product'.

8.5 Due to the intangibility of financial services products (see Unit 4), the service is what the customer is purchasing and is therefore the central focus of marketing activity. For this reason it is important to consider the service from the customers' point of view. In the view of customers the purchase of a service solves a problem: for example, using an ATM means that they do not have to visit the branch during opening hours. They will therefore select the most appropriate service for their perceived needs.

8.6 Service planning will often be about more than a single service but rather about the complete range of services on offer. It will require decisions about:

- the types of service
- the timing of services
- the volume of service.

A manager should try to have a balanced portfolio of the services on offer to meet the customers' needs. For example, there would be a balance between cashiers, customer service representatives, financial planning advisors, etc., to meet customer demand at various times throughout the day. Typical strategic choices for the services could be between:

- expanding the number of services available
- a change in the features of a service
- a reduction in the number of services
- ensuring standardisation of services
- changing the mix of services
- changing the positioning of services.

Price

8.7 Prices must be competitive but consistent with the corporate image and high enough to cover costs and maximise demand. A product will not sell unless the customer is prepared to buy. This statement highlights the following points.

- Pricing should be consistent with making the required profits at the expected level of demand.
- There should be a suitable balance between price and quality.
- Prices should be reviewed with regard to the product's positioning in the life cycle.
- Pricing should be consistent when set against the organisation's criteria.

8.8 Branch managers will have some discretion on the pricing of items – for example, loan rates (particularly for corporate customers) and overdraft fees. There are a number of influences that will reflect on a pricing strategy. These are: elasticity of demand, costs and competition.

Elasticity of demand

8.9 There is a relationship between price and demand, as demand will vary at different price levels. A manager should understand whether he is facing a position of elastic demand – a percentage change in price produces a greater percentage change in demand – or inelastic demand – a significant percentage change in price produces little or no change in demand.

$$\text{Price elasticity is measure as } \frac{\text{Percentage change in sales demand}}{\text{Percentage change in sales price}}$$

Where the figure is greater than 1, it signifies elasticity and where the figure is less than 1 it signifies inelasticity. This is shown in Figure 5.12.

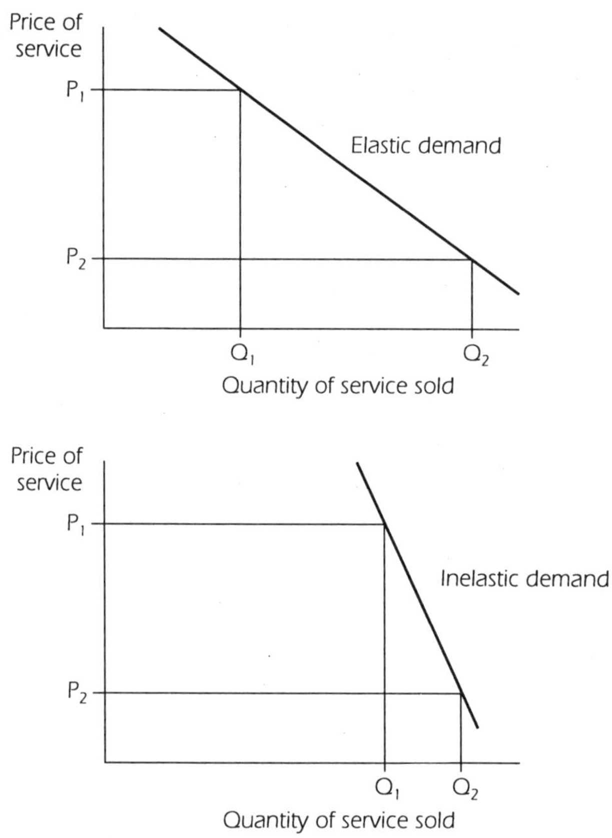

Figure 5.12 Elasticity of demand.

Costs

8.10 There are two types of major costs: fixed costs and variable costs. Each must be identified for consideration in the pricing plan. Fixed costs are those which do not vary over a period of time: for example, buildings, fixtures and fittings. Variable costs are those which will vary over a period of time: for example, expendable supplies. It is estimated that in the financial services industry fixed costs represent in excess of 60 percent of total costs. Managers need to understand how total costs (fixed plus variable) will change with different levels of output and that this has implications for both pricing and expansion.

Competition

8.11 It is essential that there is also an understanding of competitors' costs and pricing behaviour. This will allow managers to make assessments and decisions regarding their own pricing structure in relation to competitors in each market segment. Once these factors have been considered the choice must be made as to which pricing method will be used. There are a number of alternatives:

- cost-plus pricing – the total costs plus a set percentage mark-up
- rate-of-return pricing – prices set in order to achieve a given rate of return on investments and /or assets
- competitive-parity pricing – prices set at a level comparable with the market leader
- loss-leading pricing – prices set at a level below the normal profit level (this tactic is normally short-term and promotional and is usually used to recruit customers or cross sell products)
- value-based pricing – prices set at the level of perceived value to the customer within a market segment.

8.12 There is a further method of pricing which is very relevant to service industries as it is a marketing-orientated approach and takes into account the lifetime value of a customer. It is known as 'relationship pricing' and sets prices by considering the future potential profit streams over the lifetime of a customer. It can be a particularly strong method when dealing with corporate and business customers where there is ongoing contact. By assessing the potential profit over the lifetime of the customer, relationship pricing allows a manager to use any of the five pricing methods discussed above as deemed appropriate to the particular circumstances. Relationship pricing aims to position the service and reflects the fact that customers are prepared to pay extra for the perceived benefits of some services.

8.13 The pricing plan should consider all internal and external factors before a decision is made. These are: objectives, costs, competitors, potential competitors, customer attitudes, legal constraints and positioning. Once these have been considered, the typical strategic choices for price are:

- to increase, decrease or maintain price
- to alter terms and conditions
- to use price skimming
- to use penetration pricing.

Place

8.14 This is the element of the marketing mix which is concerned with distribution channels and the physical distribution of goods. With a service provider there arc three options:

- the customer goes to the service provider, e.g. visits the branch
- the service provider goes to the customer, e.g. the salesperson makes a home visit

- the service provider and the customer transact business at a distance, e.g. direct and Internet banking.

8.15 The choice of channel depends on a number of factors, including:

- the customer's motivation and the importance of the distribution channel
- how rival products are distributed
- if there is a gap in the market for exploiting new or different channels.

8.16 The decision facing managers here is the trade-off between costs and control, as the shorter the distribution channel the tighter the control. The basis of place strategy is to ensure that the customers' needs with regard to availability are met and a manager should use resources to improve availability, reduce waiting times and ensure speed of service. The strategic options available in the place plan are to:

- change distribution
- change channels
- change the service
- incorporate backward and forward integration.

Promotion

8.17 The promotion plan is concerned with communicating with the customer and is concerned with how a 'sale' is achieved. There are a number of elements which can be used in the promotional mix and these are discussed in greater detail in Unit 11. The combination used will depend on the service or product being marketed and to identify the most appropriate mix the following points should be considered. Is the objective of the communication:

- to increase sales?
- to maintain or improve market share?
- to create a brand image?
- to create a favourable customer environment?
- to inform and educate?
- to highlight competitive differences?
- to remind customers of service and product benefits?

8.18 The strategic options for promotion are:

- to change advertising
- to change selling
- to change promotion.

People

8.19 A manager must be aware of the interaction between employees and customers because no matter how the service is delivered (channels), the way in which it is delivered will be very important. This aspect is sometimes know at the 'functional quality' and includes the attitude and behaviour of employees and the interrelationships between employees and customers, taking into account the presentation of employees and their knowledge and competency. Do they appear to care about the customers? Are they positive about the organisation? Do they greet the customers? Do they appear friendly and helpful to the customers?

8.20 Rigorous selection criteria and training programmes will help to maintain quality in the people element of the plan, but of equal importance are motivation and people management itself. People play an important part in the delivery of financial services and can become a differential advantage. The strategic options in the people plan are to:

- conduct a skills analysis
- retrain where necessary
- ensure a structured career progression
- change account managers to relationship managers.

Process

8.21 This refers to the way in which the service is delivered to the customer, i.e. work activity. Therefore any decision regarding policy which impacts on customer involvement or employee discretion will impact on this part of the plan. If a process is flawed it will handicap the delivery of the service; any improvements that are made to the process should lead to an improvement in the service quality. A service which runs efficiently will have an advantage over less effective competitors. Processes can be considered from two angles:

- divergence – the variable options available to deliver the final result
- complexity – the number of steps taken to deliver the final result.

8.22 This leads to four strategic options.

- **Reduce divergence.** This involves standardising the service and placing strict limitations on any customisation.
- **Increase divergence.** This allows greater customisation and employee discretion in terms of flexibility; premium pricing can sometimes be applied in this situation.
- **Reduce complexity**. This involves streamlining the process with the ultimate aim of making it simpler and faster.
- **Increase complexity.** More services are added to the core product in an attempt to gain differential advantage and market share.

Physical evidence

8.23 Here we are looking at the tangibles that are associated with the service. It includes elements such as logos, uniforms, the layout of the branch, and so on. This affects the perception the customer has not only of the organisation but of an individual branch. It is therefore important that the physical evidence is consistent with the desired image of the organisation.

Summary

8.24 These are the seven elements in the marketing mix and it is clear that they are interrelated. When the mix is being developed it is essential that all the plans are mutually supportive, integrated and consistent. The process is shown in Figure 5.13.

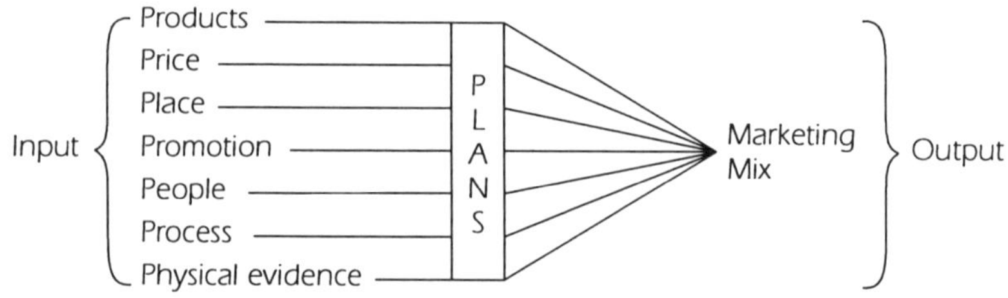

Figure 5.13 The marketing mix.

Student Activity

Discuss the usefulness of the seven Ps in categorising the marketing mix.

9 The branch marketing plan – resources and budgets

9.1 There will be resource and budgeting implications for any marketing mix. This begins the fourth stage in the strategic marketing planning process (see Figure 5.1). To assist in resource planning the following four steps should be undertaken:

1 Establish currently available and obtainable resources and detail any which are not available or readily obtainable (resource audit).

2 Estimate what resources would be required to pursue a certain strategy and decide if enough resources are available to do so successfully.

3 Assign responsibilities to managers for the acquisition, use and control of resources.

4 Identify constraints and factors which will influence the availability and use of resources (internal and external).

Figure 5.14 Resource assessment diagram

9.2 Figure 5.14 illustrates that some of the strategies can be met from existing resources, new resources or a mixture of both. Where the resources are unable to support the strategies these strategies should be reviewed and either deferred until a later time or withdrawn. Extra resources are only going to be made available if there is a sound business case to increase the spending on the marketing mix proposed and estimates will have to be made for both costs and gains.

9.3 The setting of budgets should be as realistic as the resource allocation. One approach is to use annual zero-based budgeting: the marketing expenditure is justified from a base of zero each year against the tasks that need to be accomplished. By using this approach spending on the marketing plan, which is a series of objectives derived from corporate objectives, is tied into achieving corporate objectives. In this way items of expenditure are accounted for as part of a rational, objective and task approach. It also means that should any changes be needed in the plan, funds can be allocated without damaging the organisation's financial strength. Each of the plans drawn up should carry a budget requirement and then, as with resources, if there are no funds available the strategies will need to be reviewed and either deferred for a period of time or withdrawn.

9.4 It is important to realise that the end result of the planning process is the provision of ideal strategies and plans. However, owing to the restrictions on resources and budgets which most managers will face, some streamlining of the plans is likely to take place.

10 The branch marketing plan – first-year implementation and control

10.1 Once there is an agreement for the marketing plan, the budgets and the resources, the next step of stage 4 is implementation (see Figure 5.1). Details of the tasks to be completed, timings and responsibilities should be developed. This is usually known as the one-year tactical marketing plan and it should be a detailed guide to what activities will be required in the twelve-month period if the branch is to achieve its long-term strategic marketing objectives. All staff should be made aware of the plan and what is required of them and their commitment should be sought to achieve it.

10.2 The marketing programme which is developed will incorporate the seven plans produced for the marketing mix. However, not all the plans have to have their own programme. For example, people and physical evidence may be combined. It does not matter if you choose to develop seven or four programmes; the important point is that all the elements in the marketing mix are considered. A useful method for drawing up the programmes is to produce the plan in a chart format, as illustrated in Table 5.2.

	JAN	*FEB*	*MAR*	*APR*	*MAY*	*JUN*	*JUL*	*AUG*	*SEP*	*OCT*	*NOV*	*DEC*
Skills Analysis	✓	✓								✓	✓	
Training			✓	✓	✓	✓	✓	✓	✓			
Re-train Account Managers			✓									
Career Workshops			✓		✓		✓					

✓ indicates the task to be undertaken

Table 5.2 One-year plan for strategic objectives – people.

10.3 Once the implementation programme is running, it is necessary to have some method of control. The purpose of this is to ensure that the plans are progressing towards the targets set and to quickly identify and therefore rectify any problems which may arise. The following are guidelines for basic strategic control.

- Distinguish control levels in the management structure. When managers are taking control action they need to understand what they are trying to achieve. For example, is their control measure intended to have immediate impact, such as 'firefighting' at an operational level, or is it a longer-term measure, impacting on the overall strategic plan?
- Individuals should be allocated the responsibility for different tasks and should have the authority to take control measures.
- Key factors for control and why they are critical should be identified and communicated to the managers responsible for taking control action.
- Control reporting should be timed sensibly. Depending on the level of control, reports should be regular but not so frequent that more time is spent in reporting than in carrying out the plan.
- Suitable targets and standards should be applied and should be tailored to suit individual circumstances.
- Control reports should contain only relevant information, and guidelines should be drawn to ensure that this is the case.

Student Activity

Discuss the importance of the implementation and control phase of the plan.

11 Conclusion

11.1 Marketing planning may at first appear to be a daunting task. However, once completed, it provides focus and a solid understanding of both internal and external factors that will affect the success of the branch. Even if managers are not required to undertake the whole process, it is likely that they will be required to have input at some level even if the planning is being undertaken at a regional or head office level. An understanding of how the process is carried out and what the output means is therefore essential for any manager. The temptation may be to skip some of the steps in the process, but the systematic way that this task is undertaken means that important information is not missing, and because each step develops from the previous one, it ensures that the strategic output is supportive of corporate objectives.

Self-assessment questions

1 What are the ten steps in implementing a strategic marketing plan?

2 Describe the roles of senior management and of managers at regional area offices and branches, and the relationships between them, in the marketing planning process.

3 What issues must be addressed before successful planning can take place?

4 Name the five areas that must be covered in a branch audit.

5 What is the difference between marketing objectives and marketing strategies?

6 In estimating the expected results of the plan, which financial implications must be taken into account?

7 What are the seven Ps?

8 What is meant by elasticity of demand?

9 Which four steps should be undertaken to assist in resource planning?

10 Draw up a one-year plan based on Table 5.2 for another of the seven Ps.

Unit 6

Marketing planning for branches II

1 Introduction

1.1 The purpose of this unit is to summarise the marketing planning process, as described in Unit 5, and to take students through the process of producing both a three-year strategic plan and a one-year tactical plan. The steps are the same, whether the aim is to produce a marketing plan at a branch, area, regional or head office level.

1.2 Marketing planning is about creating better value for the customer with the ultimate aim of creating a sustainable competitive advantage. The planning should not take place in isolation and it is important to consult and involve colleagues, particularly those who have direct interaction with the customer. There will, of course, be other operational plans in place and these will need to be consistent with the marketing plan.

1.3 Remember that the strategic plan should cover a period of three or more years. The tactical plan will be a detailed scheduling and costing of what needs to be done to achieve the first year's objectives of the strategic plan.

2 The stages of the planning process

2.1 The four stages of the planning process are as follows.

- **Analysis** (answer to the question 'where are we now?'): this is analysis of the market place and your own position within it relative to the competition.
- **Objectives** (answer to the question 'where do we want to be?'): from the analysis a realistic set of quantitative and financial objectives consistent with those of the organisation as a whole should be set.
- **Strategy** (answer to the question 'how do we get there?'): a broad strategy should be determined to accomplish the objectives. These need to support the corporate strategy.
- **Tactics** (answer to the question 'which way is best?'): these are detailed plans to ensure the implementation of the strategy and thereby the achievement of the agreed objectives.

2.2 It should be remembered that the strategic marketing plan is a plan of action and this should be reflected in the final document. The implementation of the plan is represented by the one-year marketing plan. In producing these plans a great deal of background and statistical information will be collected and analysed. However, the final document should contain only a concentrated commentary of these findings, providing a background for the decisions reached in the strategic planning process.

3 The marketing audit ('where are we now?')

3.1 All markets contain a number of customers but not all of these will provide a branch with the opportunity to service them profitably. To investigate which areas of the market have the potential to be profitable it is necessary to divide the market into segments and then to analyse the sales potential by type of service within each segment. The branch must therefore analyse and evaluate the key segments of their market. The same process must also take place for any further segments which are identified but which are deemed to be of less importance to branch activities.

3.2 It is recognised that all the information required may not be readily available within the branch, but additional information may be found at area, regional or head office level. The audit requires a far greater degree of information than is actually included in the plan, and it may be useful for the manager to implement a running reference file which can be used when carrying out the audit. It is very important to remember that the audit is not a marketing plan and there should never be large documents relating to the audit included in any business plans.

4 Contents of a strategic plan

Summary of the branch performance

4.1 This should provide a bird's-eye view of the branch's total marketing activities. It should include a quantitative summary of performance and a summary of the reasons for both good and poor performance. Ensure that any comparisons are meaningful and use constant revenue. Also ensure that the same base year values are used in any projections which may appear later in the plan.

Branch performance summary 1995–1997 inclusive

	1995	*1996*	*1997*
Volume of transactions			
Gross profit (%)			
Gross margin (000)			

Table 6.1.

Summary of financial projections

4.2 The purpose of this is to provide the reader of the document with a summary of the financial implications for the three-year planning period. Ideally it should be presented as a simple diagram and should be accompanied by a brief commentary. For example: 'This three-year business plan shows an increase in revenue from £750,000 to £100,000 and an increase in contribution from £175,000 to £400,000. The purpose of this marketing plan is to illustrate how these increases will be achieved.' See Figure 6.1 overleaf.

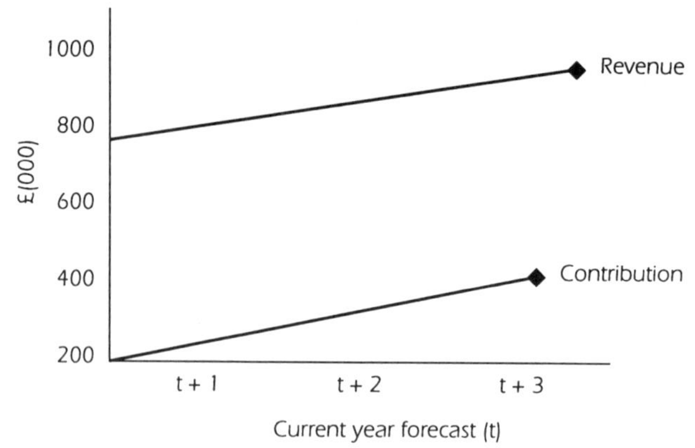

Figure 6.1 Financial projections.

4.3 To be in a position to complete this summary a manager should first have completed a gap analysis for both revenue and profit (see Figure 5.11). When completing the gap analysis it should be noted that the 'target' point should be the minimum point that would enable the achievement of the corporate objectives set for the branch.

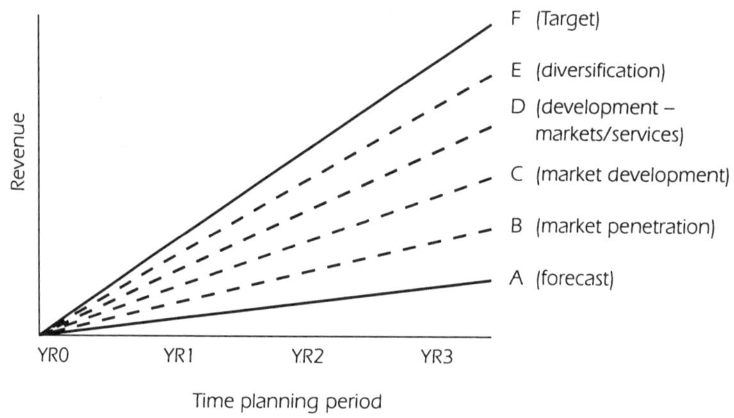

Figure 6.2.

4.4 When completing the gap analysis managers may also find it useful to complete an action chart. The purpose of this is to identify possible productivity-related tasks which can assist in closing the first gap – point B market penetration – which represents the cash and margin focus.

PRODUCTIVITY (items listed are not mutually exclusive)	*Profit*
Increase cross sales	
Increase appointment levels for financial advisers	
Improve rates for business loans	
Increase charges on overdrafts	
Reduce loan rate discounts	

Table 6.2 Action chart: activities that may close the gap

4.5 Use Table 6.2 to list any actions that could be taken to close the productivity gap; then plot the total value of these at point B on the gap analysis chart.

Market overview

4.6 The purpose of a market overview is to provide a brief picture of the market before looking in greater detail at the individual segments which form the basis of the marketing plan. It applies segmentation at a market level, dividing the latter into homogenous groups of customers – for example, high net worth customers, current account customers, and so on. Each group has distinct characteristics which can then be exploited in marketing terms. This approach is probably the most apt for branches, as it will enable managers to develop their most profitable markets. In segmenting the market, both weaknesses and development opportunities will be revealed.

4.7 There is no set way to present this section of the marketing plan, but the end result should be a summary of what managers consider to be the key characteristics of their markets. The branch manager should consider the following questions.

- What are the main services, markets or segments that are likely to provide the branch with suitable business opportunities?
- How, if at all, are these changing – are they growing or declining?

4.8 It is also helpful if the manager can present as much of the information as possible in a visual format – for example, bar charts, graphs or product life cycles.

SWOT analysis

4.9 Before being in a position to determine marketing objectives and any future strategies, a manager must summarise the audit findings into a SWOT analysis. The questions a manager should be asking are:

- What are the strengths and weaknesses of the branch in relation to the competition? Why would potential customers seek to deal with this organisation rather than a competitor?
- What are the opportunities?
- What are the threats, both present and future, to the branch business in each key segment?

4.10 The market overview will have identified the key segments, and the presentation of the plan should include a SWOT analysis for each of these segments. Each one should be concise and interesting to read. At a branch level the most useful way to set out a SWOT analysis is probably an extended version which includes implications and actions, as this will provide further guidance when strategies are formulated.

Element	Implications	Possible actions
Strengths		
•		
•		
•		
•		
Weaknesses		
•		
•		
•		
•		
Opportunities		
•		
•		
•		
•		
Threats		
•		
•		
•		
•		

Table 6.3 Layout for SWOT analysis presentation.

Key assumptions

4.11 The branch must highlight the key assumptions that will establish the basis for the setting of objectives and strategies. These assumptions should, in the main, deal with external factors that would have significant impact on the achievement of the objectives if they were to occur. They might include factors such as market growth and legislative and taxation changes.

4.12 Assumptions should be few and relate only to the key issues which have been highlighted in the SWOT analyses. If it is possible for the plan to succeed regardless of whether an assumption becomes fact, then it is not necessary to include it and it should be taken out.

Marketing objectives and strategies

4.13 Once the key strengths, weaknesses, opportunities and threats have been identified and stated and the assumptions about conditions that could affect the business have been made, the process of setting marketing objectives should follow quite easily. This is because there will now be a realistic statement of what the branch wishes to achieve as a result of the market-centred analysis.

4.14 Setting the objectives is the most important step in the whole process, as it represents the commitment of the branch to a set course of action that will in turn determine the scheduling and costing of subsequent actions.

4.15 It would be useful here to redefine the meaning of objectives and strategies in the planning process. An objective is *what* the branch wants to achieve and the strategy is *how* a branch plans to achieve it. Therefore there are objectives and strategies at all levels in marketing – for example, pricing objectives and strategies, promotion objectives and strategies.

4.16 The important point about marketing objectives is that they should be related to services and markets only, as it is only by selling something that a branch can achieve its financial targets. Pricing, promotion and other elements of the marketing mix are the means (strategies) by which a branch can succeed in achieving its targets. Therefore these sets of objectives, known as sub-objectives, should not be confused with marketing objectives.

4.17 In order for a branch to maximise its profits and cash flow, it must consider carefully how customers' needs are changing and how its products and services must change to meet these needs. The branch therefore needs to consider the two main dimensions of commercial growth: service development and market development. The marketing objectives are concerned with:

- selling existing services to existing segments
- developing new services for existing segments
- extending existing services to new segments
- developing new services for new segments.

4.18 A marketing objective should be specific, measurable, achievable, relevant and timely. For a branch, this will probably mean expressing objectives in terms of volume, value and market share. The marketing objectives should cover the full three-year planning cycle and include broad strategies and revenue and cost projections. The one-year marketing plan should contain the specific objectives for the first year of the three-year plan and the corresponding strategies for achieving these. Note that the one-year plan and the three-year plan are separate documents.

4.19 The strategies will state in broad terms how the branch is going to achieve its objectives and should consider the following:

- customer service levels for the specific market segments
- specific service policies
- pricing policies to be applied to specific market segments
- communication policies.

4.20 It is worth noting that a manager should consider a number of the options available before deciding on the 'best' one for recommendation. A manager must evaluate the most attractive strategies and assess their chances of success in a realistic manner.

Financial projections

4.21 To complete the three-year plan the manager must provide the financial projections for the full planning period under the principal revenue and cost headings as set out by head office.

5 Contents of a one-year marketing plan

5.1 This is a separate document from the three-year plan and should only be developed when the three-year strategic plan has been completed and approved. To develop the three-year plan, specific sub-objectives for the services and market segments must be set and they must be supported by detailed strategy and action plans. Forecasts and budgets should be included and these should reflect the marketing objectives and strategies. In turn the objectives, strategies and programmes should reflect the agreed budgets and sales forecasts. The main purpose of the sub-objectives is to reflect the major steps required for implementation, assigning accountability, focusing on the major decision points and specifying the allocation of resources, together with the timings.

5.2 If this system is used, a hierarchy of objectives should be built up in such a way that every item of budgeted expenditure can be related back directly to the initial financial objectives. This is known as task-related budgeting and is used by many organisations. For example, if a branch campaign has been identified as a strategy for achieving an objective for a particular market or segment, all the campaign expenditure appearing in the budget can be related back directly to that major objective. The main feature of this is that budgets are set against both the overall marketing objectives and the sub-objectives for each element of the marketing mix. The advantage of this is that the branch is able to develop a clear picture of its markets, and all items of expenditure can be fully accounted for as part of an objective.

5.3 There is no set format for a one-year plan. However, the following sets out the minimum information a manager should include. It should be noted that the one-year plan would also contain contingency plans.

- Overall quantifiable objectives including volumes, values, gross margins and market share. Show the previous year, current year (estimated) and the target for the following year. Ideally there should be a brief explanation for each one (see Table 6.4).

OVERALL OBJECTIVES										
Service/ Market/ Segment	Sales Volume			Value			Gross Margin			Comments
	Year –1	Year 0 (est)	Year +1 (forecast)	Year –1	Year 0 (est)	Year +1 (forecast)	Year –1	Year 0 (est)	Year +1 (forecast)	

Table 6.4.

- Overall strategies – for example, new customers, new services, customer service, pricing sales promotion (see Figure 6.5).

OVERALL STRATEGIES		
Outline strategy	Cost implications	Comments

Table 6.5.

Table 6.6 overleaf shows a suitable layout for the task-related budget for sub-objectives, strategies and tactics.

- Sub-objectives – detailed objectives for the services, markets or segments, as appropriate.
- Strategies – details of how the sub-objectives will be achieved.
- Tactics – details, timings, costs and responsibilities.

SUB OBJECTIVES, STRATEGIES AND TACTICS						
Markets/ Service/ Segment	Objective	Strategy	Tactics (specific actions)	Timescales	Who is responsible?	Cost

Table 6.6.

- Summary of the marketing activities and their costs. Show the previous year, current year (estimated) and target for following year. Ideally include a brief commentary (see Table 6.7).

MARKETING ACTIVITY SUMMARY				
Activity	Cost last year	Cost current year (estimated)	Cost next year (forecast)	Comments
Salaries				
Travel and expenses				
Sales meetings				
Training				
Corporate hospitality				
Merchandising				
Advertising				
Branch campaigns				
Internal costs				

This is not an exhaustive list and should be amended as appropriate to your own organisation.

Table 6.7.

- Contingency plans, which should address the following points.
  - What are the key assumptions on which the one-year plan is based?
  - What would be the effect on the operating income if the assumptions did not come true?

- How will the assumptions be measured?
- What action would need to be taken to ensure that any adverse financial effects of an unfulfilled assumption are mitigated (the end result being that the profit forecast will remain the same at the year-end)?

To measure risk, assess the negative, asking the question 'what can go wrong with each assumption that would then change the outcome?' – e.g. if an increase in mortgage lending of 10 percent is a key assumption, what lower growth rate would have to occur before a substantially different management decision on the business mix would be required?

- Operating results, which should include:
  - net revenue
  - gross margins
  - adjustments
  - marketing costs
  - administration costs
  - interest
  - operating results
  - ROS
  - ROI.

  This is not an exhaustive list and a manager will be guided by head office requirements. However, the list should include figures for the previous year, the current year (estimated) and the target for the following year.
- Key activity calendar – a summary of the key activities indicating when they will take place and for what period of time. This will assist in monitoring the progress of the one-year plan (Table 5.2).

6 Summary

6.1 Marketing planning is not an exact science and at first may appear complicated and daunting. Unit 5 deals with all the steps involved in the process whilst this unit seeks to clarify and simplify how the information should be presented when a planning document is written.

6.2 Often a branch manager will not be responsible for the production of a three-year strategic plan. His input may be sought but the production of the plan will usually come from an area or regional level. However, once the three-year plan is approved, a branch manager will usually be required to produce the one-year plan, which is the detailed information about how the set objectives are to be achieved. Having studied Units 5 and 6, you should now be in a position to produce the one-year plan.

Unit 7

Distribution: branch location

Objectives

After studying this unit you should be able to do the following.

- **Describe the importance of the branch network and the outlet location.**
- **Describe possible branch valuation procedures and their use.**
- **Explain the process of opening a branch.**
- **Explain the decisions involved when deciding to close a branch.**
- **Describe the use of centralised operational support.**

1 Introduction

1.1 Traditionally the location of the branch has been a major influence on a customer's decision to select a financial services provider. Although other factors, such as service levels, have a bearing on the decision, the position of the branch is often felt to be the single most important factor. This, together with the knowledge that a high level of loyalty exists in financial services retailing, makes the choice of a branch location an extremely important one.

1.2 The high level of capital outlay involved in the selection of a branch location and the opening of such an outlet makes it essential that such decisions are only taken following a great deal of research and strategic planning.

2 Outlet location and the branch network

2.1 Several factors must be considered when selecting a branch location. The branch must be situated in an area that is capable of sustaining the size of the planned branch; that is, there must be sufficient individual or business customers in the area to ensure its profitability. If it is intended to attract individual customers, it should be sited somewhere that is highly visible and that has a high level of pedestrian traffic. If it is intended to attract corporate clients, the branch should be close to businesses. It is also important to bear in mind the suitability of the building. Is it the correct size? Is the design suitable? Is there sufficient window, and therefore advertising, space? Taking these points into consideration from the start can minimise the costs incurred in any refurbishments undertaken.

Branch strategy

2.2 Increased competition in recent years has made it important that the branch is not viewed in isolation, and that decisions about the branch are taken in the light of the role the branch plays in the overall network. It is also important that the network operates as effectively as possible. This has led many financial services retailers to search for a branch strategy that will prove economic and lead to a marketing advantage over the competition.

2.3 Initially, many financial institutions concentrated on the commercial side of the business and located their branches in areas convenient for their business customers. However, the importance of the personal sector has grown; in order to remain competitive and profitable organisations need to compete in this sector. Many companies are therefore moving their branches to areas of high pedestrian flow, such as shopping centres. The requirements of such branches are different from those that serve a business community. They tend to concentrate more on the shoppers' needs for cash withdrawal. These branches can also be used as an advertising tool to sell such things as new accounts, mortgages and personal loans, rather than concentrating purely on servicing existing customers.

Branch numbers

2.4 The general trend among financial services institutions is currently to reassess the branch network and to reduce the number of outlets they have. The need to operate profitably in this highly competitive market has led many companies to take harsh decisions and to close their unprofitable branches. If it is felt that the lack of business is due to the current location, a branch may be moved to an area that is considered to have more potential for profit.

2.5 Many banks and building societies have recently been involved in programmes of merger or takeover, and this often leaves the company with an overlap of outlets in certain locations. This inevitably leads to a decision to close one of the branches. Where the number of customers using the branches is high, the retailer may close both and relocate to a new larger site. There are some smaller building societies who have, in recent years, undertaken a programme of network expansion in order to reach customers in a wider geographical location; however, such expansion plans are rare and very much against the norm.

Telephone banking and ATMs

2.6 We have already discussed the increase in telephone banking, and this will be considered further in Unit 8. Because this type of banking is available 24 hours a day, and provides virtually all available services except cash deposit, it greatly reduces the need for the customer to visit a branch. From the provider's viewpoint, telephone banking enables them to offer their services with vastly reduced costs and overheads. The success of the telephone banking system, particularly if it continues to develop in the future, will further diminish the role of the traditional branch and may lead to further network rationalisations.

2.7 The same could be said of the ATM network, which gives customer access to cash withdrawals, balance enquiries, etc. 24 hours a day. Traditionally located outside bank and building society branches, many retailers now offer increasing numbers of ATMs inside the branch itself. However, it is the growth in the number of 'remote' machines that causes the biggest threat to the branches. These 'cash points' are now familiar sights in all retail centres, at supermarkets, airports and even at petrol stations. The sharing agreements that are in place allow customers of one institution to use the ATMs of another, therefore increasing the availability of such machines and reducing even further the need to visit the branch.

Student Activity

1. What is the current trend among financial services organisations with regard to branch numbers?
2. Briefly describe the effect that the growth in telephone banking and the ATM networks has had on branch strategy.

3 Branch valuation procedures

3.1 Once a financial services retailer has embarked on a programme of branch network rationalisation, it will have to upgrade, downgrade and even close branches. It may also need to relocate some outlets to more profitable areas, or to open new branches. Before any decisions can be made as to whether a particular site can, or will, be profitable for any particular type or size of branch, the organisation must carry out some kind of branch evaluation. There are many different methods used in the evaluation of a branch site, ranging from the very systematic approach, relying heavily on modelling techniques and databases, to an approach based on local knowledge.

Market effectiveness

3.2 When an institution wishes to rationalise its network by reducing the number of outlets, it must look at the effectiveness of each branch. This will identify underperforming branches and enable decisions to be made as to which branches are currently unprofitable. Such decisions involve looking at factors such as

- the number of customers, both current and potential
- customer behaviour (How often do they use the branch? Do they have sufficient deposits? Do they have more than one relationship with the organisation?)
- the amount of competition in the area
- the costs of running the branch and/or refurbishment costs.

Location evaluation techniques

3.3 In the past, efforts to predict the likely profitability of a new branch site were less scientific than they are today. However, many financial services retailers are adopting the complex modelling techniques used by product retailers, and we will therefore look briefly at some of these techniques.

Checklists

3.4 The use of checklists is a qualitative approach used to assess potential branch sites. There are four categories for which a checklist of factors to be considered is made. The evaluation team need to be aware of the benefits and the drawbacks of each of the elements that appear on these lists. The four categories are: geodemographics, branch activity, centre details and premises. We now look at each of these in turn.

Geodemographics

3.5 Geodemographics provides details of the market population in the area of the possible branch site. It examines such things as the population structure and the perceived need for financial services. It uses such sources as census data, electoral registers and classification systems that have been developed by various agencies operating in the financial services sector. The type of information on a geodemographic checklist involves such things as

- population density
- population structure
- social-economic groupings
- occupation and employment trends
- economic stability of the area
- growth potential
- retail and business potential
- housing values and level of home ownership
- cultural groups
- general levels of disposable income of population.

Branch activity

3.6 Information regarding current branch activity indicates how well a particular area is being serviced, and therefore the level of potential for new branch development. Information regarding competitors' branches has to be gained from surveys and from local knowledge. The information contained on a branch activity checklist is likely to contain such things as

- number of branches and their distribution
- organisations who currently have branches in the area
- turnover and profit levels of current branches
- patronage estimates
- market share of competitors
- any development activity currently being undertaken
- brand images of current representation, and any territory overlaps
- any internal data available (e.g. customer profiles, number of product sales).

Centre details

3.7 The centre details list covers factors to be considered when evaluating centre locations. It requires detailed knowledge of a population's work and travel habits, especially when considering appropriate sites for ATMs. Institutions obtain the necessary information from such things as town street maps, pedestrian flow counts, and town plans showing the activity type of other retail units in the area. The type of information covered by this list includes

- details of primary and secondary retail and business areas
- any retail and business statistics available
- street statistics and information
- local authority policy, particularly any rules regarding use of retail units
- work and travel patterns
- shopping patterns
- any new developments planned for the area
- details of the local road network and parking facilities
- information on available public transport and pedestrian routes.

Premises

3.8 The premises list contains information that will help to determine the profitability and effectiveness of a particular branch or ATM location, and it therefore contains very site-specific information such as

- site availability and current usage
- costs involved (lease costs, possible refurbishments costs)
- frontage size and potential
- access and local parking
- expected footfall
- security
- local amenities
- activities of neighbouring retail units.

Gravity models

3.9 A more quantitative method of branch location evaluation involves the use of a gravity model. Gravity models operate on the principle that the level of use of a branch will be related to its size and the distance and time a customer will need to travel compared to other branches in surrounding areas. From this it should be possible to predict the possibility of changes between places, thereby defining the boundaries between the trading area of two branches. Complex gravity models have been developed using patterns of branch distribution, and information such as population density. The results can then be used to establish catchment areas and help to plan a branch network. This method can also be used to highlight areas of branch overlap in existing networks. The models can then predict the effect of altering a network, and a distribution strategy can be designed.

Multiple regression

3.10 Multiple regression is a sophisticated evaluation technique that involves investigating the relationship between branch performance indicators and location attributes. If a high level of correlation exists the data can be used to predict the key factors in branch performance and therefore forecast profitability. To do so requires huge amounts of data over a great deal of time and it is the quality of such data that determines the accuracy and reliability of this technique.

Spatial techniques

3.11 A number of models have been created that use a two-step approach; that is they

1 predict the gross potential of an area

2 predict the market share that could be expected from that potential.

3.12 Such techniques are used to predict promising areas in which to site a profitable branch. An alternative three-stage approach would include

1 deciding on the trading area

2 collecting the data relating to the trading area and translating the data into potential business

3 calculating from this the potential return on investment in order to make a decision about the branch location.

Student Activity

1 Explain what you understand by the term 'checklist evaluation'. Name the four categories of list.

2 Explain, briefly, gravity models and how they are used.

4 Opening a branch

4.1 A decision to open a new branch may be taken because there is an area of potential, or to replace a branch that is underperforming.

4.2 The evaluation procedure will predict which site is likely to generate the greatest sales and therefore profit. The ideal site is likely to be an area of high retail activity where traffic flows are high. Ideally the site will be single storey only with large frontage. The size required depends largely on the purpose of the branch; for example, in a large out-of-town shopping centre where the major function is likely to be cash withdrawal, the space required is small. In any event, the size required is likely to be much less than for traditional sites.

4.3 Finding a vacant unit that satisfies these criteria may be a long process. Also, these units tend to be the most expensive, and costs play a large part in the decision to open a new branch. However, finding the appropriate site is only the start of the process. The retailer then needs to obtain planning permission for the bank or building society outlet, and this can be difficult and a time consuming task. Often local authorities prefer to restrict the number of non-retail outlets in prime urban sites in order to maintain their major function as shopping centres. It is common for local authorities to divide the retail centre into two categories: primary and secondary. Generally, within a primary retail street, any application to change the use of the shop from retail to service will be declined.

4.4 Many financial institutions are aware of the possible planning department rejections and have developed strategies to deal with them. Often, such institutions have dedicated staff to support their applications and may undertake some work to canvas local support prior to the application. They may also undertake negotiations with town planners, taking time to discuss the plans for the branch network as a whole, particularly in cases where the granting of permission to open the new branch will result in the closure of two other sites. The town planners' decision may be swayed by the understanding that other sites, possibly the traditional large high-street corner sites, will be vacated.

Student Activity

1 Describe the type of site that is most likely to be selected for a new branch outlet.

2 What problems could occur when seeking planning permission?

5 Deciding to close a branch

5.1 Following a review of the branch network, the branch evaluation process may highlight a number of underperforming and unprofitable branches. The financial services retailer then needs to decide what action to take. They may identify steps to take within the branch to improve performance (e.g. a refurbishment, a change in the branch focus, a review of the branch staffing levels). If there is potential in the area, but the location of the branch is a problem, they may decide to relocate to another site nearby. If this is the case, they will need to undertake a process of site evaluation to ensure that the new branch will prove more successful.

5.2 If the retailer decides that the area has no or little potential for profit, then they may decide to close the branch without relocating and accept a subsequent loss of custom.

5.3 There are circumstances where a financial services provider may decide to allow an underperforming branch to remain, for example

- where such things as the marketing mix can be altered to bring about an increase in profitability
- where the branch can be downgraded, and costs greatly reduced in order to increase the profitability
- where, although no profit is made, the branch provides excellent advertising due to its position
- if there is due to be some change (e.g. building a shopping centre in the surrounding area) which could have a huge impact on the branch's performance.

5.4 However, in some cases the institution will decide to close a branch, either to relocate it, or simply to close it to reduce costs. If this happens, they will be keen to cause as little inconvenience to their customers as possible, and will transfer their accounts to the relocated branch, or the nearest available outlet. However carefully this is handled, there will inevitably be some negative feeling and some customers will be lost to other providers. A customer's decision to close his or her account or use the new branch will involve consideration of some or all of the following factors.

- Convenience of the new branch to which the account has been transferred.
- Extent of customers' mobility (the elderly may find even a small increase in distance too inconvenient).
- The customer's view of the service he has received (if the customer was at all unhappy with any element of the service, he may take this change as a trigger to move to another provider).
- Loyalty. If the customer has a long standing relationship with the financial institution and is a loyal customer, he is unlikely to want to change providers.
- Cross sales. If the customer has a large number of other products from the same provider (a current account, a mortgage, insurance products, investment vehicles, etc.) then he may be more inclined to remain a customer.
- Level of branch usage. If the customer uses such facilities as the ATM and only seldom visits the branch, then, provided there are still convenient cash dispensers, he is unlikely to change providers.

5.5 If customers are lost it is likely that they will be lost to other providers who have an outlet close to that which has been closed. Provided the research and business predictions are correct, this will, however, be more than offset by the new customers that will be attracted by the new branch in its new location, which is likely to offer more streamlined services.

5.6 In order to keep the loss to a minimum, the provider is likely to notify customers in advance of the move so as to keep them informed, and may open the new branch by holding an 'event' such as a reception morning that is designed to achieve local press coverage and reinforce customer loyalty.

Student Activity

1 Why might a financial services retailer decide to maintain an underperforming branch?

2 What factors might influence a customer's decision to close his or her account when a branch is relocated?

3 When closing a branch, what can the retailer do to ensure loss of business is kept to a minimum?

6 Centralised operational support

6.1 Following the large number of mergers and takeovers in the financial services industry, and also because of the increase in competition, there has been a need to increase efficiency and reduce operating costs. One of the ways to reduce costs is to introduce centralised operational support. This entails moving the processing of business and the handling of telephone enquiries away from the branch staff, thereby removing the need for such large branch staff numbers and allowing a saving in staffing costs.

6.2 The benefits of a centralised operational support system are

- specialist skilled staff are required in only a few branches, thereby saving costs
- it avoids having senior managers in all branches, again saving costs
- it allows the processing and enquiry functions to be centralised, thereby reducing costs and increasing efficiency.

6.3 Such an approach also means that the remaining staff can concentrate their effort on sales and marketing activity, altering the function of the branch from that of a servicing unit, to more of a retail outlet. However, such a radical change many not be suitable for all an institution's branches, and they may therefore find that they are able to offer a different level of service and support throughout the network, depending on such factors as branch location and customer base. What this leads to is a network with a hierarchy of branches, an example of which could be that shown in Table 7.1.

Table 7.1 A hierarchy of branches

Grade one branch	ATM and deposit facilities only (could be situated in shopping centre, airport etc.)
Grade two branch	Small number of branch staff, predominantly ATMs and automated deposit taking.
Grade three branch	ATMs and counter facilities. Small number of interview facilities; likely to have a 'shared' sales adviser.
Grade four branch	Large town branch offering full banking services.
Regional and National Headquarters	Administration and management centres offering support to the network.

6.4 This delivery system involving branches with varying levels of service provision has led to 'hub and spoke' arrangements being created, with the centrally located 'hub' branch offering a greater level of service and therefore some support to the smaller 'spoke' branches, which are located within easy travelling distance of the main branch. This allows the smaller branches to concentrate purely on what makes them profitable, but means that the organisation's full services are available to the customer if needed. See Figure 7.1.

Figure 7.1 Hub and spoke arrangement

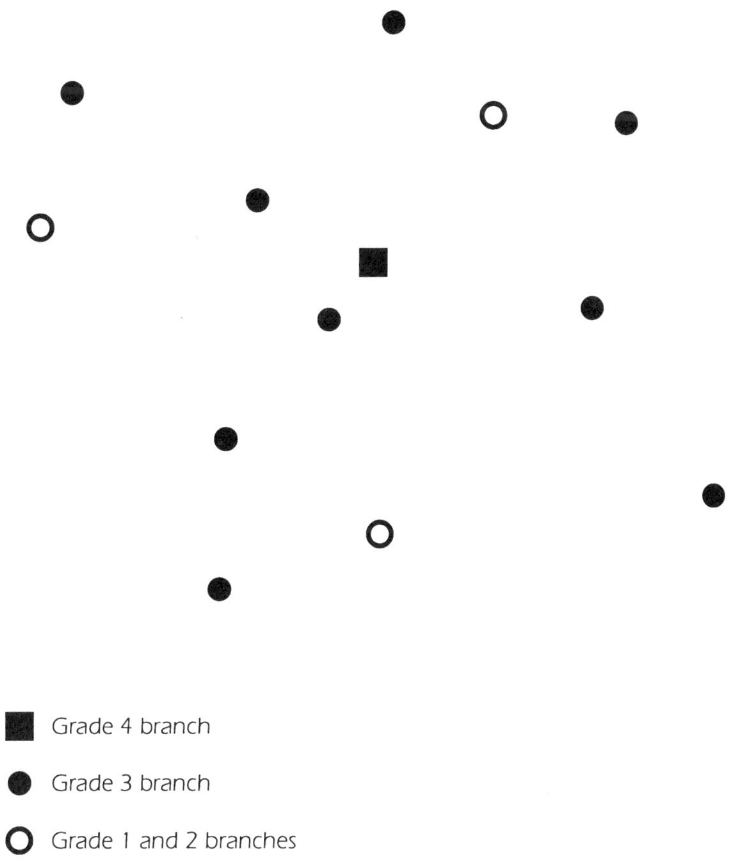

6.5 This network of smaller branches with a centralised operational support allows a financial services retailer to achieve at least a minimum level of service in all geographical areas, which otherwise would be unsustainable because of staff costs.

6.6 Another approach is to have speciality branches. Rather than operating the full range of banking services, the branch concentrates on certain elements of the bank's product and service range, which is determined by the area in which it is situated and the customers it will serve. For example, a corporate branch is designed to deal with corporate accounts and does not handle retail financial services. It offers such services as corporate cash management rather than the usual bank teller services.

Student Activity

What type of service is likely to be offered centrally when a centralised operational support policy is adopted?

7 Case study and analysis

7.1 The Norfolk Building Society is currently looking at their branch network. They have just over 180 branches, located mainly in the south. Many of these branches are situated in the same sites as they have been since they were opened, some of them having been there for over 50 years. There is also a considerable overlap in branches, with some towns being serviced by four or five small branches situated in the suburbs as well as the town centre.

7.2 Currently each branch is responsible for its own administration, and each has a number of tellers and a branch manager.

7.3 The reason for the review is an attempt to improve the effectiveness and cost-efficiency of the network. It is also desirable to free up some of the cashiers' time, to enable them to become more retail-focused, increasing the amount of time they can spend promoting the company's products and services.

7.4 Norfolk Building Society also wishes to ensure that the locations are suitable for their customers, and that the support systems operated within their branches are as efficient as possible. It is expected that the result of the review will be a recommendation to reduce the number of branches by relocating some and closing others. Obviously nothing can be decided until further investigations have been carried out.

7.5 Imagine that you have been charged with carrying out the review, and have been set the following objectives.

- To investigate the appropriateness of the current branch network by evaluating the current branch sites.
- To make recommendations as to the number and location of the branches.
- To suggest ways cost savings can be made without reducing the retailing power of the network.
- To make recommendations about the best way of handling customer queries and offering the required customer service facilities.

7.6 Explain how you would go about achieving the objectives you have been set, and assuming the review was carried out make recommendations as to what action the organisation should take. You should consider the following.

- How you would evaluate each site.
- Recommendations as to the positioning of branches.
- Recommendations as to how administrative support should be offered.
- The steps you would recommend the organisation to take when opening a new branch.
- How the organisation should go about closing branches, if that is appropriate.

7.7 Your analysis should be detailed, and your report would include the following brief information.

- You would need to evaluate each branch site, and any other sites that you feel the society might choose to occupy.

- You would use one of the evaluation techniques outlined in this unit. For example, you could use the checklist approach. Here, you would list all the factors under the headings Geodemographics, Branch activity, Centre details and Premises. Each of the points would then be investigated in order to assess the benefits and drawbacks of any particular site.
- Once all the sites have been evaluated, you will be in a position to see which are the most efficient, and where there is overlap.
- As part of the evaluation process, you should also include potential sites. For example, a town may have three small branches which you will evaluate; but you should also look at other potential sites which might be used for a new branch combining the three current outlets.
- If the branches have been located in the same sites for some years, this may mean there is potential for some to relocate.
- It may be that when first opened the branches were situated near business centres, enabling them to concentrate on business customers. Since then, the locality may have changed, so that now the branch undertakes mainly personal business. Such branches may need to be relocated.
- The shape of the town may have changed, i.e. new shopping centres may have opened, footfall may have increased or decreased in some areas if town centres have been pedestrianised. All these things will have an impact on the ideal branch location.
- Not all branches will need to offer all services. It may be that some branches can be closed if the needs of the customers can be met by installing remote ATMs.
- It is likely that a large saving could be made by offering different levels of administrative support at different branches. This would involve removing the customer services and administration functions from the branches. These services would then be offered from a centralised location, or from one large branch, which would offer these functions on behalf of several smaller branches.
- Centralising the support would mean a cost saving to the Norfolk Building Society, because fewer administrative staff would be required. Often, fewer managers would be required in these circumstances, as only one Customer Services Manager per area would be needed. It may also mean that less space would be needed for a branch. A smaller retail unit can then be used, again saving costs.
- A centralised support unit dedicated to dealing with customer queries often on the telephone should also prove highly efficient for the customer.
- Having evaluated its branches and other possible sites, and having decided to centralise its administrative support, it is highly probable that the Norfolk Building Society will wish to close some branches that are no longer profitable. It may choose to merge some branches, or move some to more profitable sites. Some may be moved onto smaller sites as fewer staff mean less space is involved. Where two branches are being combined, a larger site may be needed. Therefore, the society may find itself in the position of both opening and closing branches.

- When opening a branch, the society will need to ensure that the location is suitable for the customers it wishes to attract and for the functions it expects to perform. The size of the location will be important, as will the amount of frontage and window space.
- Consideration must also be given to the cost of the outlet and the amount of alteration or refurbishment that is required.
- As the new unit is likely to be located in a retailing centre, planning permission to convert to a building society branch will be needed. Some towns restrict the number of non-retail sites they permit. It would therefore be well worth the Norfolk Building Society ensuring that they have regular contact, and develop a good working relationship, with the town planners.
- When the branch is opened, the marketing department should take the opportunity to create as much positive publicity as possible for the company. They should hold an opening event, and ensure that they get coverage in the local papers and if possible on local TV.
- Although there are some circumstances in which the society would choose to retain a non-profitable branch, they will inevitably find themselves having to make closures.
- There may be sound financial reasons for closing a branch, but there is a danger that customers who use it may move their business to another provider.
- In order to minimise this loss of business, the Norfolk Building Society should ensure that they contact every one of the customers who will be affected by such closures. They should inform them of the location of the society's new branch, and any other branches they have in the area that the customers may find convenient. They should also tell customers about the services the company can offer over the telephone, and the location of any ATMs in their area. They may also, if simply relocating the branch, invite customers to some form of opening day party as a reward for customer loyalty.

Summary

Now that you have completed this unit, you should be able to

- ❑ **describe the importance of the branch network and the outlet location**
- ❑ **describe possible branch valuation procedures and their use**
- ❑ **explain the process of opening a branch**
- ❑ **explain the decisions involved when deciding to close a branch**
- ❑ **describe the use of centralised operational support.**

Self-assessment questions

1 Write a short essay on the importance of the branch network and outlets. Make sure that you include answers to the following questions.

(a) Why is it important to run an effective branch network?

(b) What factors determine the suitability of a specific branch location?

(c) What are the current trends for branch numbers, and what has influenced them?

2 Write a paragraph to explain how you would assess the market effectiveness of a branch.

3 Describe four methods of evaluating the location of a branch.

4 Briefly describe the steps involved in opening a new branch.

5 (a) What factors might cause a financial services provider to close a branch?

(b) What factors might encourage a financial services provider to keep an unprofitable branch open?

(c) How can a financial services provider attempt to keep the customers of a branch that closes or relocates?

6 (a) List the advantages of centralised operational support.

(b) Describe the 'hub and spoke' network.

Unit 8

Distribution: other channels

Objectives

After studying this unit you should be able to describe each of the following methods of retailing of financial services

- **direct sales forces**
- **telephone-based sales operations**
- **direct mail and direct response advertising**
- **electronic fund transfers at point of sale**
- **intermediaries, including IFAs and brokers.**

1 Introduction

1.1 Rather than relying totally on the branch for the distribution of their products, most financial services organisations use a range of distribution channels in order to reach the maximum possible number of customers. There are many reasons for this, not least of which are the disadvantages that reliance on a branch network can bring. These include

- the costs and the resources required to open and maintain a branch
- the restriction of location: there may not be a branch located in a convenient area for many customers
- branches tend to have very restrictive opening hours, typically nine to five, which can make visiting them difficult for people who work full time
- the process of making a purchase from a branch can be time consuming, compared with that of purchasing using one of the other channels of distribution.

1.2 These disadvantages, all of which can create barriers to doing business with a provider, have meant that both existing and new companies have taken a fresh look at the way they offer their products for sale to the public, It is from these problems and the customers' need to find a more convenient way of purchasing, that the many new methods of distribution have evolved. In recent years, many companies have been launched into the financial services industry without a branch network. They have gained customers and business by offering a product rather than a relationship; that is, by offering a convenient and cost-effective product rather than relying on the customer facing a branch environment. The success of these companies has been one of the major factors leading to a change of strategy from many banks and building societies. They have re-examined their marketing strategies, and many of them (while maintaining their branch networks) have introduced new methods of distribution in an attempt to reach as many customers as possible. The choice of distribution method is one of the most critical decisions in financial services marketing: it affects all other retailing decisions, and often involves long-term commitment and large financial resources.

1.3 The emergence and the success of these alternative distribution methods has meant that a typical financial services retailer now has to think in terms of a distribution mix and a delivery strategy rather than simply a distribution method. Even though one method of delivery may be dominant, the mix will need to be very carefully managed in order that they compliment each other rather than compete. The key to successfully managing this mix is to balance the customer needs with the cost of the delivery method and the potential income that will come from the sale to ensure that both the customer and the organisation benefit.

1.4 This unit will investigate both the indirect marketing channels such as EFTPOS and home banking and the direct methods of distribution such as direct mail and direct sales forces.

Indirect

1.5 An indirect method of distribution typically refers to a system which makes use of an intermediary outlet, or technology. The major disadvantage with this method is that it generally requires the customer to make the first approach i.e. it is a passive marketing method.

Direct

1.6 This describes any method of distribution by which the product is supplied straight to the customer without any involvement from a third party. Direct distribution is often divided into two categories.

- Those methods which use a sales force to deal on a face to face basis, often in the customer's home.
- Those methods using media such as newspapers and leaflets requesting a response from the customer. These methods can be used in isolation or as complementary to those in the first category. Both of these will now be examined in more detail.

2 Direct sales force

2.1 A large number of retailers, particularly insurance companies, still sell the majority of their products through a 'direct sales force'. This phrase is used to describe a team of highly trained sales professionals who work for one company to sell that company's range of products and services to the public. The company commands the salespeople's total allegiance and they can work for no other company as long as the agreement exists. Salespeople have a duty to inform customers that they represent one company only, and that they can therefore only recommend that company's products. In return for selling the company's products, the salespeople receive a salary, a commission, or a mix of both.

2.2 The sales force occupies a unique position as the link between the customer and the provider company. As far as the customer is concerned, the sales force is the face of the company. This position is made difficult by the fact that salespeople have to work in the interests of the company, but also have a duty to act in the best interests of the customer. In the financial services industry, recent adverse publicity has meant that, in order to be successful, the salesperson must be able to obtain the trust of his or her customers. Because of this, the recruitment, training and motivation of the direct sales force are crucial, and these are examined in more detail in Unit 13.

2.3 The direct sales force has traditionally been a very successful way of selling financial services products. The industrial insurance companies used their door-to-door premium collectors to sell further products to the family and friends of their original customers, thereby ensuring a stream of new business. Many insurance companies also use large direct sales forces to sell their products by means of prospecting and home visits. Here the salesperson uses anything, from electoral rolls and telephone directories to personal recommendations, to find suitable customers. The salesperson then interviews the prospective customer and completes the sale in the customer's own home.

2.4 The number and size of direct sales forces in operation has increased in recent years due to the increase in home ownership. As the mortgage market has increased, direct sales forces have been used to sell accompanying endowment products. The decrease in the number of *independent* advisors offering their services to the public (as a result of the costs and difficulties of complying with stricter regulation) has also tended to increase the direct sales forces.

2.5 While it is usual to associate the phrase 'direct sales force' with a team of full time salesmen and women who visit customers' homes, we must remember that in many financial situations the sales force will in fact be members of the branch team. These members of staff will have dual responsibilities, both to service business and customer queries but also to act as the sales point for further products.

2.6 Many banks and building societies now have their own direct sales forces to promote their insurance products. However, these have tended to be based in their readily accessible branch network rather than offering home visits.

2.7 There are many advantages in choosing a direct sales force as the distribution method. For example,

- they can be used to sell more complex products, as the competent and highly trained salesperson will be able to explain features and answer queries
- they offer the customer the individual, personal approach and develop a level of rapport and trust with the customer
- because of their depth of discussions with customers, salespeople can give valuable feedback on customer needs and input into future product development.

2.8 However, there are also drawbacks to this method. For example,

- a direct sales force is extremely expensive to operate; the recruitment and training of these sales professionals involves a large financial commitment for a length of time before any return is shown; ongoing costs can also be high, involving such things as salaries, provision of cars for home visits and ongoing training
- the regulatory environment in which most sales forces operate means that the supervision of the salesperson can be both time consuming and costly. Any rogue salespeople can damage the company's reputation and also lead to severe punishments for both the individual and the company.

Student Activity

1 Explain how the use of a direct sales force has evolved over time.

2 What are the advantages and disadvantages of selling financial services via a direct sales force?

3 Telephone-based sales operations

3.1 The growth of the telephone as a method of distribution of financial services products has already been discussed. The costs involved in the operation of a direct sales force make telephone-based sales an attractive alternative. The use of the telephone is now common practice for the purchase of general insurance, such as motor and household cover. Companies such as Direct Line lead the way, but have been closely followed by many of their competitors. Similarly, First Direct led the market in telephone banking, allowing customer access to the usual banking services without the need to visit a branch. First Direct have now been followed by a large number of other companies and banking by telephone is now commonplace.

3.2 Although it was initially felt that this distribution method would only prove popular with the more sophisticated end of the market, the public's general acceptance of the use of the telephone for the purchasing of financial services had led many companies to consider it as a viable alternative for other products within this sector.

3.3 Some building societies now offer mortgages by phone to customers who prefer not to visit a branch for an interview. Also, insurance companies and bancassurers now use the telephone as a method of selling supporting endowments and other insurance and investment products to the public. This market, that of telesales for life assurance and pension products, has yet to experience the successes described above, but is considered to be a growth market and is seeing many new entrants keen to exploit this potentially lucrative new distribution channel. The sale of life and investment products via the telephone can be done in one of two ways.

1 The provider can offer products for sale to people who telephone knowing exactly what they want. An application can be completed over the telephone and, in some cases, the first premium can be paid by debit card.

In the case of life assurance products cover can, in some cases, be granted instantly.

2 The provider can offer advice over the telephone. The regulatory requirements are the same as for giving advice face-to-face, and details must be forwarded to the customer to sign. Again, some customers can be offered cover instantly.

3.4 Some providers offer a service that combines telephone and direct sales force selling. The customer makes initial contact with the company using the telephone; then, if the case is complex, or more personal contact is required, an appointment is made for a salesperson to call at their home. This method of combining the two sales approaches has yet to achieve any major success in the industry.

3.5 There are both advantages and disadvantages to the use of the telephone as a distribution method for financial services. Some of these are described below.

Advantages of telephone-based sales

3.6 Costs are much lower than those of a 'face-to-face' salesforce. The salesperson who sells via the telephone can do so for a very large proportion of his or her working day as they are not required to travel to customers' homes. Also, calls that prove to be inappropriate do not waste several hours of the salesperson's day – he or she simply answers another call.

3.7 The customer has access to financial services outside office hours. Many telesales centres are open until 10 o'clock in the evening, allowing customers to deal with their financial affairs at a time that is most convenient to them, and from the comfort of their own homes.

Disadvantages of telephone-based sales

3.8 It allows the organisation to reach a segment of the market that would not have otherwise bought from them. Many of the people who buy via the telephone do so because they don't want to visit the branch and don't want a salesperson to call at their home.

3.9 The service offered via the telephone must be efficient, and therefore the use of technology is imperative. This can mean large initial costs for any company considering setting up a telephone-based sales organisation.

3.10 The personal contact and development of a trust-based customer relationship is much more difficult for this type of distribution, as compared with the use of a direct sales force.

Student Activity

1 What type of financial services are currently sold via the telephone, and which products may be sold using this distribution method in the future?

2 What are the advantages and disadvantages of a telesales organisation?

4 Telemarketing

4.1 The phrase telemarketing is used to cover any form of direct marketing which uses the telephone to make contact with the customer. Unlike the other forms of direct marketing, it allows immediate contact with the prospect. It can be used in many different ways, some of which are examined below.

4.2 *Maintaining up-to-date data* A financial services retailer needs an up-to-date database if they are to be successful. The telephone can be used to contact customers, to gather, update or verify the information that is held.

4.3 *Lead-generation* Probably the widest use of the telephone is the generation of leads, which can then be followed up by a visit from a member of the direct sales force. The telemarketing operator will call prospects whose names come from a variety of sources, e.g. the organisation's database, or lists bought in from specialist companies. Telephoning is a quick, and therefore cost-effective, method of lead-generation.

4.4 *Test marketing* The telephone can be used as a method of test marketing any of the retailer's products and services. It is particularly useful, as the response is immediate.

4.5 *Relationship building* By keeping in contact with our customers, we are demonstrating that we value their business, and would appreciate the opportunity to do business with them again. When we need to contact our customers, using the telephone is a more personal way of doing so than simply sending a letter. It will strengthen the relationship that the organisation has with the customers. We know that there is a great deal of customer loyalty in the financial services retailing sector, and that loyalty is a factor influencing customers when they purchase further products.

Advantages of telemarketing

4.6
- The use of the telephone gains an immediate response from the customer and is therefore quick and effective.
- It can be used as a low-cost method of generating leads for the direct sales force, whose time is better spent servicing calls rather than having to look for their own customers and operate their own leads.
- It helps to cement the relationship between the retailer and the customer, and ensure that the information held on the database is accurate and up to date.

Disadvantages of telemarketing

4.7
- There is a danger that telemarketing can seem intrusive. The organisation is reaching right into the customer's home, and may do so at an inconvenient time.
- Because of this intrusiveness, many customers dislike cold calling. If they are telephoned they may have negative feelings towards the organisation, and be inclined to go elsewhere to satisfy their next financial need.

Student Activity

1 Explain what is meant by telemarketing and how it can be used.

2 What are the possible disadvantages of using the telephone to try to generate leads for the sales force?

5 Direct mail and direct response advertising

5.1 The use of direct mail as a retailing tool for financial services products has increased substantially in recent years, and financial institutions are amongst Britain's leading users of such facilities.

5.2 Direct mail is often used to solicit sales of a particular product from a specific market place. For example, it may be used to achieve the sale of credit cards to high earners, or life assurance to families with children.

5.3 Direct mail can, for example, take the form of a mailshot included in a magazine or paper whose readership is known tc be made up of the target market. More usually, direct mail is sent to existing customers of the organisation who may require further products. The customer responds by completing the form, either to receive further details about the product, or to apply for the product itself.

5.4 The success of a direct mail campaign depends largely on the choice of the customers to be mailed. Improvements in technology have made it possible for banks, building societies and insurance companies to target their mailshots more successfully by segmenting their huge customer databases. While traditionally such segmentation was based only on geographical or demographic factors, many customer databases can now be segmented by such things as habits, attitudes, lifestyle factors or profession. The more accurate the segmentation, and the more tightly defined the recipient customers are, the greater the level of response. Selecting the customer in this way also allows the material mailed to be designed with that specific target group in mind, rather than having to adopt an approach to suit everybody. If mailshots are properly targeted they become highly cost effective.

5.5 Any direct mailing will have one of the following objectives.

- To provide customers with information about the products and services the retailer has to offer.
- To stimulate sufficient interest from the customer to encourage them to contact the company and request more information.
- To help the customer recognise that they have a need, and that they require advice, therefore arranging for an appointment with a member of the sales force.

5.6 Direct response advertising is a phrase used to cover both direct mail and press and leaflet advertising. In direct mailshots the customer is usually provided with sufficient information to be able to purchase the advertised product, usually by completing an enclosed application form. In press and leaflet form, the product is usually sold using a two-stage process. The customer is generally required to respond to the advertisement by requesting further information. The provider company then sends an information pack and the customer responds in a similar way to that outlined above.

5.7 Generally, the use of direct mail and direct response advertising means that the customer buys the product without the involvement of a salesperson, either employed or independent. If successful, this method of distribution is very cost effective. Some companies also use a combination of the distribution methods. For example, a customer who reads a direct response advertisement may be able to request an appointment with an adviser rather than an information pack.

5.8 Although a wide variety of products can be sold by this method of distribution, those that are sold most successfully tend to be the simpler products that customers feel comfortable buying without the need for advice.

5.9 There are advantages and disadvantages to this method of distribution. Some of these are described below.

Advantages of direct mail and direct response advertising

5.10 The lack of involvement of salespeople means there are no commission payments. Thus the costs of acquiring the business can be kept very low.

5.11 The use of direct response advertising can generate a huge database of customers who prefer to deal direct. These customers can then be mailed with other product offerings, so achieving low-cost cross sales.

5.12 The Financial Services Act has placed many restrictions and much regulation on the information that must be given to a customer in any advertisement for a regulated product. The use of direct mail allows a greater amount of information to be given to the customer.

5.13 Financial services products can be very complex, and customers' knowledge of them may be fairly limited. The use of direct mail allow customers to read and reread the information if they choose to, and also allows them time to come to a decision on what to do. It may therefore prove a success with people who are nervous of moving too quickly into buying.

5.14 With direct mail, the message can be personalised, sometimes merely by adding the customer's name, on other occasions by targeting them with something known to be of particular interest. The more personalised the sales message is, the more powerful it is as a sales tool.

5.15 Even if the customer does not respond to the mailing by purchasing another product, there will be additional benefits that come from regular customer contact: in other words, those of relationship building.

5.16 The results of a direct mail campaign are relatively easy to monitor. The provider simply measures the number of customers who respond and buy a product, against the numbers and costs involved in the mailing.

5.17 Direct mail is very controllable. The provider has ultimate control over who receives the mailing, what is included in the mailing pack and when it is sent.

Disadvantages of direct mail and direct response advertising

5.18 If not properly targeted and tested, response rates can be low, and therefore the return on the capital outlay will be low.

5.19 Selling 'off the page' may need a different, simpler, separately priced product range to that offered through brokers and this will involve time, effort and capital outlay to achieve.

5.20 Direct response advertising is much less easy to target than direct mail and therefore response rates may be lower.

Student Activity

1 Describe how direct mail is used in the retailing of financial services.

2 What are the advantages and disadvantages of this distribution method?

6 Electronic fund transfers and ATMs

6.1 There are many types of technology links between the financial services provider and the customer, which can be used as methods of distribution. We will look briefly at the following.

- Electronic fund transfer at place of living (EFTPOL)
- Electronic fund transfer at point of sale (EFTPOS)
- Electronic fund transfer at place of banking (EFTPOB)
- Smart cards
- Electronic purses

6.2 EFTPOL is more commonly known as 'home banking'. It can be offered in a screen-based form and a telephone-based form. The screen-based systems offer more services, and more complex services, than those offered via the telephone. However, telephone-based systems are more cost effective and more accessible. EFTPOL is most commonly used in respect of cash management, and can be used by individuals or businesses. So far, this has not proved to be very popular with individuals, compared with other electronic developments.

6.3 Electronic fund transfers at point of sale (EFTPOS) is essentially a payment method that is also often described as a distribution method. Attempts have been made to develop a national EFTPOS involving the clearing banks and some building societies; however these have failed, largely as a result of delays caused by the desire for an open membership that would allow any financial organisation to participate.

6.4 The introduction of independent, though less ambitious, EFTPOS systems, and the growth in the use of debit cards, have led to a reduction in the level of cash in circulation. They have also prompted further developments in the area of supporting technology and have slowed the growth of the level of overheads for financial services companies.

6.5 The increasing use of such systems poses a threat to the traditional branch network, as the reduction in the need for cash potentially lessens the need for the high street branch.

6.6 As we saw in earlier units, this move to a cashless society is likely to continue. The use of EFTPOS and debit cards is enabling the telesales market to grow, and this is likely to continue. We may also see the introduction of 'electronic purses' that store money, usually drawn directly from the customer's bank account.

6.7 The most familiar format EFTPOB is the cash dispenser or ATM. Marketing messages can be displayed on ATM screens, leading to the belief that these machines could also be used as a distribution channel. Many ATMs already allow the customer to complete a variety of tasks (such as balance enquiries, cheque book orders and transfers between accounts) as well as withdrawing cash. So far it has been felt that simple single-transaction machines are most appropriate for general use as they are less likely to malfunction, and less likely to lead to queues and delays for the customer. However, ATMs could be used to encourage customers to request additional services from their bank or building society in a similar way to mailshots.

6.8 Smart cards look similar to debit or credit cards. The difference is that a smart card contains a microchip which holds huge amounts of information about the customer. The card would contain all the details about the customer's account, and could be used to conduct transfers off-line. Although these are not currently widely adopted in the UK, they are much more common in continental Europe. The advantage of smart cards from a retailer's point of view is that they would allow efficient and effective information processing, and make customer information more accurately targeted.

6.9 Electronic purse is a method of reducing the amount of cash used, and therefore reducing the risk associated with it. An electronic purse would work in the following way.

- The customer is supplied with a plastic card similar to a credit or debit card.
- As a security measure, the customer is also supplied with a personal identity number.
- Money can be 'loaded' on to the card by transferring some of the balance from a bank or building society account.
- When the customer wishes to pay for goods or services, the card is swiped in a similar way to the use of a debit card.

6.10 Trials of this type of card have been carried out, but it remains to be seen if they will ever achieve the popularity currently enjoyed by credit and debit cards.

Student Activity

1 What do you understand by the term EFTPOL, and what are its advantages to the customer?

2 Explain briefly what an electronic purse is.

7 IFAs and brokers

7.1 Many companies rely on other firms to distribute their products to the end customer. In other industries it is common practice for manufacturers to distribute their products to wholesalers, who in turn distribute to retailers and then on to the ultimate customers. While financial services products have very different characteristics, and therefore require different sales methods, it is still common for a third party to be involved in sales. These third parties do not purchase the goods and sell them on, but simply bring the customer and the provider together. They receive a commission payment for doing this.

7.2 These third parties are known as 'brokers'. Before the emergence of the telesales market in recent years, this method of distribution was the method by which most motor insurance was sold, and it still accounts for a large proportion of the general insurance market. The customer details his or her need to the broker, and the broker recommends a product and a provider. In exchange, the broker is paid a commission by the provider company.

7.3 This method of distribution is also used to sell life assurance, pensions and investment products. Since the Financial Services Act and the polarisation requirements therein, brokers are required to act either solely for one company or as an independent financial adviser. These IFAs are individuals or companies who are free to enter into agreements with any number of provider companies to sell their products. This means that when a customer is seen by an IFA and explains his or her needs, the IFA must consider and recommend not only the most suitable type of product, but the best available in the whole market place. The IFA must recommend the product and provider that most clearly meets the customer's need. Such decisions can be based on criteria such as

- price
- investment performance
- claims paying history
- product features
- service offered
- financial security of the provider company.

7.4 With this method of retailing, the company depends heavily on the broker for its business, and therefore usually employ salespeople to ensure that the best possible service is offered by the IFA.

7.5 Because the IFAs are independent (that is, not employed by any of the provider companies) they are responsible for their own expenses and the costs of such things as training and complying with the regulations. This has meant that, as the regulatory requirements have become more stringent and the competition from other retailing methods has increased, the number of IFAs has decreased.

7.6 Although IFAs still represent a large proportion of the business of insurance companies, their customers tend to be at the more sophisticated end of the market. IFAs typically deal with large cases and corporate clients as well as individuals. This is likely to be exacerbated if the market for selling life products direct increases. This would mean that many of the simpler products would be dealt with directly leaving IFA's to concentrate their efforts on the complex customer needs. There is also a trend for IFAs to ask for the commission they would have earned from a product sale to be reinvested in the product, or rebated to the customer. Instead of receiving this commission, the IFA charges the customer a fee for their advice. This method of doing business is intended to increase the impression of the professionalism of the broker, who offers their services in a similar way to an accountant or solicitor. It also means that the IFA earns an income even if the customer decides not to buy. Often this means that the customer who does buy a product is better off financially. However, the introduction of fee paying to IFAs means that in years to come independent advice may only be available to those who can afford to pay for it and, more importantly, who are willing to pay for it.

7.7 There are a number of advantages and disadvantages to selling financial services products through brokers. Some of these are described below.

Advantages of IFAs and brokers

7.8 Selling through IFAs and brokers means there is only a cost where a sale is made. Although the company will pay commission for each sale, there are no salaries to pay to the brokers, as they are independent of the provider company.

7.9 There are fewer regulatory requirements. Many of the regulatory requirements surrounding the sale of life assurance and investments relate to the time of the sale and the customer contact at the time of the recommendation. This is the responsibility of the IFA rather than the provider company.

Disadvantages of IFAs and brokers

7.10 The company is reliant on the third party to introduce business. If the broker decides to favour another provider, business is lost.

7.11 There are no cross sales opportunities. The majority of IFAs require a company to agree not to cross sell other products in their range to the customer, before they will agree to introduce business to them. This means that every sale requires a new customer.

Student Activity

1 Write a paragraph to explain how the future business of the IFA is likely to change.

2 Briefly describe the advantages and disadvantages of using brokers as a retailing method.

8 How different distribution channels add value

8.1 The choice of distribution channel is an extremely important one, as the correct choice will make a huge impact on the profits enjoyed by the company. The selection of distribution method will be influenced by the type of product being sold; the knowledge and the needs of the customer; and the benefit that can be gained by the financial services provider.

8.2 *Product* We looked in Unit 1 at the characteristics of financial services products, and we will now examine how those factors may influence the choice of marketing method. The products are intangible, and therefore there is nothing physical to attract the customer to make the first move and approach the provider. This may lead the provider to feel that they would be better served by employing sales men and women to guide the customers through the sales process. We also saw that many financial services products are very complicated, and this could be another factor steering the provider towards employing face-to-face sales people to promote them.

8.3 *Customers* The whole purpose of a distribution channel is to get the product to the customer. It follows, therefore, that the needs of those customers are of vital importance when selecting which distribution channel to use.

8.4 Let us now look at some of the customer's needs and see how this will affect the decision.

- Access, for many financial services products, is a major factor in selecting a product and a provider. For such things as cash withdrawal and account transactions, the provider may decide that automation is the method to use. They might decide to install ATMs in remote sites away from branches to satisfy this customer need.
- Convenience will be a factor in the purchase of products, but will be more important for some products than others. For example, when selecting a building society, customers are likely to rate convenience of the branch as one of the highest factors influencing their decision. However, when choosing a pension product, say, they would not rate convenience nearly as high as brand of provider and their relationship with the company.
- If customers are very knowledgeable about the product and the market place, they may be happy to buy using a direct method, such as direct mail, or indirectly by approaching a third party or by using technology. However, those customers who are not confident in the understanding of the products on offer will require advice. Providers may choose a direct sales force to satisfy such people.

9 Benefits for the provider

9.1 Although the needs of the customer are extremely important, consideration must also be given to what benefits the provider will achieve by the use of any distribution method. This benefit could be in the form of profit to the organisation, but might also take the form of increased customer awareness or strengthening of the brand value.

9.2 Some of the factors which may affect the benefits of each channel to the provider company are as follows.

- Intermediary commission payments, that is, the amount an IFA would be paid for selling the product, will reduce the amount of profit available to the company. The company might then have to charge more for the product. This would have to be considered carefully.
- The low charges and low costs involved with direct mail may mean that the provider can make greater profits using this method, provided it fits with the product type, customer knowledge and customer needs.
- The organisation may benefit from increased customer loyalty and an enhanced reputation if it employs sales men and women to explain its products and handle customers' questions. It may also gain advertisement and name awareness from having a high street presence and a branch network.
- The provider must also consider the product's positioning and quality image, and see how this might be affected by selecting different distribution channels.

10 Distribution strategy of a financial services provider

10.1 Balancing all the factors mentioned above and designing a distribution strategy is a very complex matter. Getting it right can be a huge benefit to the organisation; conversely getting it wrong may be disastrous for company profits. Traditionally, banks and building societies relied totally on branch networks to sell their products. The changing environment, the increase in competition and the changing needs of customers have led most providers to re-examine their distribution strategy. As a result, most banks and building societies now use a much greater variety of marketing methods to sell their products.

10.2 Distribution channels should never be seen as being in competition, but as complementary and adding value to the organisation and its customers. By using a mix of channels, the company can increase the number of customers they reach, and therefore the profit they make. The disadvantages of one distribution method are often another method's advantages. For example, buying insurance over the telephone will appeal to those customers who require convenience, easy access to the product and speed of delivery. However, those looking for the reassurance of a friendly face-to-face visit would not be attracted to that particular channel.

10.3 Thus, by knowing and understanding customer needs, the provider can select a mix of distribution methods, to ensure they get their product to the right customers at the right place and at the right time.

10.4 To select this correct mix, the marketing manager will need to ask, and get answers to, the following questions.

- Who are the customers, and what is their knowledge?
- Where are these customers located?
- What products are they looking for?
- What is the nature of those products?
- What distribution benefits are the customers seeking?
- How are the competitors distributing their products? In other words, what other options are available to the customers?

It is these facts that will enable an effective distribution strategy to be designed and successfully implemented.

Summary

Figure 8.1 shows a summary of the different distribution methods available for financial services companies.

Figure 8.1 Available distribution methods

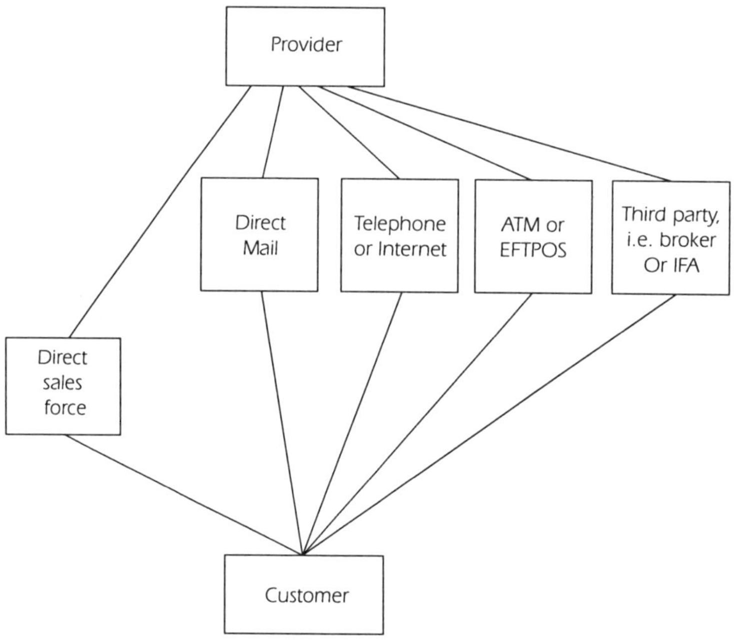

Student Activity

1 Explain briefly how the characteristics of the product may influence the provider's choice of distribution method.

2 How will such a decision be affected by the needs and knowledge of the customers?

3 How does the choice of distribution method add value for the provider company?

11 Case study and analysis

11.1 The Yorkshire Equitable Insurance company has been providing life assurance pensions and investments for just over 200 years. It is firmly established as one of the country's leading insurance companies. They have 0.75 million customers and £200 million funds under management.

11.2 They currently conduct almost all their business through IFAs, amongst whom they have an enviable reputation for products and services. They chose not to become involved in the acquisition of estate agents, even though many of their competitors entered that market several years ago. Instead they chose to concentrate on the intermediaries. This strategy has been rewarded by increasing support from the brokers. Business has increased in all areas in recent years.

11.3 To ensure continued support from the IFAs, they have agreed not to cross-sell to any of the customers they have had introduced to them.

11.4 However, last year, following an increase in customer calls enquiring about their investment products, the company launched a PEP product. This they sold on an execution-only basis to customers who telephoned them. After only a few months it was apparent that this product was a huge success, and is proving an excellent source of revenue to the company.

11.5 Yorkshire Equitable Insurance are more than aware of the direct operations currently enjoying success in the life assurance, pensions and investment areas. They have spent a considerable amount of time and effort studying their set-ups and marketing strategies. In previous years they conducted similar research into the direct sales forces operated by other companies; but after careful consideration have always rejected the temptation to follow suit, preferring instead to concentrate on their single distribution channel, thereby strengthening their standing with the IFAs.

11.6 Currently, there is growing support among the management and the board to expand, by offering a new direct distribution channel. Proposals have been put forward to offer a reduced product range to the public via the telephone. This would involve opening a call centre, where customers would telephone either to buy products on an execution-only basis, or to obtain advice from trained tele-advisers.

11.7 This would involve the company venturing into the area of direct mail, which would be new to it, but they believe it would be highly profitable.

11.8 Opposing this new venture are several members of the management team, who believe that such a move would upset some of the IFAs. It could result, they claim, in a loss of business which they think would be greater than the income the new venture would bring to the company.

11.9 Suppose that you work for one the members of the board who firmly supports the new distribution channel. You have been asked to prepare a paper for the next management meeting explaining why you feel that this move would be the correct strategy for the company.

11.10 Within the report you would need to address the following.

- Why now is the right time to enter the direct market.
- How you feel the business from the other channel would be affected.
- Your recommendations as to what actions to take to minimise the impact.
- What areas of necessary expertise the company may have to acquire.
- The methods of lead-generation you would recommend the company uses to attract customers to telephone the call centre.
- The benefits that would be gained by the company by entering this market, in addition to the purely financial ones.

11.11 Your report would need to contain the following information.

- This would be a good time to enter the direct market, as selling life, pensions and investment products using the telephone is a growing market.
- Customers' attitudes to direct buying is changing. Using a telephone to buy motor and household insurance is now commonplace, and this new-found confidence is starting to spread to other areas of the financial industry. There is also a great deal of promotional activity being carried out by other insurance providers and this is helping to raise customer awareness of this distribution channel.
- With the ever-increasing advances in technology and customer knowledge, and with the market becoming increasingly competitive, it is an ideal time to become involved in an emerging market. This will enable the company to become a market leader.
- Although there is no guarantee that the launch of an additional distribution channel will not affect business from the IFAs, these two methods of selling products should be seen as complementary rather than in competition with each other.
- It is unlikely that the type of customer who deals through an IFA would change to buying life and pensions business over the telephone. When using an IFA they will be doing so because they want the personal touch and face-to-face advice. They would not get this from a direct operation. Therefore the two different channels appeal to different customers.
- By launching the second channel, additional customers would be attracted to the company, rather than moving them from one sales method to another.
- To minimise problems, such as the IFAs' perception of the direct channel, it may help to sell the products direct to the public using a different brand.

- The IFAs are most likely to object if the public are able to buy the same product direct at a cheaper price. Because of the economies of a direct channel, the company is likely to want to price differentially. This may mean that the company needs to develop a new range of products.
- By developing new products, they can tailor these to the needs of the customers they expect to attract. For example, they may choose to make them simpler and offer fewer add-on options, making them easier to explain over the telephone.
- The company may feel they want to keep IFAs up to date with the developments of the new channel, and reiterate their agreement not to cross-sell, in order to keep any bad feeling to a minimum.
- The company may need to acquire direct marketing expertise. When dealing only through IFAs, the company only becomes involved in a sale once the customer has decided to buy the product. Any lead-generation activity is undertaken by the broker.
- The company will need to ensure that they have the right training and testing for their sales people. This is another area in which they are not currently involved.
- Although the Yorkshire Equitable currently has a team of sales men and women who service the IFAs, they will now have to have a team who will be dealing directly with the public. This will require different skills, and they may need to acquire new sales management expertise.
- The company should test a number of lead-generation methods, including:
  - outwards calling from lists or previous contacts (not those who have bought from IFAs)
  - newspaper advertisements
  - direct response advertising
  - direct mail
  - advertorials
  - radio or TV advertisements.
- Apart from the financial benefits, the company will also achieve a new brand and the opportunity to become a market leader in an expanding area.
- By collecting data on the people who call or fill in coupons, the company will be constantly expanding its database, which can then be used for further marketing opportunities.

Summary

Now that you have completed this unit, you should be able to describe each of the following methods of retailing financial services

- ❑ **direct sales forces**
- ❑ **telephone-based sales operations**
- ❑ **direct mail and direct response advertising**
- ❑ **electronic fund transfers at point of sale**
- ❑ **intermediaries, including IFAs and brokers.**

Self-assessment questions

1 Compare and contrast the use of direct sales and telephone-based sales in the marketing of financial services products.

2 Describe the operation of direct mail and direct response advertising.

3 Briefly explain how EFTPOS might be used in the marketing of financial services products.

4 Explain the advantages and disadvantages of using intermediaries in the marketing of financial services products.

Unit 9

Product management

Objectives

After studying this unit you should be able to do the following.

- **Describe the nature of market research.**
- **Explain the influences on product strategies.**
- **Describe product planning, the use of product life cycles and the use of the BCG and directional policy matrices in that planning.**
- **Describe the process of developing new products and modifying or eliminating existing ones.**
- **Explain the role of the branch in product management.**

1 Introduction

1.1 The purpose of product management within any financial services institution is to develop and manage a range of products that ensure the company remains competitive in its market. The company must attract customers and complete enough sales to make a profit.

1.2 Product management can be, very broadly, broken down into three areas.

1. The development of new products.
2. The promotion of the products.
3. The maintenance of existing products including, where appropriate, their elimination.

Underpinning this process is the necessity of having accurate information about the market. This is provided by market research.

2 Market research

2.1 Market research is a means of providing sound market information to guide business decisions. Its use has two main purposes

- to reduce uncertainty when business decisions and marketing strategy are being planned
- to monitor performance after the decisions have been taken and the strategies have been put into operation.

Both roles are essential. The costs associated with any action – such as a product development, a change in distribution channel, or a branch relocation – mean that companies can ill afford to make incorrect decisions. Performance evaluation is almost equally important, in order to learn and improve future strategies.

2.2 Market research is essential in all sectors where products are being marketed to consumers, whether the product is a financial service, a brand of toothpaste or a political party. However, the financial sector is a major research user given its size, complexity and need for continuous product strategies.

2.3 Equally, market research applies both to domestic consumers and businesses as consumers of services, although the research methods used will differ.

Information sources

2.4 Many methods are available for conducting market research, so, before starting any research project, it is essential to define the business problem to be addressed. Careful discussion is then needed on the type of research required, what should be gained from it, and the cost and value of the information gained.

2.5 The next stage is to consider how to source the required information. First, desk research reviews existing data sources: they are more cost-effective to use than collecting new data. There are several kinds of source, as follows.

Customer data

2.6 Analysing existing customers can reveal buying rates, product loyalty and usage patterns. However, it does not reveal the reasons for customer behaviour. Nor does it provide details of customers' use of competing products.

Official statistics

2.7 The Office for National Statistics (ONS) publishes a wide range of statistics covering all industrial sectors and markets and national accounts. They monitor levels of trade, consumer expenditure and demography.

Population censuses

2.8 The decennial census is the largest of the ONS sources, and provides consumer demographics at local, regional and national levels. Census data may be obtained from ONS, and more detailed data and analysis from Agencies (see *Geodemographics*, below).

Syndicated market research

2.9 Some agencies collect data continuously, tracking market movements and product shares. Within the financial sector, the leading sources are NOP (Financial Research Survey) and MORI (Financial Survey).

Geodemographics

2.10 The census agencies have developed 'added value' data and reports based on census and syndicated data. These include nationwide area classifications (ACORN and MOSAIC) which also provide estimates of consumer demand. These are invaluable for retail planning and site location, etc.

Data collection techniques

2.11 Existing sources may not provide all the information needed. When designing bespoke market research, anonymity (both for the respondent and client) is essential. Research is of two kinds: qualitative research and quantitative research.

Qualitative research

2.12 Qualitative research is used to discover how and why something is happening. It probes people's unconscious attitudes and needs. Small samples of respondents are used for in-depth interviews (one-to-one), and group discussions, or focus groups.

Quantitative research

2.13 Quantitative research supplies numbers to anything that can be measured, and often follows a qualitative study to provide hard data. There are several techniques.

- Face-to-face interviews allow interviewers to ask complex questions and use visual aids.
- Telephone interviews can be speedy and controlled centrally.
- Postal surveys are more cost effective than personal interviews, but attract a lower rate of response.
- Omnibus research adds extra questions to an existing panel.
- Panels involve the same people over a long period and are useful to establish trends.

2.14 All these techniques aim to survey a representative sample from the total population of interest. Conclusions are then drawn about the whole population from these samples. Sample size is critical, so a balance must be struck between cost and an ideal sample size. Many market research agencies can offer help in designing this research.

Methods of analysis

2.15 Qualitative researchers analyse the results of their interviews to provide an interpretation of underlying attitudes and needs. Quantitative analysis often uses cross-tabulations, comparing the various answers received, often divided into classes of respondent. Sophisticated techniques are also available for modelling, product pricing consumer preferences and forccasting. Graphs are often used for presenting such material.

Student Activity

1 Why is reserarch so important in product management?

2 Outline the different methods of research that can be used.

3 The product

3.1 The product can be argued to be the most important element of the retailing mix, as only with a reasonable product will the effort put into such things as pricing and promotion reap any rewards. The intangibility of financial services products means that, probably more so than with other products, customers do not purchase them because they want them, but for the benefits they bring. For example, a customer who applies for a credit card does so not for the card itself but for the ability to purchase goods and services instantly without the need to carry cash, and for the instant credit the card allows. This becomes an important point when looking at the skills involved in making a sale. The salesperson must always remember that the customer is not going to buy the product features but the benefits that those features bring.

3.2 In terms of financial services, the term 'product' is commonly used to cover all of the offering from the provider, despite the fact that the majority are in fact services and are intangible.

3.3 Each product is borne from a product concept that can be expressed as three levels, as shown in Figure 9.1.

Figure 9.1 The three levels of a product concept.

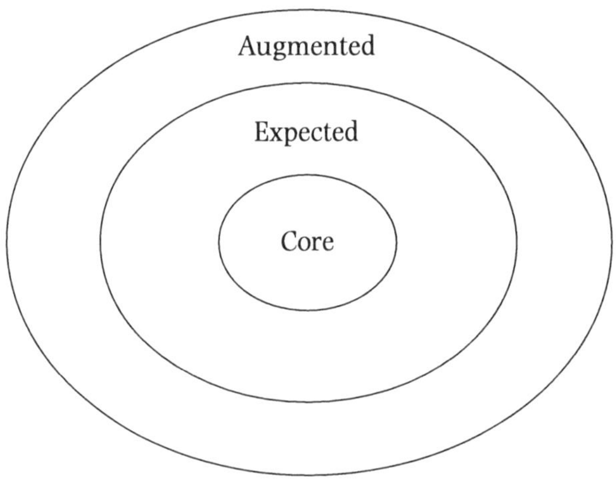

3.4 The *core* of the product is the basic essential element that all products of that nature must offer. For example, all pension plans must offer an investment element that provides the sum to pay the pension; all motor insurance must provide cover in the event of an accident.

3.5 The second layer of the concept is the *expected* product. This comprises those features that are in addition to the core element of the product but which customers expect to find, and which they consider desirable from a product of that nature. For example, the provision of a no-claims discount on a motor insurance policy. It is at this stage of the product concept that differences between providers emerge, as different companies hold differing views as to what the customer wants and expects from them.

3.6 The third element of the product concept is the *augmented* product. That is, the additional features over and above what the average customer may expect. These additions generally take the form of a service. For example, Direct Line offer to save customers time following an accident by collecting their car, shopping around for repair quotations, arranging the repairs and then delivering the car, cleaned inside and out, back to the customer. These additional extras can gain a company a real edge on the market and improve their competitive position. However, if an additional feature proves very successful it is likely that competitors will also see the benefit of it and it will soon become part of the 'expected product'.

3.7 The product concept can prove very useful when looking at various elements of product management, particularly product development and enhancement.

4 Influences on product strategy

4.1 Successful product management relies on a well planned and executed product strategy and product range strategy. We look first at some of the things that influence such a strategy.

Competitors

4.2 Competitor analysis is very important within any industry, as tracking changes to their product range and product mix can give important guidance on the way in which the market is likely to move. It also shows the type of products that competitors feel customers want now, or will be looking for in the future.

4.3 This is particularly true within the financial services industry, where it is generally accepted that the services offered by one provider are very much the same as those offered elsewhere. It is also accepted that within the industry a great deal of copying of products occurs, so that if one company finds a gap in the market and launches a new product, very shortly many others will follow, offering very similar things. This means that tracking the products offered by competitors is essential when designing a product strategy. It is now common practice for rival firms to exchange product information on a regular basis.

Customer needs

4.4 When retailing financial services it is of paramount importance to understand what the customer wants. The provider needs to know such things as

- who the customers are (age, sex, socio-economic class, demographics, etc.)
- what led them to make the decision to buy
- what influenced their choice of product

- which product features appeal to them
- how they use the product
- what influenced their choice of provider.

4.5 The provider also needs to know whether the customer, having bought a product, is happy with it. What made the buying experience good or bad? Would they buy again from the same company, or from a different one?

4.6 Only when this type of information is collected and analysed can a company properly plan their product strategy. However, understanding its present customers is not in itself sufficient. A company must also understand the needs of potential customers – people who have not yet made a decision to buy.

4.7 This need to understand both customers and non-customers can be aided by the use of the sophisticated data bases now commonplace in financial services providers. With these databases providers can record enormous amounts of information about their customers and about people to whom they have spoken but who did not buy. The databases of some companies run into millions of entries and therefore, provided they are kept up to date, they will provide a very rich source of factual data.

4.8 By manipulating this data product managers can gain a very rich picture of their customers including such things as a profile of the typical product buyer. For example they may find that the main buyers of their PEP product are married people aged between 55 and 70, who have grown up children and who fall into socio-economic groups A and B. This type of information will be extremely useful both when designing or amending the product and its features, and when planning the marketing campaign. Only by having this understanding of their target market can product managers ensure that the products they design will meet the customers' needs.

4.9 The databases will enable the user to see not only the characteristics of current purchasers, but also those of people who haven't bought. For example from the data it may become clear that a company's household insurance policies are only being taken out by people with small homes and low value of contents, or that the customer base is disproportionately skewed towards single occupants rather than families. This information will prompt the product manager to investigate what it is that these customers need that their product is not offering, and he or she can then make the necessary changes.

Future trends

4.10 It is important not simply to concentrate on the current situation. Successful retailers also attempt to anticipate the future needs of the customer to ensure that, when their requirements change, they are in a position to satisfy those needs and therefore maintain and possibly increase their market share.

4.11 Because of the importance of customer research, as discussed earlier, many organisations have dedicated research departments whose function is to ensure that the product manager has sufficient data to plan the product strategy successfully.

Changes in legislation

4.12 As the products within the financial services industry are heavily shaped by legislation, any changes or any new legislation may give rise to opportunities, both for new products and for new ways of marketing existing products. Such changes may also limit or remove a large market segment. It is therefore prudent for a product manager to anticipate such changes and plan for such eventualities.

4.13 In some instances, where the opportunity for a new product comes from a change in government policy, the product designers are given the chance to shape the new legislation that will eventually govern both the product and its distribution. For example the Labour government has indicated that it will introduce a new 'Stakeholder pension' in the year 2000/2001. Companies who are likely to be providers of such a product are being invited to submit ideas on what the product should look like and how it should operate. Such opportunities should be grasped enthusiastically by any product manager who must appreciate the chance to get ahead of the game.

Company factors

4.14 Internal factors may also influence the way in which the product strategy is designed. For example, a company that sells the majority of its products through salespeople who conduct lengthy interviews with customers, may well develop different products from one that sells its products off the page or over the telephone. When planning their strategy, companies also need to consider the type of staff they employ, the culture in which they work, and the level of knowledge and skills those staff possess.

Also, such things as brand and company image may influence the strategy. The manager may see an excellent opportunity for a new or enhanced product, but if it is in conflict with the company brand, he will be unable to pursue it.

Student Activity

1 Product management can be broken down into three areas. List them.

2 Describe the three elements of the product concept.

3 Give three examples of things that may influence a product strategy.

5 Product life cycles

5.1 In the past, the financial services industry offered the same products over many years. It was not commonly thought that a product had a 'life cycle'. However, the nature of the industry at the present time, with increasing customer awareness, the use of new technology and a high level of competition, mean that the idea of 'life cycles' for financial services products is now widely accepted.

5.2 Products are seen to go through four stages within their life cycles:

- development and introduction
- growth
- maturity
- decline, possibly leading to elimination.

The length of time taken to progress through the life stages varies from product to product, although it is fair to say that generally, the more innovative a product is, the shorter its life span.

Figure 9.2 The product life cycle

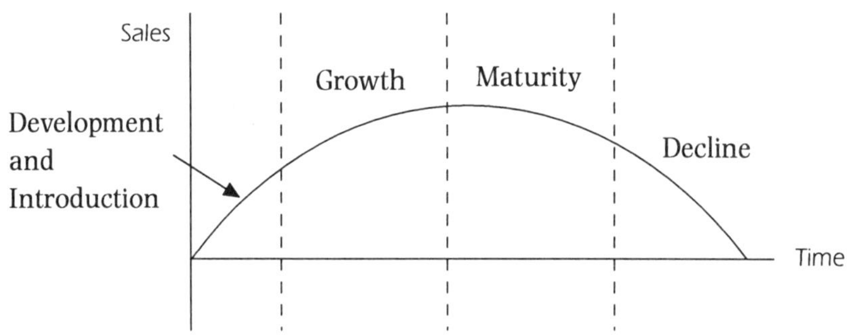

5.3 We will now look at these stages in more detail and consider them in terms of product management activity.

Development and introduction

5.4 Although there are exceptions, development time within the financial services industry would ideally be short, largely due to the intense competition and the element of copying that often occurs. During this stage, competitor analysis is important if the product is a version of those offered elsewhere. Even more important, particularly if a product is brand new, is information on the customer and their needs. Therefore the research department plays an important part before and during the initial stages of product development.

5.5 Once the customers' needs have been researched the product manager will draft an initial product design. There is then likely to be a period of discussion involving all areas of business to ensure that the design is feasible for the business. These discussions will involve representatives from such areas as legal, customer services/administration and sales departments etc, who will all study the design and make amendments. There will also need to be a great deal of discussion with the finance areas of the business. They must check that the charges within a product and the predicted sales volumes will mean that, after development costs have been accounted for, there is still the desired level of profit to the business. The majority of the products launched today will also require a great deal of technological support, and there will also be a need to ensure the product design which is being put forward can be delivered using the services and technology that the business currently has. If not then new systems will need to be bought or built, or the design amended.

5.6 Once the product is designed there is some form of trial; then the product is introduced for sale to the public. Around the time of the launch, marketing activity focuses on raising the public's awareness of the existence of the new product and promoting the product's benefits. This could take the form of any, all or a selection of the following:

- national or regional TV, radio or newspaper advertisements
- poster or cinema advertisements
- branch campaigns if the provider has a branch network
- magazine articles and advertorials
- mailing to existing customers and non customers
- magazine and newspaper inserts etc.

The provider will have estimated the level of business expected and indeed needed in the first few weeks and months following the launch for the product to be a success. In order to achieve these objectives the promotional activity will need to be carefully targeted and executed, and again this shows the importance of the correct research. Because of the nature of this stage, the company experiences a period of expenditure rather than profit making.

Growth

5.7 Following its launch the product experiences a period of growth, during which sales increase and the company recoups the outlay made during the development and introduction stage. If this is a totally new product, then it is likely that during this stage competitor companies will enter the market with similar offerings. It is therefore important to continue to promote the product during this stage to ensure that any loss of market share is avoided or kept to a minimum. Competitors are likely to have tried to improve the product when launching their versions and, therefore, during this stage competitor analysis remains vital. There may also need to be improvements to the product to ensure that it remains competitive. If the product was simply a version of those offered by other providers it is likely that the design will have tried to improve on that of the competition. It may therefore be taking market share from other providers during it's growth stage, and the marketing activity is likely to be concentrated on publicising the advantages of the new product compared to the others available in the market.

Maturity

5.8 Maturity is the stage when sales, and therefore revenue, are at their highest, although it is also the time of greatest competition. Because of this competition, this is the time when providers may try to retain their sales levels by cutting costs or by the introduction of special offers. The expenditure on promotional activity may be cut back in order to focus on other products that are within the introduction or growth stage of their life cycle and that are likely to produce greater returns on expenditure. Any marketing activity conducted during this stage of the product life cycle will be carried out in an attempt to delay its entry into the next stage.

Decline

5.9 Eventually, as new and improved products are launched which more closely meet the customers' need, the sale of the product will decline. During this stage both sales and profits reduce, and therefore little or no money is spent on promotion. The company needs to decide whether to maintain the product while incurring minimum expenditure or whether to eliminate it.

Student Activity

1 List the four stages in a product life cycle.

2 Choose one stage of the life cycle and briefly describe the activities the product management team are likely to undertake during that stage. Give the reason for each activity.

6 Boston Consulting Group (BCG) matrix

6.1 A company needs to be aware of where its products sit in terms of market size and growth within the market. There are a number of ways to do this; one of them is to use the Boston Consulting Group (BCG) matrix, as shown in Figure 9.3.

Figure 9.3 The BCG matrix

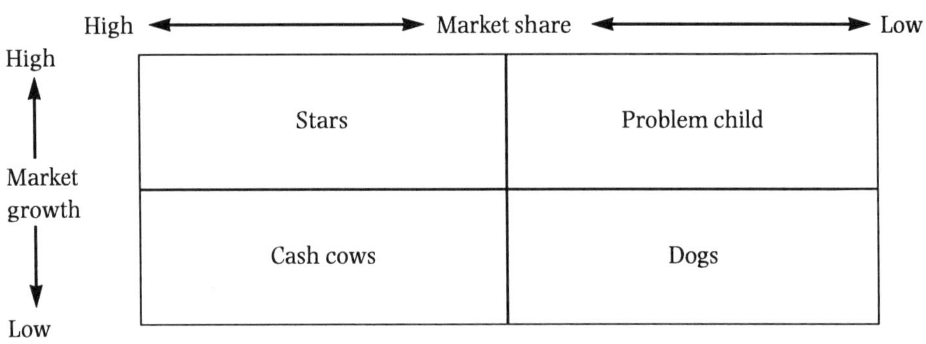

6.2 The purpose of the matrix is to classify products according to two factors: the share of the market they hold, and the growth within the market. It is then possible to use the classification to help to prepare the product strategy.

6.3 The BCG matrix comprises four categories of product. Each of these is described below.

Problem child

6.4 Problem children are products that currently only attract a small market share in a market that, as a whole, is prosperous. A company needs to decide what to do about such products: the provider is likely to want to improve their position within a growing market and will therefore undertake either product development or some enhancement activity.

6.5 To gain more market share the provider could decide to eliminate the problem child and instead develop another product along similar lines to those of their successful competitors. Alternatively, they may choose to enhance the product to bring it into line with, or improve upon, successful competitors' products.

6.6 In order to ensure that the product meets its customers' needs the provider might need to redesign the product features completely or introduce additional features onto the plan. Alternatively they may simply need to reprice the product if competitors are offering similar products with lower charges. This is particularly true of products which have very transparent charges and for which the market is very cost driven, for example personal loans. In some cases it may be the distribution of the product which is responsible for the product's poor performance in a buoyant market. In that case the product manager must investigate improving the product or introducing new methods of getting it to the customer. In some cases the lack of interest in the product may be related to the services the customer is offered once they have bought and an improvement in those may have a dramatic effect on the product's performance.

6.7 In some cases the company may decide that the problem lies not with the product itself or the service but with the public's awareness of that product. In this case they will engage in promotional activity in order to increase their market share. Any decision made regarding the future of a problem child needs to be taken after research into the market and competitors' products, and with consideration to the product's position within its life cycle.

Stars

6.8 Stars are products that are being sold in high volumes in an increasing market, bringing high levels of profit for the provider. A company with a star product cannot just sit back and hope its success will continue. A star product will inevitably attract the attention of competitors, who will be keen to copy and, if possible, improve upon it in order to gain market share. Therefore continuing market activity will be needed to protect the star product's position and to ensure continued growth and profit. The provider will need to monitor the competition closely and react quickly to any new ideas introduced. They may also undertake some promotional activity to consolidate their market share.

Cash cows

6.9 Cash cows are products that sell well but that are in a market that is experiencing little or no growth. If the market is stable, then the company may choose to undertake some marketing activity in order to consolidate their market share and to ensure the product continues to provide a valuable source of revenue. If, however, the market is in decline they may well decide that any expenditure on a promotional activity would not prove to be a worthwhile investment. Instead they will enjoy the sales and profit whilst they continue, but effort and expenditure will be concentrated on activity to ensure that a new profit stream is built to provide continued revenue should the market for this product decline.

Dogs

6.10 Dogs are products with a low market share in a market with little or no growth potential. If the low sales volumes are still profitable the company may decide to continue to offer the product, but they are likely to undertake little or no marketing activity. If, however, offering the product is not profitable it should be considered for deletion.

6.11 Although this method of classifying products cannot be used as a sole planning tool in developing a product strategy, taken in context with such things as the product life cycle and customer and competitor research, it does give some guidance when making policy decisions.

Student Activity

1 List the four classifications used in the BCG matrix.

2 Choose two of these classifications and describe briefly what they are and what decisions each classification may lead the product manager to make.

7 Directional policy matrix

7.1 The directional policy matrix is a more useful development of the Boston (BCG) matrix. The BCG matrix classifies products according to their market share and the growth within that market. However, many companies experience difficulties in accurately measuring the market share and accurately predicting the potential growth of particular markets. Because of this, the BCG matrix was evolved into the directional policy matrix as shown in Figure 9.4.

Figure 9.4 The directional policy matrix

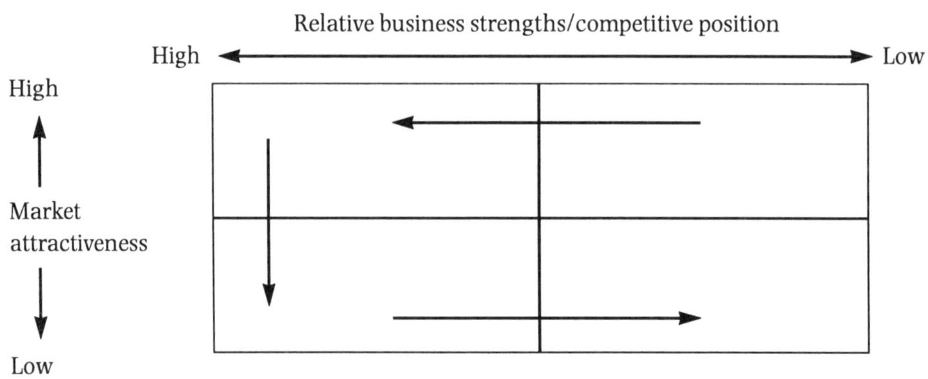

7.2 In the directional policy matrix, market share and market growth are replaced by business strength and market attractiveness. Market attractiveness is not only the size of the market, but includes such things as the expected growth, the lack of competition, the profit margins within the market and any favourable political or socio-economic conditions. Business strength is determined by such things as the number of sales, the product's reputation, reliability, service and competitive pricing. These are very practical attributes as they are more specific to an organisation whose products are in fact services. The directional policy matrix is sometimes shown as having nine segments, but the simpler version shown, developed by McDonald and Payne (1996) *(Marketing Planning for Services)*, is easier to grasp and more appropriate for the financial services product concept. To understand the practical application of this matrix, we also need to consider the product life cycle.

Upper right-hand quadrant

7.3 There would be little point in developing a new product and spending time and money launching it unless there was a market for it. The size of the market, the need for the product, the likely sales volumes and the profit margins that can be expected will all have been investigated in the planning and researching of a possible new product. The business will then make a decision as to the attractiveness of the marketplace before any new product is developed. It therefore follows that new products will only come about if they are in the 'high market attractiveness' area. As the product will be new, its market share or business strength will be low initially. Thus any service product will usually appear in this box when it is first launched.

Upper left-hand quadrant

7.4 If the correct research has been carried out and the product includes the right features at the right price, then the sales will improve. The product will become a strength to the business as it starts to bring an increasing income stream to the business and enhances the reputation of the provider. It will therefore move to the upper left-hand quadrant.

Lower left-hand quadrant

7.5 As existing customers' needs are met, and as new products and services with greater appeal to the customers are introduced by competitors, the growth of product sales may slow. Because the market becomes saturated, providers are likely to cut charges or offer special deals in order to try and maintain their market position. They may need to start or increase promotional activity and all these things will incur a cost to the business. This in turn means that profit margins are cut and so the market attractiveness declines. The product is now positioned in the lower left-hand quadrant.

Lower right-hand quadrant

7.6 As sales diminish due to the lack of customer appeal, the product's strength to the business also decreases. The company is likely to reduce or even withdraw completely any marketing support, choosing to spend resources on new or existing products that offer the prospect of greater returns on any investment made. The product is therefore now firmly in the lower right-hand quadrant.

Using the directional policy matrix

7.7 All of the products and services offered by financial services organisations should be able to be positioned within this matrix. Doing so is of great help to the product manager in the following areas.

Product planning

7.8 By positioning the product within the matrix, the product manager can predict how the sales will evolve, and therefore develop a suitable product strategy. This will be done with a great deal of information about competitors products and customer needs etc, hence the importance, once again, of accurate, up-to-date research.

7.9 The provider will need to understand not only the product and its competition, but also possible future trends in the market which will increase or decrease the market attractiveness. By placing the product in one of the quadrants and properly understanding the movement of the product within the matrix, the product manager will be able to plan where changes to the product may be needed, and where the budget for promotional activity will be best spent.

Forecasting

7.10 The directional policy matrix will help the product manager to forecast future revenue and costs and therefore assist in the management of resources. He will be able to see which of the products he controls would provide the best return following investment in such things as advertising.

Promotional activity

7.11 The directional policy matrix assists in the planning of any promotional activity. For example, while the product is positioned in the upper right-hand quadrant, a great deal of activity surrounds the launch. However, as the product moves to the upper left-hand quadrant, the product manager may expect a great deal of competition to arise and therefore decide to continue with the product promotion as long as the market attractiveness remains high.

Student Activity

1 Name the four categories within the Boston Consulting Group matrix.

2 Explain briefly the characteristics of a product in each of the four groupings and what action a product manager may take with the product.

3 How are products classified in the directional policy matrix?

4 How would a product manager use a directional policy matrix?

8 New product development

8.1 As we have seen earlier in this unit, the development of new products plays a major part in a financial services retailer's product strategy. The two major reasons for developing a new product are as follows.

- To attract customers in a market in which the retailer is not currently active. For example, the development of current accounts by many of the building societies, who did so in order to attract business in a market that had, until then, been solely satisfied by the banks.

- To increase the level of sales in a market in which the retailer is already active. For example, an insurance company may launch a guaranteed investment bond to run alongside its existing investment bond. Although the company is already active, and probably successful, in the investment market, the development of this product should increase the sales volumes by ensuring that the company's products also cater for those people who require security in their choice of investment vehicles.

8.2 Because of the importance of the products and the time and expense needed to undertake major developments, many companies have teams of people dedicated to this task. The company will set objectives for these people to meet when developing the products; for example they could include:

- to produce products with a fast 'time to market'
- to develop products which are priced competitively and yet support the profitability targets
- to have a streamlined product development process which proves effective and cost efficient
- to produce products which both suit the customer needs and reflect the brand.

8.3 The greatest challenge in the development and delivery of new products is the complexity of the process. Developing a new product to the stage where it can be marketed to the public requires input and expertise from a wide variety of areas within the business with a broad range of expertise. It requires a high level of planning, co-ordination and control. The team of people charged with overseeing the process will usually be from the marketing team, the same people who are responsible for the initial product ideas.

8.4 Once the need or the desire for a new product has been recognised the development work can begin. New product developments by financial services providers will fall into one of the following catagories.

Major new innovations

8.5 Major new innovations are products that would be new, not only to the company, but to the whole market. Because of the nature of the development the costs are likely to be high, as greater levels of research testing and promotion may be required. Although there is a greater risk of failure attached to such products, the potential rewards of being a market leader are also substantial, not only in terms of profit but also of enhanced reputation, image and brand value.

New lines

8.6 New lines are products that, although not currently offered by the retailer, are sold successfully by other providers. Although the potential rewards are lower because of the existing competition, the risks are also lower as the product is already proven to be popular with the consumer and profitable for other providers.

The process of product development

8.7 Although the reasons for the product development and the type of product being developed may vary, the process for doing so remains virtually the same. The stages of this process are outlined in Figure 9.5. Let us now look at the activities that occur during each of the development stages.

Figure 9.5 The product development process

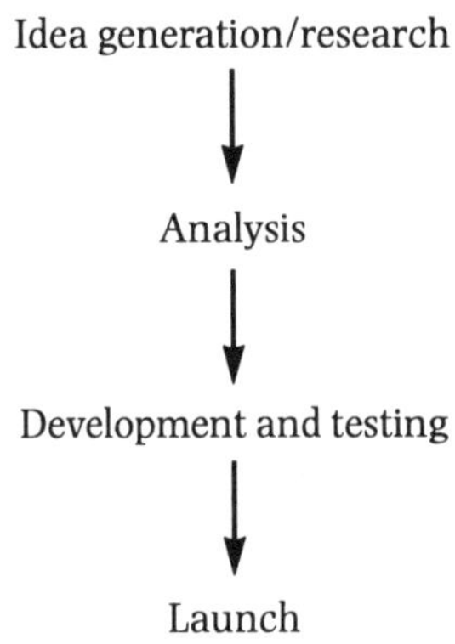

Idea generation/research

8.8 Ideas for new products can come from many sources. Within the financial services industry the opportunities often arise from changes in legislation, but this is not always the case. Ideas can come from within the company, and most organisations employ product development teams whose responsibility it is to suggest and develop new lines. Often such teams employ agencies to assist in the generation of ideas, as well as to assist in other stages of the development process. Another rich source of ideas are the company's staff, particularly branch staff and salespeople. Because of their daily contact with the purchasing public, these people are in an ideal position to advise exactly what customers like, dislike, or would find appealing in a new offering.

8.9 We have also seen earlier in this text how new developments and original ideas are often very quickly copied by other companies. Therefore it follows that in many cases the idea will come from the research that is carried out into other companies' products.

8.10 Another reason for a new product development being undertaken could be that the company's research into the customers' needs and the opportunities in the market may reveal an opening that the business wishes to exploit. For example, the company may feel that they would prosper by developing a new distribution channel. If they decide to pursue this business venture it is reasonable that they would want to develop new products which are designed specifically to suit the new method of sale.

Analysis

8.11 Not every idea can be developed into a new product offering, and therefore there needs to be some form of screening process. The ideas are screened to ensure that they fit with the company's current brand and existing products and to ensure that they satisfy the customers' needs and requirements. The analysis will also ensure that if the idea moves into the development stage it will prove cost effective and profitable. This stage is likely to involve the use of market and customer research.

8.12 The amount of time and effort dedicated to this stage of the development will depend on the type of product being developed and its complexity. A major new innovation will undergo substantially more analysis than one which is simply an updated version of one which is currently offered. It is also at this point in the process that the new design will be tested against the various areas of the business. For example, can the current sales people sell it or will they need additional training and testing? If technology is used in the sale, is it adequate to support the new offering? If so, how much work is required to ensure that this can be done, how long will it take and how much would it cost? The provider will also need to check on the methods of administering the customers' business once it is obtained, and ensure that all the necessary processes are also designed so they can be built and be available when the product is launched. They will also need to consider the branches and investigate any necessary changes that the new product would necessitate.

8.13 It is only when all these aspects have been considered, planned and costed that the product manager and the business management can properly evaluate the plans, and therefore make a decision as to which ideas are developed and which are not.

Development and testing

8.14 Those ideas that move favourably through the analysis stage are turned into a product development project. The product features may need to be continually refined bearing in mind those offered by the competition as well as the needs of the customers. In addition to the basic product features, the development stage also includes the design of the packaging. For example, in the case of an insurance policy this will include such things as the policy document, the plan brochure and the plan conditions. The company also needs to design any promotional material it intends to use to launch the product to the public.

8.15 It is during this stage that all the changes identified during the analysis stage will be developed. This is likely to involve a high level of resource, although this obviously depends on the complexity of the product. Because of the increasing use of technology within the industry, the development of any new product will entail technology changes. Although we saw earlier that ideally products should be developed and launched as quickly as possible, the amount of technology changes required often places restrictions on the speed with which this can be done. When the industry becomes more and more competitive the pressure to deliver new product solutions in the shortest possible time will continue to grow.

8.16 In other industries it is common practice to undertake 'test marketing' at this stage in the development; that is, marketing the product to a specific geographical location in order to measure the response. This will enable them to make any adjustments needed so that the launch of the product to the general public is as successful as possible. However, within the financial services sector this type of testing is a very under-used marketing tool, particularly where the new product is classed as a major new innovation. The reason for this appears to be a fear that such testing could allow the competition see the product and copy it, thereby stealing the benefit of being the first with a nationwide launch.

8.17 Prior to the launch of the new product there will also need to be a period of training. Again the extent of training required will depend largely on the type of product and its complexity. This training must encompass such people as the salespeople who will be required to sell and explain the product to the public, and the branch staff who may be required to promote the product. There will also need to be some training for the people who will administer the product and any centralised customer support facility. If the product is a regulated product there may also be a requirement to test the people who will be authorised to sell it.

Launch

8.18 This is the final stage in the process and the true test of whether the idea is a successful one. Around the launch, marketing activity is concentrated on such things as the most opportune timing and the most appropriate media for the target market. The scale of the launch and the amount of the resource and expenditure allocated to it will depend on the product. A major new innovation may command a large-scale public launch with a high level of media advertising as well as branch promotion. However, a streamlined or modernised product development may be launched with only a promotion to the company's sales staff.

8.19 Following the product launch, the company is likely to carry out some form of evaluation to measure the success of the new product, although they must bear in mind that it may take some time for the product to move from the first (development and launch) stage to the second (growth) stage of its life cycle.

8.20 The results of the evaluation are likely to lead to refinements in the product design or amendments to the marketing strategy to ensure that the sales targets set at the design and analysis stage of the new product development are met.

8.21 Following the launch of the product the team of people who have carried out the development process will conduct a review of the development process. The purpose of this review is to check their performance against the objectives they have been set and particularly to check the following:

- the amount of time spent on the project by each of the business areas involved
- the length of time between the recognition of an opportunity or customer need, and the product being available to market
- the costs involved.

8.22 In order to gain accurate information, anybody who works on the project will need to record their time and effort. This is an additional task, but the benefits are significant. An accurate picture of the three areas outlined above will help the marketing department to improve the product development process and the way in which these projects are managed in the future. Another advantage is that the review will help when planning future product developments. The information will enable future projects to be more accurately estimated when looking at the resource and capital outlay required, and will mean that the estimates for such things as delivery time are realistic.

9 Product modification

9.1 The initial designing and development of a product through to launch and then growth in sales does not mean that the work of the product development team is finished. We saw earlier, when looking at the use of a product life cycle, that it is often necessary to make amendments to products in order to maintain or improve their appeal and competitive position.

9.2 Product modification can take the form of

- adding additional features to an existing product
- improving the service or making the service easier for the customer to use
- improving the way in which the product is delivered
- amending the pricing of the product.

9.3 The modifications may occur in the early stages of the product; that is during the introduction or early in the growth stage following staff and customer feedback. Equally, the need to make amendments may occur during the maturity stage, particularly if competition is strong and other companies have launched products with additional benefits. If these additional benefits are proving popular with the customers, then modification will be necessary in order to protect market share and profits, and to prolong the product life (that is, delay the onset of the decline stage).

Costs

9.4 Although the costs involved in product modification are likely to be much lower than those incurred in the original development, there are inevitably some costs involved. These will be for such things as changes in the technology used, staff costs, and any promotional activity undertaken to advertise the improved product to the customer.

9.5 The anticipated cost needs to be balanced against the expected improvement in profit resulting from the enhancements, or the potential loss of business the company is likely to suffer if the improvements are not made. The position of the product within the BCG matrix and the directional policy matrix will assist the retailer when making such commercial decisions: the company is more likely to pay product enhancement costs for a product classified as a problem child, or to maintain the position of a star, than they are for a dog. However, this is only a general guide – there are always exceptions.

9.6 Once the opportunity to make an improvement has occurred, the process is very similar to that involved in product development, namely idea generation, analysis, development and testing and then launch, although each stage is likely to be on a smaller scale and therefore the time spent on each stage will be shorter.

10 Product elimination

10.1 As we have seen, gone are the days when a financial services product had an unlimited life span. In today's innovative financial services environment products have a natural life cycle and will reach a point where their popularity and ability to meet customers' changing needs (and therefore the profit they generate) will decline. When this happens, the provider has to make a decision. Should they make enhancements in order to prolong the life cycle or should they withdraw the product? As we saw earlier, costs will be a consideration, but so will such factors as the feelings of the staff, the feelings of the customers and how such a withdrawal will reflect on the company and the brand if such a product is no longer available.

10.2 Once a decision to eliminate a product has been made the company must decide whether simply to withdraw the product from sale (allowing existing customers to continue with the product) or eliminate it entirely. The feeling of existing customers must be carefully considered, especially as organisations within the financial services sector, such as banks, tend to experience a high degree of customer loyalty. However, the cost of maintaining the product purely for the benefit of existing customers also needs to be borne in mind. Often when a retailer eliminates a product they replace it with a new product designed to meet the changed needs of customers. If this is the case, they may decide to offer customers with the old product the opportunity to move to the new product on enhanced terms, therefore removing the costs associated with the maintenance without losing customer loyalty.

Student Activity

1 List the stages involved in product development.

2 Describe the marketing activities likely to take place during each stage.

3 List the reasons that may influence a provider to decide to enhance an existing product.

4 Describe the decisions that need to be taken when a product reaches the end of its life cycle.

11 The role of the branch in product management

11.1 As mentioned throughout this unit, the branch has a vital role to play in product management. The majority of financial services companies rely heavily on branches for their contact with customers. With the current competitive environment leading to numerous take-overs and mergers, most now have a nationwide network of branches offering easy access to their services. These branches are staffed by the people who have daily contact with the buying public. These individuals' up-to-date knowledge of the market place can assist the product manager in the following areas

- influencing product strategies and product planning
- development of new products
- product modification and deletion.

11.2 The branch staff are able to feed back to the product manager any information they gain about customer needs and the customers' preferred ways to meet those needs. This will help in the planning of new products and the development of a product strategy for existing lines. Branch staff are also in an ideal situation to find out what customers like about other company's products. They can therefore inform the product development team about any product or product feature that customers request. The product teams can then recognise the common requests, spot developing markets and develop products to meet such demands.

11.3 Branch staff are also vital to the success of a product once it has been developed and is being launched. Success depends on the customer being made aware of the product and the benefits it can offer, and much of this promotion is focused on branches. Branches are also able to give a great deal of initial feedback following the launch, which will enable the product manager to establish what enhancements may be necessary, or what further promotional activity is needed.

12 Case study and analysis

12.1 Yorkshire Equitable has been a leading life assurance, pensions and investment provider for many years, conducting virtually all of their business through IFAs. They have recently decided to launch an alternative distribution channel, selling products direct to the public.

12.2 In order to minimise the possible conflict between the two distribution channels, they decided that the direct operation would develop its own set of products, independent of the broker division.

12.3 Initially they will launch with one pension product, one life assurance product and one investment product, although these will be added to very quickly following the launch.

12.4 Imagine you have been recruited to develop the three new products for launch, and the other products which will follow. You would need to consider:

- what research you would conduct before starting the product developments
- how you would decide on the product design
- who would need to be involved in the product development project
- an outline project plan
- how you would support the product launch
- any further actions you would take after the launch.

12.5 Your analysis would include the points below.

- You would have to conduct research into your customers, such as:
  - who they are
  - what their buying habits are
  - what would prompt them to buy by telephone

  - what products and features they are looking for
  - how much money they are likely to spend.
- You would need to conduct research into your competitors, and find out as much as possible about the following
  - what do their products look like?
  - what charges do they make?
  - what options do they offer?
  - how successful are they?
  - how are they marketing their product?
  - do they use any other distribution methods?
  - how do they generate leads?
  - what is their typical customer profile?
- You would also need to conduct some research into the direct market, in an attempt to gain as much information as possible. For example:
  - is the market growing, and at what rate?
  - are there any external factors, e.g. political, which may affect the market growth?
  - how attractive is the market?
  - how many competitors would you have for your new products?
  - what are the expected profit margins?

12.6 You would then use all the research to decide on a product design. This should be tailored to meet the customer needs and to suit the distribution method chosen. It will also need to be competitive, so the design must be able to stand comparisons with its competitors.

12.7 The product design would then need to be tested, to ensure that it is capable of being produced and administered by the company, and that it fits with the brand values.

12.8 The people who would need to be involved would be drawn from the following areas of the business.

- Marketing
- Actuarial/finance/accounting
- Systems
- Administration
- Customer services
- Sales
- Field operations/branch
- Underwriting

12.9 The project plan can take various forms but should follow Figure 9.6.

Figure 9.6 The project plan flow diagram

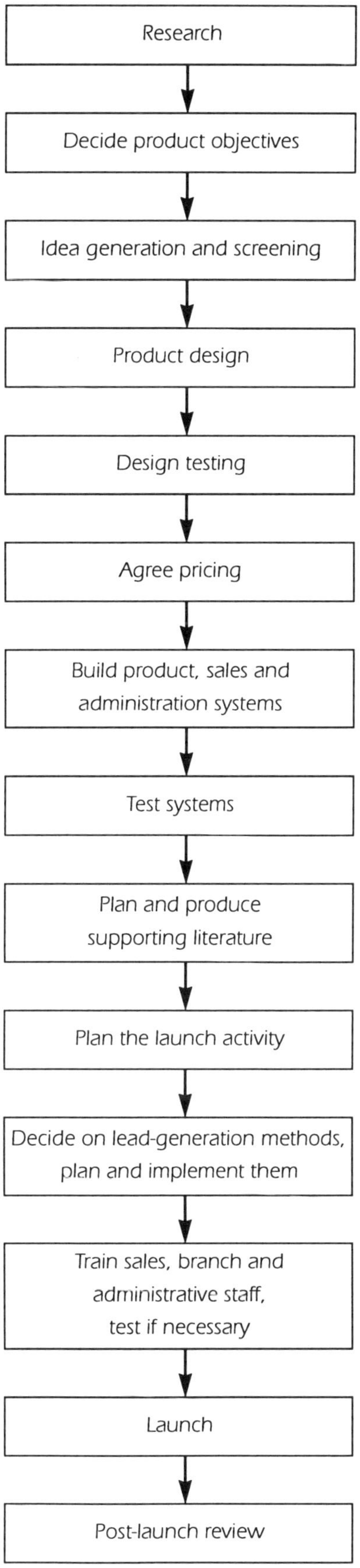

12.10 The product launch will be supported using one or more of the following.

- Information to all staff
- Awareness-raising among the public by means of advertising
- Use of special offers for a limited period
- Lead-generation activity, such as outbound calling, direct mail, direct response advertising, etc.

12.11 Following the launch, a post-launch review should be conducted. This would involve:

- checking that the product has met the objectives set at the start of the project
- checking sales volumes against the business predictions made
- analysing the cost of production against the budgets set at the outset of the project
- looking at customer profiles
- analysing the product against the typical customer, and making any changes to the product that are necessary.

Summary

Now that you have completed this unit, you should be able to do the following.

- ❑ **Describe the nature of market research.**
- ❑ **Explain the influences on product strategies.**
- ❑ **Describe product planning, the use of product life cycles and the use of the BCG and directional policy matrices in that planning.**
- ❑ **Describe the process of developing new products and modifying or eliminating existing ones.**
- ❑ **Explain the role of the branch in product management.**

Self-assessment questions

1 (a) Explain why market research is carried out.

(b) Briefly describe the various sources of information available for market research.

(c) Describe the market research techniques that can be used.

2 Describe the four key factors that influence product strategy.

3 (a) Draw a diagram to illustrate a product's life cycle.

(b) Briefly describe each of the stages in the life cycle.

(c) Describe two matrices that can help with product planning and explain how they are used.

4 Draw a diagram to show the stages in the development, modification and elimination of a product. Briefly describe each stage.

5 Write a paragraph to explain why branch staff have a vital role to play in product management.

Unit 10

Pricing

Objectives

After studying this unit you should be able to do the following.

- **Describe the process and factors that need to be considered when pricing services and products within the financial services industry.**
- **Explain the relationship between the pricing and retailing of such services.**
- **Describe the role of the branch in the pricing process.**

1 The pricing of services

1.1 The pricing of services is always a complex issue. There are several elements that the provider needs to consider when setting a charge. These include the following.

Costs

1.2 The provider must carefully calculate all the costs involved in offering the service to the public, including such things as staff costs, the costs involved in the use of any technology, and any promotional outlay. Although it is possible to cross subsidise (that is, use income from a profitable service to cover the costs of providing an unprofitable one), generally this should be avoided.

Competitors' prices

1.3 A major consideration must be the charges being made by competitors in the market for similar services. In doing this, the company must bear in mind any additional features of their product that are not included in the products offered by the competition. Conversely, they must consider any deficiencies of their product as compared with those of their competitors. A direct comparison can only be made on a like-for-like basis. Competitors' prices are most important for services where competition is strong and charges are easily identifiable.

Customers' willingness to pay

1.4 The point at which a customer agrees to purchase a service from a provider can be expressed as the point of agreement: a mutual acceptance between the two that the price and the service represent a fair exchange. The level at which the customer is happy for this to take place will depend on the benefits they perceive they will receive from the service. Many factors influence the customer's willingness to pay. One is the reputation of the provider – a customer may be prepared to pay a little more to buy from a reputable provider exactly the same service available more cheaply from an unknown supplier.

2 Financial services pricing

2.1 In the financial services sector, pricing can take many forms. In stockbroking it takes the form of setting a transaction cost; in general insurance it involves rate setting; for building societies it takes the form of setting mortgage rates and loan interest rates; and in banking it takes the form of deciding on a fee structure for accounts.

2.2 Because financial services are intangible, it could be argued that the customer is less able to judge whether a price is fair – whether it represents value for money. However, the combination of the regulations in some areas of financial services requiring providers to clearly state all charges and the increasing level of customer knowledge of the industry, mean this is no longer strictly true. Although the public may not understand how the charge for a product is arrived at, they frequently make direct comparisons between rival companies when looking at its cost.

Student Activity

1 State three things a provider may need to consider when providing a service.

2 What forms does pricing take in the financial services sector?

3 The pricing of deposits and savings

3.1 The price of a savings account is essentially the difference between the interest rate that could be paid if no costs were involved and the interest rate that the financial services institution actually pays.

3.2 In terms of deposits and savings, price is an important element of the marketing mix. However, product and promotion are also extremely important and are often used by providers to compensate for a higher price than that charged by their competitors. For example, many banks and building society accounts are marketed on the basis of their product features such as withdrawal facilities, accessibility and minimum investment levels. Customers may choose a bank account that offers significantly lower interest than its competitors if it provides 24-hour telephone banking, a bill paying service, or has a branch near their home or work place.

3.3 When setting a price for deposit accounts such as a bank account, the institution must take account of the mix of customers they will attract and the way in which those customers will conduct their accounts. For example, ABC Bank decides to allow free banking for customers in credit, and to pay interest on credit balances. However, it charges for transactions made while a customer is overdrawn and charges interest on the amount of the overdraft. With this type of charging structure the bank makes a profit from customers who are overdrawn, particularly if they make a large number of transactions. The bank makes a loss from customers who remain in credit by a small amount. That loss will be greater, the larger the number of transactions made. For customers who have a very high credit balance, the bank again makes a profit, as they are in effect being loaned money at a low rate of interest. The amount of profit will again depend on how often the customer uses the account – the lower the number of transactions, the higher the profit margin.

3.4 Therefore the provider needs to predict and monitor the mix of customers it attracts and, if necessary, amend either its promotion (to attract a different mix) or its pricing.

3.5 When looking for a new deposit or savings account a customer is quite likely to check the price in the form of charges and interest rate. However, many customers do not move their business even if the price subsequently becomes less competitive. This may be because a general lack of interest in finance means that they are unaware of the account's decreasing competitive position, or it may be due to the high levels of customer loyalty within the industry. Some organisations now use this customer behaviour as a marketing tool; a practice known as 'cascade marketing' as shown in Figure 10.1.

Figure 10.1 Cascade marketing

Attract customer by offering a competitive price

↓

Accounts are unprofitable for the provider

↓

Increase prices gradually

↓

Account becomes profitable

↓

Some customers are lost

↓

Many customers remain

3.6 When using the cascade marketing technique, the organisation attracts a large number of customers by offering a particularly competitive interest rate, even though this will yield no profit and may even make a loss. Gradually, the price is increased in the form of interest rate reductions, to the point where the organisation is making the desired level of profit. Although some more financially aware customers are lost as they transfer their investments to organisations offering more competitive rates, a large number remain. This technique can also be used in the marketing of debt, for example personal loans, where a very low rate can be offered and then gradually increased over time.

Student Activity

1 Explain why a bank would need to consider the way in which it expects its customers to conduct their deposit accounts when setting the charges.

2 What is cascade marketing and for what products within the financial services industry is it sometimes used?

4 The pricing of shares and mutual funds

4.1 The price of a share in a quoted company or a government debt (known as gilts) is governed by the forces of supply and demand. Each sale needs to be matched by a purchase and vice versa. If the demand for a particular share exceeds the number of shares available, then the price of the share rises until sellers appear or buyers disappear so that supply and demand are again equalised. Similarly, if there are large numbers of people wanting to sell shares in a particular company, this brings down the price until a balance is restated.

4.2 In addition to the actual cost of the share, the marketmaker through whom the deal is made charges a commission for that deal. Typically, a broker would charge a percentage of the sales value, subject to a minimum fee for any deal. For certain shares there may also be VAT, contract levy or stamp duty; these need to be considered by the investor as shares must experience a rise in price before these costs can be recouped.

4.3 Brokers and share dealers may manipulate the charges they make so that they attract the buying or selling of a particular share. For example, if a broker knows that he or she has an order for 500 shares in company A, he or she may attract customers who are selling these shares by offering to buy the shares free or for a reduced fee. The broker can afford to buy at a reduced fee as she or he will make a full fee on the sale. The double cost of both buying and selling shares makes small deals expensive and has discouraged small investors from purchasing equities.

4.4 This cost, and the desire for wider share ownership, led to the birth of unit trusts or mutual funds. With unit trusts, although there is no commission charged on the purchase or the sale, there may be a price involved and this is known as the 'bid/offer spread'. The offer price is the price at which the customer buys units in the trust, and the bid price is the price at which the provider buys them back. Traditionally there was a 5 to 7% difference between the two. However, the increased competition from direct business writers and increased customer awareness of costs has meant that many providers have now reduced or dropped the up-front charge. There is also likely to be a charge for the management of the fund, as a fund manager will actively buy and sell for the unit holders. It is this expert fund management and the spread of shares that attracts smaller and more cautious investors.

5 The pricing of mortgages and loans

5.1 A mortgage is simply a long-term loan that is secured using the customer's home. It is either repaid at the end of the term, in which case the customer simply pays interest throughout the term, or both capital and interest are repaid monthly so that the full loan has been repaid by the end of the mortgage term. The price, in either case, is mainly the interest rate charged by the lender. Some lenders do, in certain cases, also charge a setting-up fee.

5.2 Until the breakdown of the Building Societies Association Cartel in 1983, the pricing of mortgages was relatively unimportant for building societies as interest rates and mortgage rates were fixed by the Cartel. The rates provided a large enough margin to allow all expenses to be covered and for the building society to still make a reasonable profit.

5.3 In the early 1980s banks began to offer mortgages in direct competition with the building societies, and this led to building societies taking a much greater interest in the pricing of their mortgage products, as a way of regaining market share.

5.4 The way in which a customer can obtain a true charge for credit is by checking the APR (annual percentage rate). The concept of the APR is to provide a common base upon which the various credit products could be directly price compared. APR is calculated using a complex formula that takes into account any up-front charges made by the lender, and the fact that capital may be being repaid and therefore the interest rate is increasing. (However, APR is not fully understood by all customers and is sometimes considered to have confused customers more than it has helped them.)

5.5 Although not always understood, the introduction of APR figures has meant that the customer can see exactly how one company's charges compare with another's. The majority of promotional activity for mortgage products is price based, therefore any provider whose charges are too high will price themselves out of the market. The 'bank base rate' is the minimum lending rate for banks and is set by the Bank of England. Building societies also have a base rate known as the 'mortgage base rate', which fluctuates following any changes to the bank base rate. The mortgage base rate that the building societies offer on their mortgage products is set by each individual society – it is not decided by any industry-wide body.

5.6 Not all products are offered at the building society's base rate. Some may be seen to bring a greater risk of non-payment, such as higher income multiples, higher loan-to-value mortgages, or when customers are permitted to self-certify their incomes. To allow for these greater risks the building society will make higher charges in the form of increased interest rates.

6 The pricing of credit cards

6.1 For many years customers were able to receive credit cards without paying any price at all. If the card was used purely as a method of payment (that is, the customer paid the full balance each time a statement was received), then no charge was ever made. If the customer used the card to obtain instant credit, then a rate for that was calculated as for other loans. The problem for the card issuers was that many people did not borrow using the card, and many of those who did were unreliable in making repayments. Thus offering such cards was often costly. Because of this, card issuers began to charge an annual fee for the use of a credit card, and now such a fee is almost universal.

6.2 Many people subsequently moved to using debit cards, such as Switch, as these are free. Many customers now also use just one credit card, where previously they may have had two or three. The introduction of card fees has therefore led to much more profitable business for the issuers.

Student Activity

1 What influences the price of an equity share?

2 What is an APR and why was it introduced?

3 What effect has the introduction of annual fees on credit cards had on the retailing of them?

7 The pricing of life assurance

7.1 The price paid for a life assurance policy is the premium (usually paid monthly) throughout the term of the plan. The premium is determined by the company's 'rate' for a person of that age, for that product and that term. Rates are calculated by the company's actuary to ensure that the life fund has sufficient assets to cover its liabilities at all times. When setting a rate, the actuary needs to consider costs, simplicity, claims and profit, as described below.

Costs

7.2 The rate must bring sufficient premium to cover the operational costs: such things as staff costs, promotional activity, ongoing administration costs, and commission paid to the salesperson. Commission must now be disclosed to the customer in the form of 'cost of advice' which they are informed of when buying the product. This means that the customer can see exactly how much of their premium is being taken each month for this purpose.

Simplicity

7.3 The public like the cost of their life product to be simple to understand. Simplicity also makes the salesperson's job easier when they are trying to ensure that the customer understands the product they have bought. Although some companies now offer reviewable rates, whereby the costs can increase and decrease, the majority of life assurance premiums are set for the full term of the plan. This simplicity means that the actuary must provide for possible inflation for the term of the plan when setting the rate.

Claims costs

7.4 The actuary has to predict the number of claims the company will experience, and must ensure that there are sufficient reserves to cover them. The actuary sets a rate for the average person of any particular age. The underwriting process identifies any customers who are considered to pose a higher than ordinary risk, and special increased rates are quoted for them. The actuary must also make allowances for the fact that fraudulent claims will be received, even though the company will make every effort to ensure these are detected.

Profit

7.5 As well as ensuring that there is sufficient money to cover costs and claims, the actuary will set a rate that allows a fair level of profit for the company. The level of profit a company can make on a particular product is influenced by the factors discussed at the start of this unit, such as competitors' prices and the customers' willingness to pay.

8 The pricing of pensions and endowments

8.1 Both pensions and endowment policies may contain an element of life assurance, and this will be costed and charged for as outlined above. However, the principle purpose for these type of products is that of saving, either for a set period of time or until retirement, and the provider company therefore makes charges for the services involved in this savings and investment element. For unit linked contracts, the way in which these charges are taken has become fairly standard across the industry, although the amounts of the charges can vary substantially between products.

Bid/offer spread

8.2 The bid/offer spread is the charge made for the cost of buying units in a unit linked contract. The bid price is that at which the units can be purchased; the offer price is that at which the units are sold back to the fund manager. Traditionally there is a difference of around 5% between the two, so there is a 5% charge to the customer.

Allocation

8.3 Not all of the payment made by the customer is used to buy units in the selected funds. By fixing the allocation rates the provider is again able to make a charge. The setting of an allocation rate is usually used to cover the setting up costs (that is, the cost of offering advice, issuing the plan, etc.). There are two ways in which this can be done.

1. The costs can be recouped up-front by giving nil allocation for a set period of time. For example, nil allocation for 12 months, thereafter 100% allocation.
2. The costs can be taken across the whole period of the plan by offering reduced allocation. For example, 98% of all premiums are used to buy units.

Management fee

8.4 Companies usually charge a fee for managing the funds in which the customer has invested. This is generally expressed as a percentage of the value of the investment and typically ranges from 0.25% to 1% per year. This charge is taken from the fund before the unit price is calculated.

Plan fee

8.5 A plan fee or policy fee is usually taken to cover the costs of administering the product, and this is expressed as a set amount per month. For example £2 per month. This is taken from the plan by cancelling units and increases annually in line with costs.

One-off charges

8.6 It is also possible for companies to include additional one-off charges for specific events. For example, a single set-up charge, or a charge for switching investments between funds.

8.7 Because of the number and variety of charges that are made on this type of contract it has in the past been very difficult for a customer to compare one product's costs with another's. However, companies are now required to disclose all charges to the customer, including details of how the charges affect the value of the plan, and how the charges will reduce the yield.

8.8 When setting the charges, the product team needs to consider such things as the following.

- What costs will they will incur in obtaining and administering the business?
- What is the customer profile? How long will policies be in force? How large will the premiums be?
- How much profit do they wish to make?
- What are the charges made by the competition?

8.9 When this information is known, decisions can be made as to how charges should be applied. They may be made up-front or throughout the term, as set amounts or as a percentage of the fund, etc. The setting of a charge is extremely important as these are long-term contracts: unless the contract states that the charge may increase, they will be set for the full term of the plan.

9 The pricing of general insurance

9.1 The term 'general insurance' covers a wide range of products – anything from accident and sickness policies to insuring a ship and its cargo. However, the two most commonly known products are probably motor insurance and house contents' cover. In all categories of general insurance the customer pays a premium to obtain a set level of cover against a certain event occurring. In order to set that level of premium the insurer calculates a rate using their past experiences of offering cover of that nature. This method of setting a rate can be either an advantage or a disadvantage, depending on the company's experience. For example, if a company has suffered a number of claims by young drivers, it may find it has to charge more for this cover the following year and so prices itself out of the market. Alternatively, if their experience is particularly good, they may be able to charge less and therefore attract more customers and make more profit.

9.2 In recent years some companies have tried to move the buying decision away from being totally price focused by offering additional benefits on their product. For example, they offer free hire cars with their motor policies for customers whose cars are garaged following an accident, or 24-hour emergency help lines on their house contents policies. However, despite these initiatives, the general insurance market continues to be very price driven. This is borne out by the success of such companies as Direct Line, who, by the nature of their operation, were able to offer lower rates and attracted vast numbers of people to use them for first motor, and then home contents, insurance. The price-driven nature of the market can also be seen in the number of companies whose promotional activity concentrates on price, and the emergence of companies such as Premium Search whose business is to find the cheapest rate possible for the customer.

9.3 As previously, the insurer must also cover costs and, in general insurance more than in life assurance, must make provision for fraudulent claims. It is felt that a large proportion of house contents insurance claims are either fully fraudulent or exaggerated, and provision for these increases the cost of everyone's cover.

10 The role of the branch in pricing

10.1 For a large proportion of financial services products sold, the branch cannot set the charge. The costs are almost always predetermined. For example, the rate charged for credit or mortgages, the charges made on a bank account, or the charges applied to an investment product are decided centrally. In some circumstances the branch may have the ability to waive certain charges, but this is usually only done within given guidelines.

10.2 In some circumstances an organisation will act as an intermediary. For example, a building society may not offer its own life assurance products, but may sell the products of another company. In this case the branch is likely to have no influence on how those products are priced.

10.3 However, if the products and services offered are their own, then the branch does have a role to play. Staff who have constant contact with the customers who pay for the service are in an ideal position to contribute to the pricing process. We saw at the start of this unit that one of the factors influencing pricing is the customers' willingness to pay; staff who are branch-based should be a valuable source of research as to how customers will react to costs and charging structures.

Student Activity

1 Describe the factors an insurance company needs to consider when setting a rate for life assurance.

2 Describe the costs involved when a customer invests in a pension plan.

3 What role does price play in the retailing of general insurance products, and what have providers done to try to alter this role?

Summary

Now that you have completed this unit you should be able to do the following.

- ❑ **Describe the process and factors that need to be considered when pricing services and products within the financial services industry.**
- ❑ **Explain the relationship between the pricing and retailing of such services.**
- ❑ **Describe the role of the branch in the pricing process.**

Self-assessment questions

1 Briefly describe the three factors that influence the pricing of financial services.

2 Explain how these three factors influence the pricing of each of the following, and describe how charges are made for each.

(a) Deposit and savings.

(b) Shares and mutual funds.

(c) Mortgages and loans.

(d) Credit cards.

(e) Life assurance.

(f) Pensions and endowments.

(g) General insurance.

3 Does the branch have any role to play in the pricing of financial products? Explain your answer.

Unit 11

The Promotion

Objectives

After studying this unit you should be able to

- **describe the steps to follow when developing a promotional mix**
- **describe the different elements that can be used in the promotional mix**
- **explain the role of the branch in promotional activities.**

1 Developing the promotional mix

1.1 The promotional mix comprises a number of different elements. Each element exhibits certain strengths and weaknesses. The development of a successful promotional mix demands the careful integration of each of these elements.

Figure 11.1 Decision framework for marketing communications.

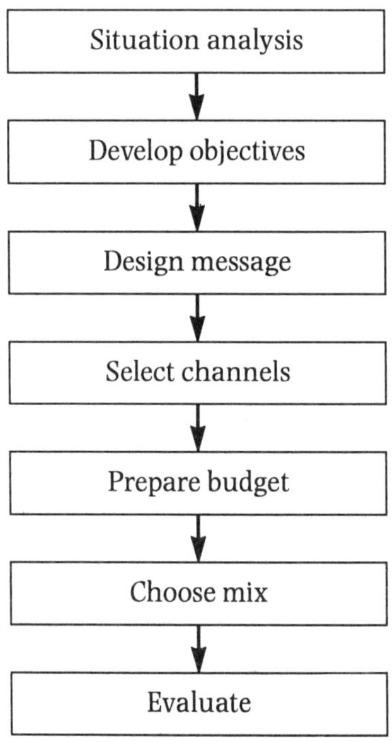

1.2 This process can be made easier by the development and use of a framework for marketing communication, as illustrated in Figure 11.1. The key stages in this framework are described below.

Analysing the situation

1.3 The first step, before starting any promotional activity, is to carry out an assessment of the current position of: customer features, the competitive situation and the environment.

Identifying customers – the target audience

1.4 An assessment of the target audience should cover

- demographics and lifestyle
- life stages
- usage levels
- understanding and perception of services and organisation
- the buying process.

The competitive situation

1.5 An assessment of the competitive situation should cover

- the industry structure
- competitive groupings
- the strength of competitors
- the threat of substitutes
- the perceived differentiation among competitors.

The environment

1.6 An assessment of the environment should examine

- the internal environment (organisation objectives, resources, other components of the mix)
- the external environment (political, economic, social and technological).

Developing objectives

1.7 Once a target audience and any limitations have been identified, a range of promotional objectives can be devised. The ultimate goal of any communication programme is for the customer to make a purchase or use a service. On the way to achieving this goal the customer passes through a series of decision stages. The communication issues are different at each of these stages.

1.8 For example, using the hierarchy of effects model (Lavidge and Steiner, 1961) the desired response is to place something in the mind of the prospect (cognitive), to alter attitudes (affective) or to create action (behavioural). At the cognitive stage the promotion aims to create an awareness and knowledge; subsequently the affective phase looks to create desire, preference and conviction; leading prospects to the purchase phase is the objective of the behavioural stage.

1.9 In most cases a promotional strategy is designed to increase sales; however, there are now an increasing number of promotional campaigns that are designed to create, reinforce or change an organisation's image.

1.10 The objectives of each element of the promotion mix require careful integration and co-ordination with the other components in the marketing mix. There should also be a basis for evaluation of the effectiveness of a promotional campaign; this can be achieved by specifying the target audience, the level and nature of change and a timescale for each objective.

Student Activity

1 State the seven activities undertaken when developing marketing communications.

2 List the two key objectives of a promotional campaign.

Designing the message

1.11 The nature of the message depends upon the desired outcome. The message must be designed to promote the required response.

1.12 Financial services products are not usually actively sought, so advertising messages tend to appeal to emotions and morals and are not often based on rational argument. If a rational appeal is made it is usually at the point of sale, in the form of detailed product information, or in the actual sales presentation.

Emotional messages

1.13 Appeals to the emotions either stress the negatives of not using a product or stress the positive feelings associated with the purchase of a product. This sort of appeal is often used when selling protection policies (life insurance); for example, by asking how a family would manage in the event of the death of the breadwinner.

Moral messages

1.14 Moral messages appeal to the customer's sense of right and wrong.

Rational messages

1.15 Rational messages explain the benefits of the product.

The use of humour

1.16 Humour is occasionally used in advertising. However, it must be used with great care: humour can trivialise an issue; it can also distract the audience, who then fail to understand the message.

1.17 Once the appeal factor has been decided upon, thought must be given to the structure, format and source of the message. These must be such that they ensure acceptance and credibility with the target audience. This stage is usually undertaken by an external agency in conjunction with the marketing team.

Selecting channels

1.18 A message can be communicated via one of two channels: personal channels or non-personal channels.

Personal channels

1.19 Personal channels are face-to-face or word of mouth. Kotler (1993) drew a distinction in personal channels between *advocate* channels (an organisation's sales staff focusing on the target audience) and *expert* channels (reinforcement by independent authorities). He also referred to *social* channels (which can include word of mouth through friends, family and other social groups).

1.20 Personal channels are probably not only the cheapest, but also the most believable, type of promotion. Word of mouth is recognised as being particularly significant to the small-business sector. A benefit of establishing and maintaining satisfied customers is that each such customer becomes an unpaid advocate of the organisation. Word of mouth is also useful when a product is seen as expensive, risky or is infrequently purchased – as is the case for a great number of financial service products.

Non-personal channels

1.21 Non-personal channels are the above-the-line and below-the-line communication channels, such as print, broadcasting, electronic and media display.

1.22 Both personal and non-personal channels have inherent strengths and weaknesses and need to be evaluated against the promotional objectives.

Preparing budgets

1.23 Budget setting varies greatly, not only between companies, but also between industries.

1.24 When a sale is made the marginal revenue generated can be identified. However, when this is derived from a number of variables it becomes difficult to identify the appropriate percentage of an individual variable, such as promotion.

1.25 There are a number of methods commonly used to set promotional budgets. They are described below.

Percentage of sales (actual or anticipated)

1.26 The budget is worked out as a percentage of the sales that a company either anticipates making, or has made in the previous year.

1.27 This type of budgeting is based on what a company can afford. However, it restricts long-term planning as it requires current or past sales figures; it also restricts reactive promotion due to the limiting of funds.

Competitive parity

1.28 With competitive parity the budget is based on what is believed to be the average spend in the industry. The problem here lies with the validity, or otherwise, of the assumption that competitors have made the correct level of promotional spend.

Affordable/residual

1.29 With affordable/residual budget setting, the budget is set either on the basis of what the company thinks it can afford, or on the surplus money left on the balance sheet after all other costs have been paid. This method can be short sighted, as it tends to treat promotional activity as a luxury rather than a necessity. It can also make long-term planning difficult.

Objective and task

1.30 The objective and task method identifies the company objectives and assesses the tasks required to achieve them. It then estimates the costs involved and allocates the appropriate budget.

1.31 This type of budgeting can form part of the long-term planning of an organisation but may not always be affordable.

Choosing the mix

1.32 The choice of the elements of the promotional mix varies. It not only depends upon the organisation, but also on the type of product being sold. For example, advertising can be a key element when there is a requirement to communicate simple messages to a mass market. Where a product is more complex and requires explanation or demonstration, then personal selling is more appropriate.

1.33 Other considerations when deciding on the promotional mix should include the stages in the life cycle, characteristics of the product, the current competitive environment, price and distribution decisions.

Evaluation

1.34 It is vital that any promotional activity is assessed for the effectiveness of the elements of the promotional mix. This can involve both pre-testing and post-evaluation. The process is not always simple, as several factors may interfere with the final results. For example

- competitor activity
- trying to achieve multiple objectives
- a carry-over effect from earlier activities.

1.35 There are a number of techniques and measures that can be used in the evaluation process. The measures can be: awareness, exposure, sales effectiveness, or recall levels. Information can also be gained from continuous tracking during a promotion, and from measuring sales levels before, during and after a campaign.

1.36 Pre-testing should attempt to predict the likely effectiveness of a campaign and to eliminate any weaknesses; but pre-testing does not guarantee success.

Market research can test levels of recall and understanding, but these types of survey can only show whether a communication link has been established and not whether a desire to purchase has been created. Statistical analysis can be used to assess the effectiveness of a campaign by comparing before and after sales levels; however, while this method can identify correlations between a promotion and sales, it is of limited use in proving that a promotion *caused* an increase in sales.

1.37 Ideally, the evaluation of a promotion should be organisation/product specific, and the objectives and measures should be clearly defined in the planning stages.

Student Activity

1 What measures can be used in the evaluation process?

2 Describe the four methods suggested for allocating budget to promotional activity.

2 Types of promotion

Advertising

2.1 We discussed the characteristics of services in Unit 4. A service can also be described as 'an act performed for a specific person'. Hill and Ghandi (1992) developed a number of advertising guidelines based on the characteristics of services; these are summarised below.

Intangibility and concreteness

2.2 Advertising should present services more tangibly by including physical evidence and artefacts showing service delivery points. For example, houses are often used to highlight mortgage facilities.

2.3 Advertising should use concrete specific language and symbols and establish credibility through word of mouth endorsements.

Inseparability/perishability and reputation

2.4 The service deliverer and the customer should be included in the advertisement.

Heterogeneity and documentation

2.5 By documenting the scope, characteristics, performance record or effects of the service with concrete information, advertising can substantiate credibility and confirm consistency of performance.

Characterisation as sequence of events

2.6 Advertising should highlight the sequence of events that comprises the service experience. For example, mortgage advertisements often show a couple looking at house details, having a mortgage interview and ultimately moving into their dream home.

2.7 Hill and Gandhi (1992) then extended the guidelines and suggested that

- the more intangible the service, the greater the requirement for concrete clues in the advertisement
- the greater the inseparability, the greater the requirement to show participation of customers in service production and delivery
- the greater the heterogeneity, the greater the requirement to stress quality
- the greater the specificity of context, customers and service settings, the greater the requirement to characterise the service through the illustration of a sequence of events.

2.8 These guidelines can be refined further by taking into consideration the relationship of the guidelines with the nature of the service, the organisation's relationship with customers, service delivery and demand and supply relationships.

2.9 Hill and Gandhi (1992) recommend that where the nature of the service delivery is continuous and a formal relationship with customers exists (for example, in insurance), advertising should emphasise concreteness, representation and sequence of events and, to a lesser degree, documentation. If the nature of the interaction between the customer and the organisation is at arms length (such as by mail) and the service delivery is focused on a single location (for example, credit card companies), then high levels of concreteness and documentation are suggested and limited emphasis is given to representation. For such products the emphasis on sequence of events is usually inappropriate.

2.10 For press, television, radio (indeed all above-the-line activity) it is important that the messages given are clear and unambiguous. Where possible, large amounts of technical detail should not be included. However, financial services advertising is governed by the Financial Services Act 1986, and this restricts the content of such advertising.

2.11 Most television adverts usually fall into category A advertising and have a simple format of announcing and drawing attention to the product or company. (For example Allied Dunbar's 'There May be Trouble Ahead' series of advertisements.) An advertisement that is designed to sell a product must provide full details of the small print surrounding that regulated product. These compliance requirements can demand that substantial amounts of copy are included in the advertisement, particularly where press advertising is involved. As a result, much financial services advertising is moving to category B – advertisements that invite customers to request a pack containing further information – thereby reducing the need for large amounts of compliance copy.

2.12 Internal marketing (that is, marketing to employees) is also an important part of the advertising process. Customer-facing staff need both to understand and to be convinced of the benefits of a product/service before they try to sell it to a customer. If staff are unaware of the target audience or are not fully aware of a product specification, or if they do not become advocates of the benefits of the product/service, they may not identify potential sales or may not perform effectively in the sales process.

2.13 The majority of customers are not continually in the market for financial services, so it may be that by using a common theme in advertising an organisation 'brands' itself into the mind of an infrequent purchaser. As a result, when a purchase is to be made the customer recalls the organisation and associates it with the service/products they are looking for. A number of organisations have successfully implemented 'branding' (for example, Lloyds and the black horse and Direct Line and the red telephone).

2.14 Advertising is also recommended to reduce post-purchase anxiety, particularly for financial services where no tangible object exists for customers to evaluate after purchase and where benefits from any purchase may not be realised for years (for example, PEPs or life assurance policies).

2.15 A large part of the role of advertising in financial services involves providing new information on services/products or offering new services/products (for example, the launch by the Halifax of the Tax Free Home Plan). When this is the case, advertising is seen as working in the traditional manner: new, relevant and interesting information sets a process in motion that leads to an increase in sales in the short-term.

Public relations

2.16 Public relations (PR) was initially associated with sending out press releases and seeking positive publicity for an organisation. In today's organisations however, PR is a sophisticated tool and uses a number of methods to enhance a positive image of an organisation and its services.

2.17 Effective PR may include

- annual reports/surveys
- mergers and conversions
- speeches
- charitable donations
- in-house magazines
- press releases.

2.18 An example of this type of activity is the Halifax's House Price Survey. PR seeks to establish and maintain mutual understanding between the organisation and its publics. An organisation's publics are made up of customers, employees, suppliers and intermediaries.

2.19 To maximise the effectiveness of PR it should be deliberate, planned and continuous, as opposed to a series of ad hoc damage limitation exercises designed to minimise the negative publicity generated by a particular situation.

2.20 PR is quite often handled at a corporate rather than functional level, to ensure that the organisation presents a consistent image and delivers a consistent message. A corporate image is particularly important to financial service organisations because, as we have previously discussed, one of the evaluation criteria customers use when judging the quality of an intangible service is the assessment of the corporate image. Customers may also revert to perception to differentiate an organisation when faced with a profusion of similar and complex offers.

2.21 The development of a clear corporate image is an important element of competitive strategy and can be a valuable marketing asset. However, progress in this areas has been hindered by a lack of clear terminology for PR. Mintel (1993a) provided the following descriptions.

- Corporate identity is not merely a company logo. It is about what the organisation is, its personality: the sum total of its expertise, history, philosophy, culture, strategy and structure.
- Corporate image is how an organisation's publics perceive its corporate identity.
- Corporate communications is the way in which an organisation projects its identity (or what it would like its identity to be) to the world outside via the media.
- Corporate manifestation is the way an organisation presents itself through its visual identity, staff, buildings, sponsorship, etc.

2.22 Building societies have attempted to establish corporate identities based on culture, but have met with little success. The financial services industry has experienced problems promoting a positive image. The industry suffered very negative publicity in recent years over a number of issues. Banks were accused of foreclosing on small businesses; building societies were accused of having a callous attitude to property repossession and negative equity, and life companies were faced with a media outcry over the mis-selling of pension plans. These cases are only a few from recent years and serve to highlight why a planned PR campaign should be an important element in any promotion plan.

Sponsorship

2.23 Sponsorship is not a form of advertising that should be used to generate sales, instead it is a method that is used to build brand/product/corporate awareness or corporate image. For it to be most effective it should be integrated with other advertising and promotional media.

2.24 Sponsorship can contribute to a wide range of objectives at a corporate, local or brand level. It achieves this by

- increased media attention
- increased corporate and brand awareness, and image
- increased new product awareness
- corporate hospitality opportunities
- involvement in the community.

2.25 Sponsorship also has the benefit of being able to target large numbers of an organisation's publics in one go.

2.26 However, there are 'hidden' costs involved with sponsorship: it is usually necessary for the sponsor to market an event in an effort to gain maximum attention and publicity for both the organisation and the event.

2.27 Financial services organisations have sponsored sporting events for many years, but recent years have seen the emergence of the sponsorship of cultural events and specific items on TV. For example

- Halifax: Rugby League World Cup
- Nationwide: Division One football
- NatWest: cricket
- Lloyds: Clothes Show and Fashion Awards, Young Film-makers
- Midland: television dramas
- Cornhill: Test Match.

2.28 In the past, sporting events have been felt to offer high levels of visibility and the advantage of presenting a message to a full range of demographic segments.

2.29 Lloyds bank used their sponsorship in the fashion industry to target three specific markets: the general public, the youth sector and affluent adults. Lloyds' objective was to reposition the bank towards a modern approachable image, without prejudicing their existing quality image, and to differentiate the bank from other financial services organisations.

2.30 Many organisations carry out sponsorship on a local or regional level, again with heavy involvement in sporting events. For example,

- Axa Equity & Law: Sunday Cricket League
- Brittanic Association: county cricket
- Halifax: Opera North.

2.31 There are also many community programmes receiving sponsorship awards. Barclays Bank provided head offices with discretionary limits to spend in their local communities, with the aim of strengthening relationships and marketing the organisation at a specifically targeted audience.

2.32 Setting clear objectives for sponsorship at a local or corporate level is an important factor, but one that many organisations find difficult to do as measures tend to be qualitative rather than quantitative. However, without any objectives there is no basis for evaluation, and sponsorship may become ad hoc and removed from the communications strategy.

Sales promotion

2.33 Sales promotion is one of the principle tools used to encourage trial, and thereby generate brand changing. However, unless it is supported by other elements of the mix, it is unlikely to be strong enough to generate brand loyalty. This is because sales promotions are aimed at breaking down any brand loyalty the customer may have for another organisation's products/services; advertising is used to build brand loyalty.

2.34 Several promotional tools used by financial services organisations have proved popular. However, this is not a static market, and specialist sales promotions agencies exist to assist in the development of new ideas. Current examples include

- music/cinema and book vouchers to young savers
- travel bags and novels with travel money.

2.35 In the mortgage market cashbacks and incentives, such as solicitors and survey fees being paid, are now commonly used by the building societies and banks.

2.36 Credit cards have seen high levels of sales promotion activity, particularly as the number of new entrants in the UK market has risen. Here there are a plethora of examples including

- Air Miles (NatWest)
- Profile Points (Barclays)
- fee free cards
- cashback for transferring balances from other card issuers.

2.37 First Direct initiated a scheme whereby points are awarded for spending. These points can be redeemed for specific items such as breakdown cover or as a discount against First Direct products.

2.38 Competitions and prize draws are also being increasingly used, particularly by the banks, and are often associated with personal loan applications where the market is very competitive.

2.39 Sales promotion is not just a tool for customer activity; it can also be used to provide an incentive to staff and intermediaries, and to encourage sales staff to increase their level of activity.

Direct marketing

2.40 Direct marketing consists of a number of elements and should not be confused with direct mail, which is just one of those elements. The US Direct Marketing Association describe direct marketing as:

> **'An interactive system of marketing which uses one or more advertising media to effect a measurable response and/or transactions at any location'.**

Betts and York (1994) explained it further by stating that:

> **'It [direct marketing] aims to create and exploit a dialogue between the service provider and the customer and offers several potential benefits:**
>
> - **Targeting precision**
> - **Testing (markets, offer, services, timing, creative, format)**
> - **Is measurable and accountable**
> - **Provides new distribution channels and supports existing ones**
> - **Cost effective advertising'.**

2.41 Betts and York (1994) go on to say that, although these benefits exist, they are not always recognised and the image of direct marketing has suffered. They suggest the following reasons

- poor targeting
- unscrupulous operators

- incorrect personalisation
- misuse of sensitive information
- association with down-market mail order
- historically poor self-regulation
- inadequate training and education.

2.42 Direct marketing has grown considerably during the last decade and financial services organisations have embraced the concept with almost all areas showing an increase in usage.

2.43 The most significant growth has been in telemarketing, which offers a number of benefits in terms of building and maintaining databases, developing lists, market measurement and testing, generating retail traffic, direct selling and customer care. This type of marketing is no longer the domain of general insurance companies (Direct Line) and banking (First Direct), but is also used by life companies such as General Accident and Scottish Widows.

2.44 The rules and regulations regarding advertising complex regulated products have generated a rise in off-the-page advertising by financial services organisations. This method of direct marketing is used to generate leads, qualify prospects and encourage requests for either further information or appointments. It is also used for selling products on an execution only basis, such as Income Bonds.

2.45 Thwaites and Lee (1994) illustrated the rise of direct marketing methods in the chart shown in Table 9.1.

Table 9.1 Use of direct marketing media

	Institutions using the media (%)		
Media	*1989 Firth and Lindsay (n = 70)*	*1992 Thwaites and Lee (n = 77)*	*Percentage increase*
Direct mail	97	97	0
Leaflet inserts	67	85	27
In-house piggybacks	60	78	30
Off-the-page press advertising	63	76	21
Two-stage press advertising	59	73	24
Door-to-door leaflets	41	52	27
Third-party piggybacks	33	47	42
TV direct response	23	35	52
Telephone marketings	21	57	171
Radio direct response	20	26	30

Source: Thwaites and Lee (1994)

2.46 Cost is an issue when undertaking direct marketing, but remember that costs should have a direct relationship with results. If we compare direct mail with television, we may find that it costs £1 to reach a household of two people. The same amount spent on TV advertising may reach 100 people. However, the two people reached with the direct mail pack will be carefully targeted; the message content and style of the pack will be designed specifically for the target group, and therefore the response rate for TV advertising is unlikely to be greater than that for direct mail.

2.47 Direct marketing should be seen as a part of the promotional mix and, depending upon the strategic objectives of an organisation, should be an integral part of the planning process.

Personal selling

2.48 Personal selling is used by most of the organisations in both corporate and personal sectors. It is an important tool in financial services because of the complexity of the nature of many of the products. Personal selling can assist by

- gaining acceptance of new products by existing customers
- attracting new customers for existing products
- maintaining customer loyalty
- facilitating future sales by the provision of advice to prospects
- gathering market information.

2.49 The advantage of personal selling is that it provides a platform for dialogue and has the benefits of a focused approach with the ability to obtain immediate feedback. However, the benefits of this method must always be compared with the costs involved, as personal selling is an expensive method, particularly when compared with other elements of the promotional mix. There are also the issues of organisational culture, training and the remuneration of the sales force.

2.50 Morgan (1994) highlighted three different approaches to the operationalisation of bancassurance and the role of personal selling. The key distinctions are control, location and remuneration of the sales force. In each case the organisation had its own branch network and owned its own life company. Insurance products are sold almost exclusively to the organisation's customer base.

2.51 In the first approach general insurance and mortgage product enquiries go to the customer service representatives in the branch network. Investments regulated under the Financial Services Act 1986 are referred to representatives of the life company. Interviews are arranged to take place in the branch or at home. Customer service representatives are remunerated according to the organisation's salary scale, with small amounts of commission, and the life company representatives operate on commission only.

2.52 The second approach is similar to the first except that customer enquiries are screened by branch staff who then refer the prospects to either the in-branch sales force or the life company representative. Both groups are qualified to deal with the full range of insurance and investment issues, but the more complex products usually go to the life company representative, who operates through home visits only.

2.53 Company representatives receive a small salary with a high commission element, in contrast to the in-branch sales force who are paid in accordance with the organisation's salary scale plus marginal commission.

2.54 The third approach is different in that specially trained branch staff traditionally dealt with enquiries, predominantly from the branch and on a no commission basis. This approach has not proven successful and a revised format is being investigated.

2.55 The three approaches described have changed in the evolution of financial services. Many bancassurers have established a life company and are therefore represented by a tied sales force, often through a branch network, with minimal home visits and the remuneration package taking the form of a basic salary plus commission. To ensure that the organisation remains a full service provider, many also operate an independent financial advice subsidiary. The sales people from these subsidiaries are usually not branch based and operate through home visits.

2.56 Integration of a sales force within an organisation can be difficult. The traditional banking culture may not be conducive to the development of a sales culture, and problems may arise when two sets of staff are remunerated in different ways (branch staff on salaries and sales staff on salary plus commission).

Student Activity

1 Name the six types of promotion

2 What are some of the methods used by PR to create a positive image?

3 What is the principle tool used in promotion to encourage product by trial?

3 The role of the branch in promotional activities

3.1 It is important that any promotional activity that takes place is announced internally, before launch, and that any staff who will be affected by the activity have time to prepare themselves.

3.2 The nature of financial services is such that a high degree of interaction with the customer is essential. If a customer requests a service or product that has recently been promoted and the staff member is not aware of it, then the customer is likely to lose faith in both the staff member and the organisation they represent; this may lose a sale.

3.3 All branches must ensure that all members of staff understand the promotion and feel confident in conveying their knowledge to the customer.

3.4 We have previously discussed the fact that sponsorship can be carried out at a local level; so too can other elements of the promotional mix. Advertising initiated at branch level can be carried out in local newspapers and on local radio, thus raising the profile of an individual or small group of branches. Sometimes a head office will supply sets of copy-ready adverts and allocate a budget; the adverts are then placed in local publications at the branch manager's discretion.

3.5 G mapping is currently being investigated by a number of organisations. Using this method market information such as geographical location, customer base and competitor positioning is gathered branch-by-branch. The ultimate aim is to support branches in flexibility of point of sale materials where specific opportunities and needs are identified, and to assist branches in achieving their business targets.

3.6 Branches are the front-line of communication with the majority of an organisation's customers. They experience market trends at a local level and are seen as part of a community, particularly in smaller towns and villages. This provides some scope for 'bottom-up' planning when the promotional calendar is planned. It also provides opportunities for ad hoc activity at a local level. Guidelines can be issued from head office to ensure that corporate branding and image is maintained if any activity is undertaken. A level of budget can also be allocated at a local level to allow a branch to be proactive. This is particularly useful where branches wish to sponsor local events to build their brand image within a community.

3.7 Ultimately, input from a branch level should be encouraged and viewed by an organisation as an asset.

Summary

Before any decisions can be made about which elements to use in developing the most appropriate promotional mix, a number of steps need to be undertaken. These are important tasks and aid in the identification of both the current situation and future plans. This in turn allows for the most appropriate allocation of resources within the business.

After reading this unit you should appreciate the importance of careful selection of the types of promotional tools that can be used and understand why 'doing a little bit of everything' is not the way to achieve results. In particular, you should be able to

- ❑ **describe the steps to follow when developing a promotional mix**
- ❑ **describe the different elements that can be used in the promotional mix**
- ❑ **explain the role of the branch in promotional activities.**

Self-assessment questions

1 (a) Name the seven steps involved when developing a promotional mix.

(b) Write one or two paragraphs to describe each step.

2 Briefly describe each of the six elements that can be used in promotion.

3 (a) Why do branch staff need to know about a promotional activity before it takes place?

(b) How may promotions be carried out at branch level?

Unit 12

Service quality

Objectives

After studying this unit you should be able to do the following.

- **Define service quality.**
- **Understand how customer expectations impact upon an organisation.**
- **Monitor and measure service quality.**

1 Introduction

1.1 In providing and delivering financial services there has to be interaction between the organisation, its staff and the customer. Service quality encompasses the delivery of a service to the customer, operations, customer relationships and the internal relationships between management and staff.

1.2 In the past decade financial services organisations have become increasingly marketing orientated as the environment has become ever more competitive. This has led to them developing strategic marketing plans which respond not only to business and economic conditions, government legislation and technological advances but also to customers' needs, attitudes and behaviour.

1.3 This changing and competitive environment has meant that organisations must seek to establish a competitive advantage, and high levels of customer service are viewed as a way to pursue a differentiation strategy and therefore sustain a competitive advantage within the industry.

1.4 Customers have become increasingly aware of the range of financial services providers and products available to them. When faced with such a plethora of suppliers, customers' expectations rise and they become increasingly critical of the service they receive. Because it is so much more expensive to recruit a new customer than it is to retain an existing one, organisations must aim to provide excellent service and develop long term relationships.

1.5 With a focus on service quality the organisation seeks to build customer loyalty through satisfaction. Customer loyalty is aimed at generating opportunities for repeat business and cross selling, and ensuring customer retention and the cost savings derived from this.

1.6 Satisfied and loyal customers can also become advocates of the organisation and may attract new customers through positive word of mouth communication.

1.7 Organisations should also show commitment to staff. In recent years many financial services providers have undertaken large cost cutting exercises, and many have had to reorganise following mergers and takeovers. These types of activities impact on staff morale, motivation and performance.

1.8 Commitment to and communication with staff benefits the organisation in terms of increased morale, job satisfaction and loyalty to the company. This all contributes to reducing staff turnover and thereby the costs of recruitment and training. Also, committed and competent customer-facing staff should make fewer mistakes and therefore provide higher levels of service, which in turn means fewer customer complaints.

1.9 A focus on service quality also enhances the corporate image and can provide some insulation from price competition and so aid the pursuit of a differentiation strategy.

1.10 Successful service will lead to a reduction in costs and an increase in production and sales, which in turn lead to an increase in market share, profitability and overall business performance.

1.11 We can see why service quality is such an important issue and service quality initiatives have now become high priority with many of the leading financial service providers. Organisations take the view that the expenditure involved in this initiative is long term and key to future growth and profitability.

1.12 To develop successfully a service quality plan an organisation must have an understanding of the interaction between itself, its customers and its staff. An example would be the service encounter which affects the customers in terms of their perception and evaluation of the experience and on staff in respect of their motivation, performance, role and rewards.

1.13 The first step in achieving this understanding should be to identify the key elements of service quality as perceived by customers and employees. These would take into account their needs and wants in relation to

- the services being offered, covering core and supporting services as well as the augmented service offering, which includes the service process and the interaction between customers and the organisation
- the delivery systems and procedures – their efficiency, effectiveness, reliability and whether they are responsive
- the delivery environment – its design and access as well as the emotional impact or 'ambience' experienced by customers and employees
- technology – its impact on customer-organisation exchanges and service levels and delivery
- staff – the role they play in service provision and their personal qualities: this should include knowledge and skills and the ability to understand and service customers' needs.

1.14 The next step is to measure the importance of service quality dimensions using a method known as SERVQUAL alongside other tools. The end result of this exercise is that any service quality 'gaps' will have been identified. It also highlights the problems that can occur when attempting measurement of service quality.

1.15 This identification exercise ensures that the key elements in the service quality plan are the development of

- services to meet customers' needs
- systems and procedures which are both customer and employee focused
- a suitable delivery environment
- the use of technology in systems and services to ensure speed, efficiency and accuracy.

1.16 A service quality plan must also focus on internal marketing if it is to be successful. Here the plan must look at the internal customer – the staff – and investing in people. This is normally undertaken by Human Resource Management and includes the development of policies which cover recruitment, training, appraisals, remuneration and recognition.

1.17 Once the organisation has identified and assessed the key elements of service quality, converted them to set standards and systems, and recruited and trained the staff, it must then ensure delivery of the processes.

1.18 Potential failure points must be noted and service guarantees developed, for example, the Mortgage and Banking Codes of Practice, and procedures set in place for service recovery if it is ever required.

1.19 Monitoring the service plan is also important and requires the development of methods to research and evaluate customer satisfaction and dissatisfaction and employee performance and satisfaction. This should be planned as a rolling programme, and not an ad hoc activity, to enable a speedy response to any dissatisfactions which are identified.

1.20 Finally, as with all activities undertaken by an organisation, the development of service quality will not be possible without management support. The organisation may require cultural changes to achieve the staff orientation to the organisation and everybody's orientation to the external customer. Change must begin at the top and senior management should be seen to be committed to staff and customers alike.

2 Defining service and service quality

2.1 A service can be described as a 'service encounter', sometimes also known as a 'critical incident'.

2.2 This encounter is the direct interaction between an organisation and its customer and can occur in a number of ways. For example, a bank customer who wishes to withdraw money may choose between an interaction with an ATM located at the bank, a remote ATM or a cashier in the banking hall.

2.3 Each time a customer comes into contact with any aspect of the bank or one of its staff he or she is has the opportunity to 'form an opinion' of the bank and the service received. For example, a remote ATM which is out of order may leave the customer with negative feelings towards the bank, whereas a friendly smiling cashier will leave the customer with a positive feeling.

2.4 Service encounters, especially the interactions with bank staff, have a high level of impact on the customers and so the quality of the interaction is an essential element in the service quality experienced by the customer.

2.5 Service encounters also have an impact on the staff in relation to their motivation, job satisfaction, performance, rewards and recognition. Therefore financial service organisations must manage service encounters effectively for the benefit of the customers, the staff and the achievement of corporate goals.

2.6 The service encounter concept was developed further by Lewis and Entwistle (1990) who proceeded to illustrate the variety of encounters which take place for a financial services retailer and which, combined, impact on both customer service and service quality.

Figure 12.1 Service encounters – Lewis and Entwistle, 1990

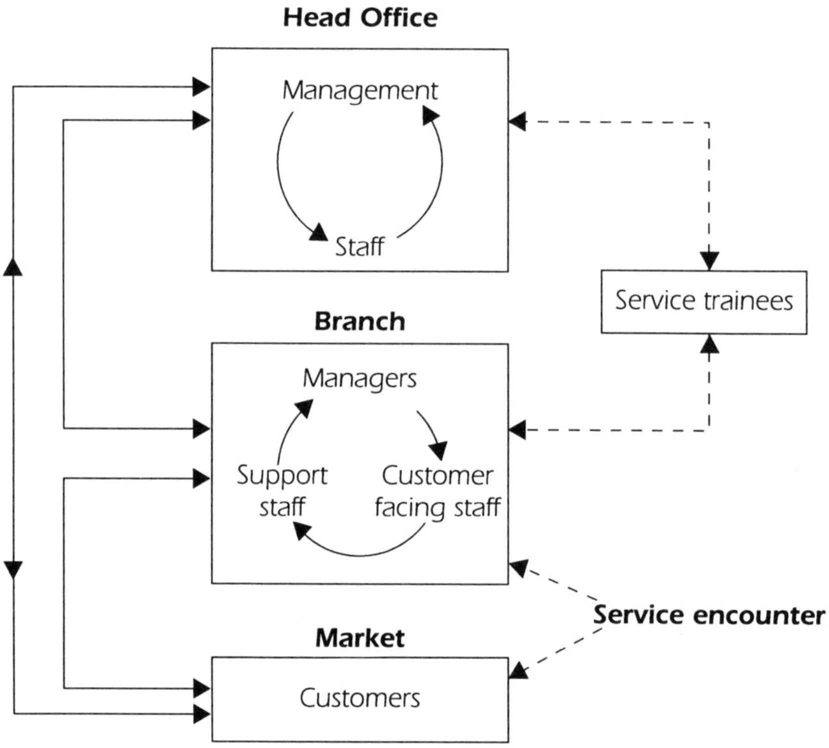

2.7 There are a number of ways of defining service quality; however, the essence of such a definition should relate to meeting a customer's needs and requirements and how well the service actually delivered matched the customer's expectations.

2.8 In the context of service quality, the definition of customer expectations means the desires and wants of the customer and would relate to what a customer feels the service provider should offer. It is not based on what a service provider *actually* offers. These expectations are derived from previous experiences with an organisation and its marketing mix, as well as competitor experiences and word of mouth communication.

2.9 The outcome is that customers make judgments on quality which result from a comparison between their expectations of the service required and their perception of the service received. If a shortfall exists then this is known as a 'service quality gap', which an organisation should aim to close.

2.10 The service quality gap was a concept developed in the late 1980s by Berry, Parasuraman and Zeithaml. They defined service quality as a function of the gap between customers' expectations of the service and their perceptions of the actual delivery by an organisation.

2.11 They suggested that this gap is in turn influenced by several other gaps which can occur in an organisation. This concept is illustrated in Figure 12. 2.

Figure 12.2 A conceptual model of service quality, Zeithaml et al 1990

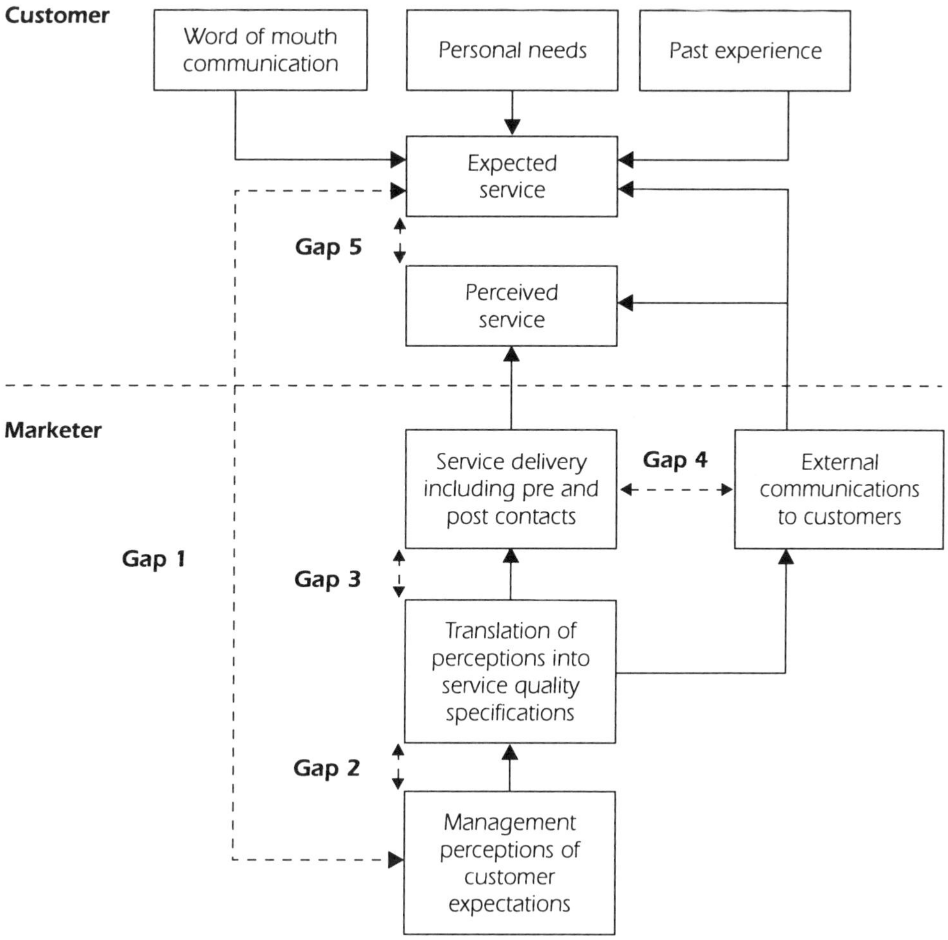

Gap 1: customer expectations – management perceptions

2.12 Managers do not always know what customers (both external and internal) want or expect from an organisation. Insight can be gained through market research such as customer satisfaction surveys, focus groups and complaint monitoring, and through better communication between managers and staff at all levels in the organisation.

Gap 2: management perceptions – service quality specifications

2.13 Even when customers' expectations are identified, lack of resources or lack of management commitment to service quality and a service culture may result in the failure to set the necessary service quality specification.

Gap 3: service quality specifications – service delivery

2.14 This is the service performance gap and occurs when the level of service delivered is less than the management's specifications for that service because of variations in staff performance, i.e. staff being unable or unwilling to perform at the desired level.

Gap 4: service delivery – external communications

2.15 This occurs when what is said about a service differs from the service delivered. For example, advertising can influence a customer's perception and thereby expectation of a service. It is therefore important that promises made can be delivered. Information and communication should be appropriate and timely and should be directed both externally and internally.

Gap 5: perceived service – expected service

2.16 When the customer has experienced the service, the feeling of how the service was delivered may not always match what they felt the service should have been.

2.17 It is difficult for an organisation to manage customer expectations but it is important that expectations do not greatly exceed perceptions.

2.18 Gaps 1 to 4 contribute to the customers' expectations and perceptions which are identified as Gap 5, and it is important that financial services providers identify which of the gaps exist in their own organisation, determine the factors responsible for them and then develop the necessary solutions.

Student Activity

1 What are the key elements of service quality?

2 What benefits can an organisation derive from having a service quality programme?

3 Customer care

3.1 Having defined service quality it becomes obvious that the major elements of perceived and expected service and the gap which can exist between them probably exists, to some degree, in all organisational operations. The customers' expectations are not always easily identifiable. However, understanding these are key for an organisation, because expectations set the level of service and thereby the minimum levels of customer care.

3.2 In a major research project carried out by Lewis and Smith, 1989, 39 service quality criteria, divided into four areas (see below) were evaluated in terms of customer expectations and customer perceptions for both banks and building societies.

3.3 It became clear from the results that customers did not always expect the same service from banks and from building societies. Sometimes expectations were met or exceeded but in some instances they were not reached.

Physical features and facilities

3.4 Customers felt that these were important elements, particularly location, privacy, equipment and physical safety.

3.5 For the most part customers were satisfied with features and facilities and the highest ratings went to convenient location, appearance of staff and appearance of buildings. One element which was rated as 'poor' for both banks and building societies, was parking facilities. Given the central city locations of many branches this was perhaps understandable, however, given the number of out of town sites which now exist this particular element may well score differently if the exercise were to be repeated today.

Reliability

3.6 All the elements of this area – accuracy of transactions, ability to do things right, ability to keep promises and competence of support staff – were felt by customers to be 'important' and they were all seen as 'satisfactory' for both banks and building societies.

Staff customers come into contact with

3.7 In this area customers were most satisfied with honesty and trustworthiness, a characteristic which was also identified as being 'very important' and so their expectations were met.

3.8 Also listed as being either 'important' or 'very important' were confidentiality and discretion, which given the nature of financial services is not surprising, and staff knowing personal needs, which received a poor evaluation.

3.9 This perhaps highlights a desire by customers to receive what they perceive to be a personal service and in the early nineties Barclays bank established personal bankers as a method of relationship marketing, the ultimate goal being to engender loyalty in the customers.

3.10 This was progressive marketing for an organisation, and in the late nineties, when the environment is becoming increasingly competitive, many organisations promote themselves as offering services which meet the individual's needs.

Responsiveness to needs

3.11 The two most important elements of this area were felt to be willingness of staff and management to help with problems or queries, and speed of service.

3.12 With this part of the research a number of open ended questions were also asked and the responses provided some interesting and valuable additional data.

3.13 They highlighted some of the positive aspects related to the service, such as staff qualities, but also highlighted some of the negatives. These included aspects such as low staffing levels at peak times, slow service, inattentive staff, poor knowledge, mistakes and poor complaints handling. All these are service qualities which, if felt to be missing by the customer, can lead to account closure.

3.14 It is well documented that customer inertia is prevalent when it comes to changing a financial service provider. However, banks such as First Direct capitalised on the growing customer dissatisfaction in respect of responsiveness to needs and have successfully recruited large numbers of customers from competitors.

3.15 The criteria evaluation indicates the levels of customer care which an organisation must undertake to satisfy its customers. Customer care can be further measured at three levels

- shortfall of expected levels
- meeting the expected levels
- exceeding the expected levels.

3.16 Falling short of the expected levels of customer care carries the risk of customers taking their business elsewhere. However, customers will sometimes accept lower levels of service in one or two elements if they feel the rest of the service meets their needs. Organisations must be careful not to become complacent and accept this as an operational norm. In the increasingly competitive financial services sector any customer dissatisfaction is a potential account closure.

3.17 Meeting the expected levels of customer care will be viewed by many as being completely acceptable. Organisations must acknowledge that this is a minimum level of service, which can also be exceeded by competitors, and that complacency here can lead to a falling level of service if it is not monitored and reviewed regularly.

3.18 It is probably felt that exceeding levels of service is the most enviable position to be in, but this can also bring its own problems. After a period customers no longer feel that their expectations of service levels are exceeded as they become perceived as 'the norm'. The organisation is then seen as meeting the expected levels of service and will have the problems inherent in this position.

3.19 Another group of customers who should also be considered when studying levels of service and customer care are businesses.

3.20 When Margaret Thatcher led the Conservatives, individuals were encouraged to establish their own business and so the banks were presented with an expanding market segment.

3.21 Providing the correct services at a level expected by these new owner/managers was key to establishing relationships which would continue as the businesses grew, hopefully, into large companies.

3.22 Smith (1990) carried out further research into this and identified the following four key areas.

Bank personnel

3.23 The major criticism was the inability of bank staff to understand the business and make informed judgments relating to a client company's potential needs.

Organisation and structure of banks

3.24 Small businesses felt that the oligopolistic nature of the UK banking market was reflected in apparent bureaucracy and remoteness of policy-makers from managers in the field.

Pricing policies

3.25 It was felt that the banks had policies which created problems rather than solutions for small businesses, i.e. high interest payments, charges, collateral requirements and raising additional – or even initial – finance.

Product offerings

3.26 Products which were felt to be relatively simple by the banks were not always seen as such by the small business manager. This illustrated the need for greater levels of information.

3.27 Smith included 55 service factors questions in the research, which also provided valuable data on expectations, perceptions and satisfactions.

3.18 The most important factors were found to be

- accuracy or competency aspects
- confidentiality and trustworthiness of the manager
- promises kept
- reliability of both branch and head office
- speed in decision making, transactions, being dealt with in the branch or on the telephone, resolving problems and queries.

3.29 All these elements reflect the need for responsiveness and competence in a banking relationship.

3.30 There has been a great deal of criticism levelled at the banks over the past decade, particularly during the recession, about how they have treated small businesses. A major criticism is that the banks do not 'care' about the business customers themselves; they are only interested in the business these customers bring to the bank.

3.31 Many banks now have specially trained business managers who look after a small number of accounts. This enables the bank to develop a relationship with individual customers and understand their needs.

3.32 In the survey some of the important factors listed in relation to the bank manager were an understanding of the business and having the authority to make decisions which affect the business, having an interest in the customer's business, availability and personal qualities. Many of these have been addressed as a result of the introduction of the business manager.

4 Measuring and monitoring service quality

Measurement

4.1 Service quality is not easily measured, particularly when the measurement relies on customer perceptions.

4.2 It is, however, important that some degree of measurement must take place if any financial provider is to understand not only the customers' expectations, but also whether the customer feels the organisation is meeting those expectations.

4.3 There are many tools for measurement, each with its advantages and disadvantages, but one of the most frequently used methods is the SERVQUAL questionnaire.

4.4 SERVQUAL is a 22 item scale based on six dimensions: tangibles, reliability, responsiveness, assurance, empathy and recovery. The first five categories were established by Parasuraman et al (1988) after factor analysis and testing had taken place. The sixth dimension – recovery – was added by Gronroos (1988) following further work.

4.5 The questionnaire is formatted into 22 pairs of Likert style scales. The first 22 questions seek to measure the customer's expectations of the service and the following 22 aim to measure the perceived level of service provided by the organisation.

4.6 The SERVQUAL questionnaire is felt to be reliable and valid and is used by researchers investigating service quality in many industries. It can be used to track service quality trends and improve service, categorise customers, compare an organisation with its competitors, and compare branches of a bank or building society.

4.7 The limitation of this questionnaire is that it can only be used for current and previous customers as the respondents must have had knowledge and experience of the organisation to answer the questions.

Figure 12.3 Example of a SERVQUAL questionnaire

Service expectations:

e.g. 'Customers should be able to trust bank employees'

'Customers would not have to queue'

'Banks should have up to date equipment'

'Banks should tailor loans to customer requirements'

Strongly agree					Strongly disagree	
1	2	3	4	5	6	7

Perceptions:

e.g. 'I can trust the employees of my bank'

'I do not have to queue at my bank'

'My bank has up to date equipment'

'My bank tailored my loan to meet my needs'

Strongly agree					Strongly disagree	
1	2	3	4	5	6	7

4.8 The SERVQUAL tool is not without its criticisms and, as we previously stated, all tools have advantages and disadvantages. The criticisms levelled at SERVQUAL are

- the absence of weighting of the variables – which, by their very nature, will vary in importance
- the use of negatively worded statements, which can be confusing to customers
- apparent repetition of scales (in the eyes of the respondent)
- the two separate lists of statements
- the number of dimensions being assessed
- the timing of measurement activities – before, during or following a service experience.

4.9 Zeithaml et al (1991) have acknowledged some of these criticisms and provided a number of refinements to SERVQUAL, although it is felt that they are quite limited.

4.10 It has also been suggested that this type of questionnaire incorporates *desired*, rather than *adequate* levels of service expectations. One of the changes that Parasuraman made, therefore, was to alter the wording on the questions to reflect what a customer would expect from an organisation claiming to deliver excellent service quality. For example,

'excellent banks will have up to date equipment'

'an excellent bank will tailor a loan to meet my needs'

Strongly agree					Strongly disagree	
1	2	3	4	5	6	7

4.11 As you can see, changing the slant of the question now enables an organisation to see the minimum a customer will expect. These expectations can then be compared against current service delivery and allow service gaps to be identified.

Monitoring

4.12 Of equal importance to measurement is monitoring, and an organisation should ensure that systems are in place to undertake this task. Methods of monitoring include research and evaluation amongst customers and staff using surveys, focus groups and discussions. Mystery shopping exercises can also provide information and collection; analysis and categorisation of both customer complaints and letters of praise are also useful.

4.13 Many organisations offer service guarantees and these are monitored to provide key indicators regarding service delivery. For example, Blockbuster Video chain offers some new releases free if, when you visit a store to rent a video, the one you want is unavailable; some companies offer cash compensation if they are unable to resolve an issue within a set timescale.

4.14 Some organisations offer service guarantees as a permanent part of their service strategy whilst others use them as tactical promotional tools.

4.15 These types of guarantees are not used a great deal by financial service providers but as competition increases they may well choose to follow this route. UK banks and building societies do, however, have codes of practice for both banking and mortgages, although these are currently voluntary.

4.16 The aim of the codes is to outline to customers their consumer rights and provide information on customer service and complaints; in other words, explain to customers the minimum levels of service delivery they should expect from an organisation.

4.17 Service guarantees should involve everyone and the whole organisation should focus on excellent service as well as examining current service delivery for potential problem areas.

4.18 If an organisation decides to pursue a service guarantee strategy it should take into consideration the following points.

4.19 A good service guarantee should be

- unconditional
- easy to understand
- simple to communicate
- easy to invoke and collect on
- meaningful

4.20 Customer complaints provide valuable data which can be analysed. Organisations are aware that if they have a large number of dissatisfied customers only a small percentage of them will actually complain.

4.21 There are a number of possible reasons why a dissatisfied customer may be reluctant to complain.

- Finding it too much trouble to complain or fear of hassle if they did.
- No easy way to communicate, no set channels and no one to complain to.
- Feeling that no one cares and that complaining would not do any good.
- Not knowing where to complain.
- Customers feeling that they caused the problem in the poor level of service delivery.

4.22 There is evidence that if a customer's complaint has been dealt with efficiently and satisfactorily, the customer has a higher degree of loyalty to the organisation and will be more likely to engage in positive word of mouth communication; i.e. will become an advocate.

4.23 Providers of financial services should aim for a level of nil defects in service delivery, which means getting timings right from the beginning.

4.24 In an attempt to achieve this, many banks and building societies devise service quality systems which are quite rigid and use sophisticated techniques and structured personnel policies. But problems will occur, for example incorrect debits or unwarranted charges, and there will be staff absences. The challenge is to recover the situation with the customer and ensure that mistakes and problems do not happen a second time.

4.25 Service recovery should be a planned process which ensures that a customer who is dissatisfied or irritated is returned to a state of satisfaction, with the organisation making a concerted effort to make things right for the customer.

4.26 Service recovery also has economic value for organisations because when it is successful, it engenders customer loyalty, helps identify organisational problems and improves service quality awareness.

4.27 If something does go wrong, a customer will have recovery expectations. He or she will expect things to be put right, receive an apology, be treated well and, if appropriate, receive financial compensation.

4.28 This means that, when related to customers, service recovery is an 'emotional and physical' repair and organisations should first fix the customer and then fix the customer's problem.

4.29 There are a number of ways an organisation could facilitate this. For example,

- acknowledge the problem and accept responsibility
- believe the customer and avoid taking a defensive stance
- 'fix' the problem – respond to a customer and personalise the response
- compensate if applicable.

4.30 An important success factor in service recovery is the empowerment of customer-facing staff. They need to have the responsibility, authority and incentive to identify, empathise with and solve customers' issues and complaints.

4.31 Knowing that the management has the confidence to empower staff helps to create a positive attitude and good relationships between both staff and customers. It increases staff commitment to jobs, which is reflected in attitudes to customers.

4.32 Service recovery is not just about 'fixing' things after they have gone wrong. It should also focus on critical service encounters and anticipate potential problems. An organisation should then develop strategies for responding to such problems should they occur.

Student Activity

1 List and briefly describe the four areas of customer care.

2 What is SERVQUAL and how can it be used?

3 What are the main criticisms of SERVQUAL?

5 Service delivery and the role of the branch

5.1 An organisation must avoid Gap 4 – the failure to deliver a service as promised.

5.2 Once customers' needs have been identified, analysed and turned into the appropriate service systems and standards and staff have been recruited and trained, the next step is to ensure that 'promises' are managed and delivered.

5.3 Advertising and promotion will be used to communicate the service to the customer. This will set a level of expectation, followed by perception after a service experience. It is therefore important that promises made can be delivered.

5.4 It is in the delivery that the branch will have most impact. As head offices are usually responsible for advertising and promotion, the key element of branch input will be through the staff, both customer-facing and back office support.

5.5 Ensuring that the service delivery matches the specifications set is dependent upon the performance of all staff, who must be both able and willing to deliver the required levels of service.

5.6 The contribution made by staff to ensure customers' needs are met is paramount. The success of a service delivery strategy will therefore depend on the development of personnel policies for staff recruitment, training, motivation, recognition and rewards.

5.7 Internal marketing sees the staff as internal customers and their roles as internal products. Before selling a service to customers the organisation must sell its internal products to the staff. By doing this the wants of the internal customer are satisfied, which leads to an upgrading of the capability to satisfy external customers' needs.

5.8 It was stated by Gronroos (1981) that there are three identifiable objectives of internal marketing.

- Overall – to achieve motivated, customer-conscious and care oriented staff.
- Strategic – to create an internal environment which supports customer-consciousness and sales-mindedness amongst staff.
- Tactical – to sell service campaigns and marketing plans to staff – the initial market place of the organisation – via staff training programmes.

5.9 Recruiting and selecting staff who are 'right' for the role is important. Some key characteristics which may indicate a person's ability to perform effectively may be

- process and technical skills
- interpersonal communication skills
- flexibility and adaptability
- empathy with the customers.

5.10 Emphasis may be placed on different characteristics depending on the capacity in which the person is employed.

5.11 The ability to deliver the service at the required level may lead to the identification of training needs for both new and current staff. This will probably cover areas such as technical and interpersonal dimensions. Further training can then be developed for more specific areas e.g. product and systems knowledge and communication skills.

5.12 Elimination of Gap 3 in the branch environment will depend on the following.

- Teamwork – demonstrated by a caring management and involved and committed staff.
- Employee-job fit – the ability of staff to perform a job.
- Technology-job fit – are the 'tools' appropriate for the staff and the job?
- Perceived control – are staff empowered to deal with customers? If not stress levels may rise and performance decrease.
- Avoidance of role conflict for staff – in satisfying staff expectations of the organisation and expectations of customers.
- Avoidance of role ambiguity – staff should know exactly what is required of them and how their performance will be evaluated and rewarded.

5.13 The correct recruitment and training encourages a customer service orientation and aims to create an environment where everyone in the branch is working towards a common goal of excellent service delivery.

5.14 By encouraging staff to take responsibility for their actions and giving them the authority to respond to customers' needs the branch will work more effectively.

5.15 The staff also require supervision and systems for evaluating their performance. Some financial service providers also have reward and recognition schemes for employees who have performed particularly well, e.g. employee of the month.

5.16 Branches are an important part of service delivery as they are representatives for the whole organisation and a customer's perception of a service encounter at branch level will determine how the customer reacts to the organisation as a whole.

5.17 One of the most difficult aspects for branches to manage is the reconciliation of resources with the service delivery promises made by head office in its communications to customers. This will sometimes leave a manager in the position of having to decide which service he or she feels is most important when faced with limited resources. For example, is it more important to have a greater number of cashiers at a busy period, thereby reducing customer waiting times, or fewer cashiers and more staff available to answer customers' telephone enquiries?

5.18 Branches are also in a position to elicit comments from customers regarding service delivery. Any trends which are identified can be passed to the appropriate department for action. An organisation which has a true service delivery culture will actively encourage staff to put forward proposals which enhance customer care and service delivery.

Student Activity

1 What are the implications for staff management in service delivery?

2 What is meant by 'internal marketing'?

Summary

- **Customers have expectations, which may or may not be realistic, and which have to be managed so that customers' perceptions (what they felt about the service) following a service encounter match up to their expectations.**
- **The model of service quality illustrates possible gaps in the service delivery process with regard to these expectations and perceptions.**
- **Internal customers (staff) and external customers are of equal importance in service quality.**
- **For a service quality culture to work in an organisation, staff must be motivated and committed, and their efforts recognised. This can be achieved through enlightened personnel policies which will also cover selection and recruitment and reward and recognition.**
- **There are two sets of external customers – general consumers and businesses – who have different needs and wants – and therefore different expectations.**
- **Customer service strategies need commitment from the whole organisation, starting with senior management.**
- **Service quality plans need to be continually monitored and reviewed.**

Self assessment questions

1 Describe the steps involved in developing a service quality plan.

2 How can customer care be measured?

3 What is the 'service quality gap' and how can an organisation go about closing it?

4 Describe methods of monitoring and measuring service quality.

5 What should be taken into consideration when developing a service guarantee?

6 Why are many customers reluctant to complain about bad service?

7 Describe ways of facilitating service recovery.

Unit 13

Sales management

Objectives

After studying this unit you will be able to do the following.

- **Describe the characteristics that make a good salesperson.**
- **Describe the process involved in making a sale.**
- **Explain the role of sales training and what it involves.**
- **Describe the elements that make up sales management, including recruitment, remuneration and motivation.**
- **Describe the role of the branch in sales management.**

1 Introduction

1.1 You have seen throughout this book that the financial services industry is changing, and so is the way in which it sells its products to the public. There has been a great deal of interest in the use of the telephone to sell such things as motor and household insurance, pensions, home banking and share dealing. However, the majority of companies still sell most of their products by face-to-face meetings with a member of staff, i.e. their sales force. Even for companies who deal via the telephone, each call needs to be answered by a competent member of staff who is trained to sell their goods to the public. Because of this, the salespeople are a critical part of any financial services company, and personnel remain the most expensive resource in the retailing of their products. Because of the level of expenditure involved and the importance of the part they play, it is essential that such a sales force is managed effectively, so that the company receives the maximum possible return for the outlay involved.

2 Characteristics of successful salespeople

2.1 The sales force is vital to the company and it is costly; it is therefore important to ensure that companies select the most appropriate people for the job. To do this they need to identify the characteristics that are displayed by the most successful salespeople and then either select people who possess similar characteristics or train people to have them.

2.2 Within the broad title of financial services there are many different products and sales methods: the exact nature of the selling role is different for each. For example, a salesperson who deals with a customer who applies for a product in response to an advertisement performs different tasks to a salesperson who has to look for his or her own customers. The latter is likely to spend a great deal of time prospecting and will therefore need different skills and attributes to the former.

2.3 Having established that sales roles can vary, let us look at some of the basic core requirements for any successful salesperson within this industry.

Intelligence

2.4 The financial services industry is both complex and highly regulated; therefore anyone who offers advice in this area must possess a certain level of intelligence. They must understand the workings of the industry in general, and also be able to understand and explain all of the products and services that their company has to offer. Because of the level of regulation within the industry, many salespeople need to pass external examinations in order to be allowed to sell to the public, and the majority are required to sit the companies' own tests on a regular basis to ensure that their knowledge is accurate and up-to-date. Salespeople therefore need not only to be intelligent, but also able to demonstrate that they can use their intelligence in examination conditions.

Numeracy

2.5 'Financial services' was defined at the outset of this workbook as an 'activity connected with money', and so it follows that salespeople not only need to be relatively intelligent but also need to be numerate. As these people deal directly with customers, and represent the company by whom they are employed, it is vital that mistakes are avoided. Salespeople must therefore be comfortable dealing with numbers in the form of such things as charges, interest rates, and taxation.

Interpersonal skills

2.6 Whether the salesperson deals with the public face-to-face or via a telephone, they are the point of contact between the company and the customer. As far as the customer is concerned they *are* the company. Because of this, it is of the utmost importance that the salesperson has excellent interpersonal skills. Customers are often uncomfortable discussing matters of finance with total strangers, and the seller needs to make the customer feel at ease. Because of the complex nature of some of the products available and the public's general lack of interest in matters of finance, many customers need help in understanding the products on offer and in making a reasoned decision to buy. The salesperson must be able to explain, at an appropriate level, the details of their products and have patience and empathy with the buyer.

2.7 As more companies diversify into new markets there has been an effort to promote relationship selling, i.e. to persuade the customer to have an ongoing relationship with a financial services provider and to use them for all of their financial needs rather than going to a different company for each product. The salesperson plays a major role in relationship selling, as it is often the relationship and trust built up between the salesperson and the customer that will persuade the customer to return. It is fair to say that in many cases the customer needs to buy the salesperson before they will buy a product.

Drive and motivation

2.8 Whatever form the role takes, the salesperson must be motivated to succeed. No selling job is easy, and particularly in jobs that require a high level of prospecting, the salesperson is likely to suffer frequent rejection. They must be able to accept the rejection and be motivated to carry on trying until they identify an appropriate customer. In addition, the really successful salesperson will be someone who is not satisfied with just doing their job, or even with doing it well, but will want to be the best, and will therefore display the motivation to do that bit extra to ensure their success. A good sales manager needs to understand what motivates different members of the sales team and needs to help them to harness that motivation and use it to improve their performance.

Student Activity

Name two characteristics that the successful salesperson will display and explain why they are needed in the retailing of financial services.

3 The selling process

3.1 Before we can successfully manage salespeople we need to thoroughly understand the job they are employed to do and the different elements of that job. In order to do this, we will look at the elements that make up the sales process. At the same time it will also be useful to understand the sales process from the customer's point of view, as this will help us to shape the way we deal with the customer.

3.2 The sales process can be broken down into the following stages

- identifying potential customers
- identifying the customer's needs
- selling the solutions
- dealing with queries
- ongoing service.

Identifying potential customers

3.3 Not all salespeople who work within the financial services industry are involved in identifying potential clients. Those who work in banks or building societies often have customers sent to them from other areas of the business. Those who answer telephone calls from customers replying to advertisements do not need to spend time finding prospective leads. However, for those who do need to find their own customers, this is a difficult and time consuming part of the sales process. We have already discussed the general lack of interest amongst the public when looking at financial matters; this adds to the difficulty of this task. The need for a salesperson to identify their own prospects is most commonly seen in the life and pensions sector and is likely to account for the very high staff turnover rate in this area.

3.4 There are many different methods that can be adopted in order to identify potential customers. At its most basic, this stage can involve the salesperson knocking on doors in order to speak to people, or telephoning people whose names and numbers appear in the electoral role and telephone directory.

3.5 It is expected that for every customer who agrees to talk to the salesperson, there will have been a large number of people who will have said 'no'. This can be very disheartening for the salesperson who faces dozens of rejections every day. However, this is an essential part of the sales process: only when the salesperson has a customer to talk to do they stand any chance of making a sale. Because of this, it is paramount that the sales manager offers help and support during this stage of the sales process, particularly for new salespeople who, without such support, may find the task too demoralising and leave.

3.6 During this stage of the process, the customer may be completely unaware that they have a need for a financial services product and has not sought advice about their situation. They have simply been approached by a salesperson asking to speak to them. The salesperson needs to understand the customer and adapt his behaviour to suit the customer. During this stage the salesperson will need to find something that will persuade a member of the public to give up his time to talk to a salesperson who is selling something the customer doesn't yet realise he needs.

Identifying the customer's needs

3.7 Once the customer has agreed to discuss his situation, the salesperson needs to help him to identify what his needs are. The depth of this investigation will depend on the types of financial service the company retail. For example, the salesperson who is selling car insurance will limit their investigations to the facts relating to the product (i.e. who will be driving the car, will they want a hire car whilst theirs is repaired, do they want to protect any no claims bonus, etc.). However, in certain parts of the industry, such as the sale of life assurance, the salesperson should understand the customer's full financial situation, so this part of the process can be fairly lengthy.

3.8 Throughout these discussions the salesperson will learn exactly what the customer needs and what he is looking for in a financial services product. The salesperson will decide which, if any, of the products available most closely match these needs.

3.9 During this stage the customer, who was unaware of any need, will be made aware of it. This recognition of need is an important element of the process and requires a great deal of skill from the seller, but it is again vital if the customer is to progress any further along the sales route. The customer who entered the discussion already aware of a need will, during this stage, be clarifying in his own mind what that need is and what sort of solution is appropriate.

Selling the solution

3.10 Once both the customer and the salesperson clearly understand the customer's need, the salesperson will then present the solution to that need: the product they are offering. Because the products are intangible the salesperson cannot show them or demonstrate them, and therefore this stage also requires a degree of skill on the part of the salesperson, who will need to sell the benefits that the product offers the customer, always relating these to the needs the customer expressed.

3.11 During this stage the customer will be looking at the solution offered, weighing up the benefits against the cost, ensuring it meets his needs exactly and making a decision as to whether to buy or not.

Dealing with queries

3.12 Very few people will make a decision to buy without asking questions, and therefore the salesperson is likely to be involved in answering these questions, and even in modifying the solution they have suggested if need be. Following the sale the customer will often have queries about the product, and will go back to the salesperson to ask them. To maintain an ongoing relationship and create some customer loyalty it is important that the salesperson sees that dealing with these queries is an important part of their role, even though they may happen after the sale is completed.

Ongoing service

3.13 With many financial services products the customer will require service throughout the life of the product. This may be given directly by the salesperson or by other members of staff within the financial services company. This service is still a part of the sales process as whoever offers it is in an ideal position to see when the customer's needs are changing and when they may benefit from a new product, therefore starting the process again.

3.14 During this stage, customers will be forming opinions of the company, its products and its staff. These opinions are likely to influence heavily both the things they look for when next buying a financial services product, and the decision as to whether they would use the same company again.

Student Activity

1 Briefly outline the process involved in the sale of financial services products.

2 Select one stage of the sales process and explain what the salesperson should be doing during this stage.

4 Selling skills

4.1 A good salesperson needs to display a number of qualities, including such things as intelligence and numeracy. However, a successful salesperson will also display a range of skills often described as 'selling skills'. These skills can be described as follows.

Questioning skills

4.2 The salesperson needs to be skilled in asking questions. This may appear to be a simple task, but the questions must be worded in such a way as to get the maximum amount of information from the customer in the shortest possible time; i.e. the questions must be designed to encourage the customer to talk rather than just to give short one word answers. This is particularly important for people selling regulated products; such people have a duty to 'know their customer'. They therefore want to obtain the maximum possible information in a way that is interesting rather than interrogational for the customer.

Listening skills

4.3 Having asked the questions it is very important that the salesperson listens carefully to the customer, and can pick up the factors that are important to them. It is all too easy to ask questions and hear the answer without actually listening to exactly what the customer is trying to tell us.

Interpersonal skills

4.4 The salesperson must have good interpersonal skills for a number of reasons. Customer knowledge, although increasing, is still relatively low when discussing financial services products, and therefore the customer will, in some circumstances, need the salesperson to be able to explain what can be a complex product in very simple, plain English terms. Also, some areas of financial services are still prone to some mistrust by customers, for example, pension products. The customer is more likely to buy such a product from a salesperson who has developed a rapport with the customer and where there is therefore an element of trust between them.

Organisational skills

4.5 Successful salespeople need to be very organised as many of them are left to manage their own time. When dealing with regulated products, where the rules regarding documentation and record keeping are strict and punishments for non-compliance severe, an ability to manage time and organise the workload is of vital importance.

Telephone skills

4.6 Many of the contacts that salespeople have with customers take place over the telephone. With the current growth in telephone selling this is often the only form of customer contact. Where salespeople are involved in prospecting for customers this is also usually done with the aid of the telephone. It is therefore vitally important that the salesperson is comfortable using this method of communication and can do so to their best advantage.

Coaching skills

4.7 Often, particularly in large organisations or companies that still rely heavily on their sales force for the majority of their business, the line management approach is such that senior salespeople are responsible for the activities of others. When this is the case, as well as the other skills mentioned above, the individual will need to be able to recognise a weakness in their employees, and be able to coach those skills in order to improve their performance.

Student Activity

1. List the skills you would consider to be important for an individual who is to be successful in the retailing financial services sector.
2. Briefly explain why such skills are relevant.

5 Sales training

5.1 When a sales manager first recruits an individual they do so because they believe that the individual has the right skills, knowledge and attributes to be successful. However, that individual will still require a great deal of training if they are to reach their full potential in this field.

5.2 For regulated products this training is governed by the rules set out by the regulatory bodies, and each company must document their training and competency procedures. All training must be carried out in accordance with T&C guidelines and documented as a record that this has taken place. However, whether or not the training is regulated, it will generally need to consist of the following elements.

Technical knowledge

5.3 The salesperson will need to be able to display the required level of technical knowledge of the area of the industry in which they will operate. The amount of training given will depend largely on the amount of knowledge needed and the current knowledge and experience of the individual. In some areas of the industry the salesperson is also required to pass examinations set by industry bodies such as the Chartered Insurance Institute; if this is the case the company may well offer training to enable the candidate to sit these examinations.

Product knowledge

5.4 As well as technical and industry knowledge, the salesperson will need to be given training on the products that are offered by their company. They will need to be well equipped to describe these products to customers, explain how they meet the customer's needs and answer any questions the customer has on the products and their features.

Application of knowledge

5.5 This is a vital area of any salesperson's training and must be included in any sales training plan. Often technical detail or product features can be taught using such techniques as distance learning or computer based training packages. However, what is important is whether the salesperson can take the knowledge they have gained and apply it to everyday sales situations. It is this application of knowledge that may require most time and assistance.

Skills training

5.6 Once the salesperson has acquired all the necessary technical and product knowledge and is able to apply that knowledge, they will need to be taught the skills that ensure success. Often the skills element of the training gets overlooked or receives less attention than is necessary, as most of the sales skills we have identified take a great deal of time and practice before they become a natural part of the salesperson's behaviour. If skills training is given insufficient emphasis within the training programme, then the salesperson will be technically competent to do their job (and is therefore unlikely to give bad advice to customers), but is likely to continually underperform in relation to sales targets and potential sales activity.

5.7 Such underperformance could lead to a drop in the drive and motivation of that individual and eventually lead to staff turnover.

On job training

5.8 Not all the sales training needed for new salespeople can be carried out in a classroom environment. Once the basic level of knowledge and skill has been achieved the salesperson is permitted to start the job for which they were recruited. This should not be the end of their sales training; the training should be continued once the new recruit is actually selling. This will ensure that their knowledge remains at the required level and is kept up-to-date, and will allow them to further develop the skills that were introduced during the initial training period.

6 Training

6.1 The training that the salespeople undergo is likely to be developed by a central training department, in order to ensure that the training they receive is suitable and will achieve the required objectives. The training department will go through the following four stages.

1. Training needs analysis
2. Design
3. Delivery
4. Evaluation

Training needs analysis (TNA)

6.2 A TNA should be undertaken prior to any training event. The format of the TNA will vary according to the individual situation and the variety of methodologies being used. This analysis can take many forms, for example it could be carried out by interviewing supervisors, or by questioning the salespeople themselves. Alternatively it could rely to some extent on factual information or on feedback from customers.

Design

6.3 The results of the TNA will outline the extent of the training need and will be used as a basis for deciding which method of training will be most appropriate. For example, if the need is simply for a refreshing of factual knowledge the trainer may decide that the best way to do this is by writing and issuing some distance learning material followed by a brief test. Alternatively if the need is for a widespread improvement in selling skills, the trainer may decide that this can only be achieved by writing and delivering a week-long training course followed by on job training on a regular basis.

6.4 Whatever is selected as the solution to the need will have to be written. The written material will then need to be validated to ensure that it will meet its objectives. The validation process is undertaken in order to ensure that the materials are technically correct and that the methodologies used are adequate and suitable for the people who will be receiving the training. The validation will be carried out by various experts from within the company, or by an external resource.

Delivery

6.5 The method of delivery will again depend on the results of the TNA and the extent of the training. The sales managers could carry it out, or it could be carried out by trainers employed by the company. For some training it may be necessary for experts from within the technical areas of the company to undertake a 'train the trainer' course first to ensure that those who carry out the training are fully equipped to do so. For large deliveries, there will need to be some form of monitoring to ensure consistency.

Evaluation

6.6 The type and extent of the validation will depend on the purpose and the nature of the training. Below are some of the methods that can be used.

Reaction	The sales people's opinion of the training that they have received.
Learning	A measure of the knowledge and skills that each sales person has learned because of the training.
Behaviour	The change in the behaviour of the salespeople whilst they are doing their job because of the training they have undergone.
Results	The effect on each sales person's results, and the results of the company, following the change in behaviour of the salespeople.

6.7 The results of the evaluation will determined how successful the training was and will be used to ensure that future training is a successful as possible.

6.8 Because of the level of regulation within many areas of retailing financial services the training programmes for new salespeople who are to work in this industry are lengthy and extremely thorough. An example of an induction training programme for a new salesperson can be seen overleaf in figure 13.1.

Figure 13.1 Example outline training programme for a sales person.

Distance learning in preparation for external professional examinations

External examinations

Training within their area with their manager. This is likely to cover such things as introduction to the branch staff, information on working methods etc.

Training at the company's head office covering all technical and product knowledge that the salesperson will need to do the job. This can cover a period of up to eight weeks depending on the company, the complexity of the job and the experience of the salesperson. It is likely that it will be interspersed with periods back in the area where the individual may be required to observe more experienced colleagues. The sales person will also need to be tested on each of the areas in which he undergoes training.

Skills training course covering all the skills required to successfully generate leads and convert those leads into satisfied customers. There will also be some form of skills assessment

Assessment of the salesperson's ability to put into practice all that has been learned and of ability to deal with customers in the required manner

Ongoing on job training and continuing development.

Student Activity

1. What key elements should be included in the training programme of a financial services salesman?
2. Explain briefly the stages that are involved in the production and delivery of sales training material.

7 Sales management

7.1 So far we have seen how important the salespeople are is to financial services retailing organisations, and how skilled they need to be to be successful within their role. It follows that such salespeople need to be managed carefully so that they operate as effectively and as profitably as possible. To this end, the provider companies invest a great deal of time, effort and money into sales management to enable them to achieve the maximum from their sales force.

7.2 The job of sales manager covers many areas and involves many tasks. Figure 13.2 shows three areas of responsibility for a sales manager.

Figure 13.2 Core responsibilities of a sales manager

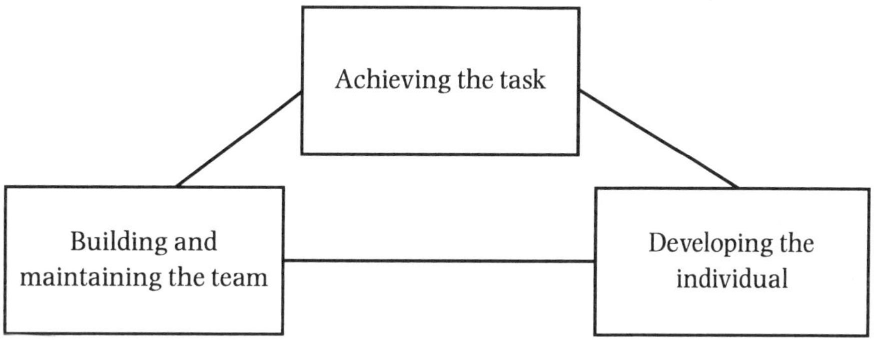

7.3 The sales manager is ultimately responsible for achieving the sales targets that the organisation has set for his team of salespeople, and therefore that has to be his primary concern. However, in order to do this the manager also needs to concern himself with building a team of good salespeople and ensuring that they continue to produce the sales required. In order to maintain and develop that team, the sales manager needs to address the needs of each of the individuals within the team and to try to ensure that each one is happy and making progress. A good manager will work on all three areas of responsibility to achieve the required results.

7.4 We now look at three tasks within the role of management that have a great impact on the performance of a sales individual, the team and therefore on the performance of the manager.

They are

- recruitment
- remuneration
- motivation.

Recruitment

7.5 Recruiting suitable people for the sales role is important for the following reasons.

- A successful salesperson will improve branch sufficiency, customer relations and ultimately create greater profit for the organisation.
- Employing the right person for the job will reduce staff turnover and the time and expense involved in the recruitment and training of a replacement.

7.6 Within most organisations the first stage of the selection process is carried out by the personnel department. They advertise, either internally or externally, with or without the help of an agency, for suitable staff, and carry out the initial screening. Having identified the characteristics that are present in good salespeople, the personnel department will test the applicants to ensure they have the required level of education, intelligence, numerical ability and mental diligence.

7.7 As well as these easily measurable criteria, we know that the successful salesperson will also display certain character traits such as drive, enthusiasm, self-discipline, patience and empathy. It is the presence of these characteristics that is likely to make the difference between success and failure; so detecting them during the recruitment process is important. Many companies now use personality questionnaires to assist in this detection, although these are not guaranteed to be accurate. It therefore often falls to the sales manager to spend some time talking to the potential recruit, getting to know as much as they can about that person and using their knowledge of the job and their experience to judge whether the individual has the necessary attributes.

Remuneration

7.8 There are two basic ways of rewarding salespeople for the job they perform. They can either be paid a salary regardless of what they sell and in what volumes, or they can be paid commission, i.e. they are paid only if they are successful at making sales. There are advantages and disadvantages to both methods when applied to the retailing of financial services.

Salaried sales force

7.9 If the salesperson is offered a salary for the job, then this has the advantage of attracting more people to the role. These may be people who, because of financial commitments, would be unable to take a position that offered no guaranteed income. A salaried sales force also has an image advantage with the public. If the customer knows that the salesperson is salaried and does not therefore receive money per sale, they may well feel more comfortable with their product recommendations. The company may also feel that the salesperson will be less tempted to oversell (to sell more products than the customer actually needs) if there is no financial incentive to do so.

7.10 On the down side, the company will be rewarding everybody equally, and therefore there is little incentive for the salesperson to make any extra effort. Because of the nature of the job, the type of person who is likely to take the position will need to be very motivated, and extra financial reward is a great motivation for salespeople.

Commission only sales force

7.11 The arguments above apply in reverse for this method of remuneration. Because they are only being paid for the business they produce, salespeople are motivated to work harder and see more customers. Performance related pay makes completing a sale much more exciting for the salesperson. It also means that the company does not pay someone who is not producing any business. However, the company may struggle to recruit the right calibre of person because of the lack of guaranteed income. They may also need to be careful how they position the remuneration package of their sales force with the public, particularly following the requirements to disclose commission payments on the sales of life and investment products.

Combined salary and commission

7.12 Because of the arguments for and against each method, many salespeople within the industry receive a remuneration package that is a combination of both, i.e. a low basic salary, with commission paid for the products they sell once they have reached a stated threshold. This achieves the best of both worlds, giving a level of security to the salesperson but offering them the motivation to succeed.

7.13 Many companies also use other forms of reward as well as cash to remunerate their sales force. These additional rewards, such as vouchers, merchandise or travel, are often used as incentives for very high achievers and as recognition for extra performance.

Motivation

7.14 The word motivation gets its origin from a Latin word meaning 'to move you to action'. Thus to motivate someone else is to give them a motive or an incentive to do something. In other words the manager must stimulate the salesperson's interest in a particular activity.

7.15 This is a much easier task if the salesperson is a naturally motivated person, and therefore the recruitment and selection processes are very important. A well motivated individual will show an evident and definite desire to do something and will show signs of energy, determination, drive and strength of purpose. The job of the sales manager is to deepen and develop this motivation.

7.16 There are tasks within any sales role that the salesperson will find difficult, repetitive or boring, and it is the sales manger's responsibility to ensure that the individuals are sufficiently motivated to see that these tasks are completed. To do this the manager will have to do the following.

- Be motivated himself, set an example to the team and show enthusiasm for success.
- Create positive feelings about the job in all the members of the team. In other words, the manager must make them feel good about what they do and help them to see that the job they do is worth while and of great value to the customer.

- Set challenging but realistic targets. If, for example, a salesperson hates the task of telephoning customers to make appointments, the manager should set him a target for the number of successful calls he must make per day or per week. The target must be challenging in order to give the salesperson a real sense of achievement when the job is successfully completed, but must be realistic so as to avoid the demotivation that would be caused by constant failure.
- Give the salespeople regular feedback on their performance. This works by showing individuals that they are important, and that the manager has a real interest in their performance and well-being. These regular discussions will also give an opportunity for the manager to inspire the salespeople to achieve more. Knowing that the manager is going to make the time and effort to discuss their progress should motivate the salespeople to make that bit more effort.
- Treat each person as an individual. What successfully motivates one person will be totally different from the thing that motivates another. Motivating factors can take the form of a 'carrot' or 'stick': for some people it may be a potential reward that stirs them into action whilst for other people it is the threat of punishment for not completing a task.

7.17 For those people who are motivated by potential reward this can take many forms. For example the motivation could be

- a sense of achievement
- recognition as being successful by peers or by management
- an advancement in status or the possibility of promotion to a higher post
- the promise of additional responsibility if a task is completed
- additional financial reward.

7.18 A good sales manager will know the team well enough to understand the factors that motivate each individual so that the appropriate method can be used to improve their performance.

8 The role of the branch in sales management

8.1 Most salespeople are based in an organisation's branch network, and even those who make a large number of home visits to customers still tend to be based at one of the company's branches. It is therefore only to be expected that such branches have a role to play in sales management.

8.2 Many of the salespeople will have been recruited from the branch staff — a rich supply of people with the right knowledge and experience who have the added advantage of a working knowledge of the organisation and its customers. Some salespeople will still be a part of the everyday running of the branch, with additional sales duties.

8.3 Often the branch staff play a significant part in the sales process. Although some salespeople are responsible for finding their own customers, many are not, as this part of the process is performed by branch staff. Often, counter staff in banks and building societies are required to identify potential customers and make the initial approach. They then direct the willing customers to the salesperson. This is an extremely important job as this must be seen as a seamless transition from counter to salesperson. Without this lead-generation there would be no sales at all.

8.4 If the salesperson is based in a branch, the staff at that branch will also play a large role in the motivation of that salesperson. If the branch staff are motivated, trying hard to produce leads for the salesperson, and keen to see the results, then the salesperson will also be keen to succeed. The feeling of belonging to a team will also serve to motivate a salesperson to perform well in what can otherwise be a lonely profession.

9 Management information

9.1 A successful sales manager needs a great deal of up to date management information if he is to keep a working knowledge of the success of the sales people in his charge and help them improve. The availability of meaningful management information is a key priority in order to deliver quality business. In order to achieve this requirement the business will need to decide what it considers to be the key performance indicators and ensure that up to date information on these is easily accessible. The company is likely to use some form of technology to ensure that this information is available.

9.2 Although the exact nature of the information the manager requires will depend largely on the nature of the business, they are likely to cover such things as:

- information as to who the customers are and what they require in a salesperson
- information about the number of customers their salespeople are seeing and the number of sales they are making
- information about the sales, for example what products they are selling, what level of premium or investment they are achieving etc.
- information relating to each individual's activity, for example how many customers do they see each day, what is their conversion from interview to customer rate, do they have any complaints made about them?

Student Activity

1. What are the three core responsibilities of a sales manager?
2. Why is it crucial to recruit a person with the right attributes for a financial services salesperson?
3. What are the benefits and drawbacks of having a sales force who are remunerated on a commission only basis?
4. Why would a sales manager need to understand what motivates each of the salespeople who work for him?
5. What is the purpose of management information?

10 Management training

10.1 A sales manager will also require a great deal of training. As with the salespeople he 'manages', it is important that an individual with the right attributes is recruited. Once sales managers are in place, they will still need to be trained to ensure that they do the best job possible. A sales manager's training programme should include the following elements.

- Technical knowledge
- Product knowledge
- Skills training
- Understanding of the salesperson's role.
- How to correctly observe a sales person in action and how to give the correct, constructive feedback.
- Coaching skills.
- How to recognise what motivates different individuals and how to use this knowledge to ensure the salespeople are motivated to do the job.
- How to identify individuals' training needs and how to deal with them.
- How to ensure he or she gives the maximum support to new employees during and immediately after their induction training programme.
- How to ensure that each salesperson has development plans and knows how to operate them.
- Sales management techniques including how to interpret management information and use it constructively.

10.2 After an initial training course has been carried out and the sales manager has been tested and judged to be competent in all the areas outlined above, he or she will then be free to supervise the salespeople in their designated area. However it is likely that initially the new manager will be closely monitored by a more experienced sales manager, who will be able to offer guidance. All sales managers will be required to complete periodic refresher training.

Case study and analysis

11.1 You are a sales manger for a large building society and have just been moved to an area where the salespeople are underperforming. You have been told that the eight people within your charge are not meeting sales targets, even though it is felt that they have the potential to do so. They are employed by the society to promote their range of life, pension and investment products in the main, but also have targets to sell current accounts and credit cards.

11.2 They are given large numbers of leads by the counter staff within the branch who refer customers from the building society branch, although they are also expected to find customers of their own if they are not kept fully occupied by the counter staff's leads.

11.3 The targets they have been set are realistic and are easily achieved by other sales people within the company.

11.4 Consider the steps you would take in order to ensure that the sales people within your area reach their maximum potential. You should think about the following points.

- The manager needs to remember the three key deliverables of individual development, team development and delivery of business targets. In order to deliver the required levels of business to the company the manager will have to look at each of the sales people as individuals and understand them, but he or she will also look at how they interact as a team and ensure that they each make a contribution to the team's performance.
- The first thing the sales manager should do is to ensure he or she has as much management information available as possible and interprets it properly. This will ensure that a clear picture of the current performance of the sales people emerges.
- The manager will need to understand the sales career history of each of the people, i.e. is this under performance a recent downturn or do they have a long history of low sales figures? This will help determine whether it is a recent change in their work pattern which is responsible for the poor results.
- Once the management information has been analysed, the sales manager will be in a better position to know where the problem lies with each of the individuals. Patterns will become evident within their work, which will give guidance as to how to deal with them. For example, sales person A may be fine at selling mortgages and credit cards but fall badly behind on the sale of investments. The manager will then need to check that A has the required level of technical and product knowledge in this area. If this is the problem, the manager can arrange further training and support A through this in order to solve the problem.
- Another valuable method of determining the problem would be for the manager to observe the salespeople as they speak to the customers. He or she should observe them in several sales situations, and ensure that the individual knows what areas of their performance they are going to comment on. The manager should then give constructive feedback on the main areas of deficiency. To resolve the problems the manager will need to put together a development plan showing how the individual can improve and how this will be measured.
- Rather than being a lack of knowledge, the reason for the deficiency may be identified as lack of sales skills. Again this could be addressed by training. Alternatively the manager may have a particularly skilled sales person within the team, and hence the need can be best addressed by allowing one team member to shadow the other and learn from the other's experience. This will also have the added value of increasing the team spirit: the feeling of the sales people that they are part of a team.
- The manager will need to examine all areas of the business to ensure the maximum potential is reached. For example, is the branch supplying the required number of customers from the counter? If not, is there something that the salespeople can do in order to improve the situation? It may be that some simple training for the branch staff as to what type of

customer should be referred to the sales people will improve the number and quality of leads enormously and therefore the business levels.

- The problem may lie with the fact that the salespeople are responsible for generating some of their own leads, and many sales people find this difficult and demoralising. If this is the problem the manager will need to find ways of making this task less gruelling for them. He or she will need to find out what motivates each of the individuals and use that knowledge to enthuse them to completing this task. The manager should also set them realistic, achievable yet stretching targets; and each time they attempt the task and feedback praise must be given each time they undertake their lead-generation activity.
- As well as making sure that sufficient management information is available, the manager should also ensure that the individual salespeople have a constant supply of up to date information about their sales figures. This may be a motivating factor for some of them, and will enable each of them to see what they need to do to reach target.
- As discussed above, an increased feeling of team membership will have a beneficial effect on the results of the salespeople. So regular team meetings and possibly the introduction of team competition will be beneficial.
- If the manager has the authority to do so, he or she may decide to alter the responsibilities of the salespeople to ensure that the business requirements are met by the team as a whole rather than by each individual. For example, it may be possible to allow each sales person to specialise in an area where they are most capable and skilled, provided that all areas are covered by the team.
- Again, provided he or she has the authority, the manager may reorganise the geographical areas that the individuals cover in order to get better results. It may be that the customers differ between the areas and are therefore more suited to one salesperson rather than another, or that travelling distance is taking too great proportion of the salespeople's time.
- All the above points assume that the individuals concerned are of the right calibre to perform the sales role. This is vitally important and the manager should always bear this in mind. Whilst every effort should be made to assist the salespeople to reach their full potential, there should always be a limit to the amount of time and resources spent on people who are not capable.

Summary

Now that you have completed this unit you will be able to do the following.

- ❑ **Describe the characteristics that make a good salesperson.**
- ❑ **Describe the process involved in making a sale.**
- ❑ **Explain the role of sales training and what it involves.**
- ❑ **Describe the elements that make up sales management, including recruitment, remuneration and motivation.**
- ❑ **Describe the role of the branch in sales management.**

Self-assessment questions

1. Name the four characteristics that make a good financial products salesperson. For each of these, briefly describe why it is important.
2. Draw a diagram to illustrate the five stages of the sales process. Write a paragraph to describe each of these stages.
3. List the 'selling skills' and write a sentence to describe each one.
4. Give two reasons for training sales people. Describe the five key elements of sales training.
5. Name three areas of responsibility for a sales manager. Explain why recruitment, remuneration and motivation are important to a sales force, and explain how a sales manager can influence these.
6. Write a paragraph to describe the role of the branch in sales management.

Unit 14

The changing environment

Objectives

After studying this unit you should be able to do the following.

- **Describe the changing role of UK branch design.**
- **Explain the purpose and process of reconfiguration programmes.**
- **Describe the key considerations in branch design.**
- **Explain how to measure design performance and evaluate the branch environment.**

1 Introduction

1.1 Creating the right branch environment for financial services is a very important and complicated area. The branch needs to be an effective area for the sale of products and services, and must also be a pleasant and suitable working environment for the staff. The branch has a major role to play in conveying the company's brand and establishing its image with the public. A well designed branch can also greatly improve the efficiency of the retailer, which leads to customer satisfaction, enhances the company's reputation and so attracts new or repeat business.

1.2 Designing and establishing the right environment for the sale and service of financial services products is now recognised as extremely important in attracting and retaining business. In this industry there is generally little scope to differentiate products from those of the rest of the market in terms of product design and pricing, branch service and reputation; the environment is one of the areas where it is possible to gain a competitive advantage. In today's environment of fierce competition there has been a great deal of activity among financial services retailers, aimed at creating an attractive, user friendly, customer focused environment in which people can do business. This has resulted in an evolution of the design of UK branches.

2 The changing role of UK branch design

2.1 The branch has traditionally been the major method of retailing financial services providers' products. This is still so in the majority of cases (excluding such companies as First Direct and Direct Line). This does not mean that the role of the branch has stayed the same. As the industry has changed, so has the role of the branch. The design of the branch must therefore change to meet the new demands that are placed upon it. The increased use of centralised operational support, as discussed earlier in this text, means that the branch is no longer required to carry out every service that the customers demand. Many of them can be carried out via the telephone to a customer services department, or even by the customers' use of ATMs.

2.2 What the branch can provide is the personal touch, which many customers still value. The branch will always have a role to play servicing those customers who demand the individual touch or who prefer to deal face to face with someone they can build a business relationship with.

2.3 In today's competitive environment there has been a general switch in the branch role from servicing customers to attracting new customers; that is, to a sales role. This need to attract new business has led many organisations to investigate and attempt to exploit the branch's potential as a sales and marketing tool. The idea is to turn branches into a true distribution outlet. Many financial services organisations are using the kind of marketing tactics previously more frequently associated with retail merchandising in order to attract and retain business. Such a radical change in focus necessarily requires a different branch design and explains, to a large extent, many of the changes in branch design that we have seen in recent years.

2.4 We must remember the increased areas of business now undertaken by many retailers of financial services products (as discussed in Unit 1), and consider the effect that these have had on branch design. Many banks, for example, are increasingly involved in the provision of mortgages and life assurance products. This type of sale requires a private consultation between the customer and the staff member, therefore demanding the availability of private interview rooms.

3 Evolution in branch design

3.1 Over the years the design of a typical financial services branch has changed significantly; we are now going to look at what those changes have been. While doing so it is important to remember that the overall objective of any significant change in branch design is to improve efficiency, thereby improving customer service and increasing new sales and profitability.

3.2 Traditionally bank branches were situated in impressive buildings with large stone fronts with ornate architecture. This helped to create an image of a business built on firm foundations; it portrayed security and reliability. These days most organisations have moved away from these traditional corner sites in favour of more open fronted shop type buildings. The interiors of the buildings have also changed dramatically from those of the traditional branches.

3.3 The changes aim to allow closer contact between the customer and the branch staff and to create a more welcoming environment – one that is tailored to the customers' needs and that reflects the changing role of the branch. Most retailers have now moved to an open plan design, and using screens to divide the customer area from the staff area is becoming less popular. This open plan approach allows different parts of the branch to be dedicated to different types of transactions, thereby improving customer service. For example, an area of the branch, usually near the entrance, may be designated as a self-service area, where customers use ATMs to withdraw cash, make deposits, or request statements. Many organisations have designed their branches so that automated entrance vestibules are accessible outside normal banking hours, thereby increasing the customers' perception that the branch is convenient and tailored to their needs.

3.4 The increased use of ATMs means that fewer staff are needed: the traditional approach to branch design with long rows of tellers is no longer required in all branches. Many retailers have also attempted to improve service by adopting a sectioned approach, whereby different desks deal with different requirements. For example, one area may deal with simple transactions, one may deal with the opening of new accounts and enquiries, and one may handle more complex requests, such as mortgage applications and requests for a full financial review. The main problem associated with this segmented and open plan approach is the lack of privacy: the inclusion of private interview rooms is essential.

3.5 The ratio of branch space dedicated to the customer as compared with branch space occupied by staff has increased significantly. One cause of this is the reduction in numbers of staff required as a result of increased automation and centralised operational support; a second cause is the need to reflect the branch role as a true distribution channel. This means that as much space as possible must used for the purpose of selling and advertising rather than as back office space.

3.6 The increased focus on the branch as a marketing tool has led more attention to be paid to the use of window displays. In traditional corner sited branches the windows were relatively small and were not considered an important feature in the sale of services. In the new style branches, often situated in prime retailing sites, there are usually very large expanses of window or glass frontage. These large windows present the image and brand values of the organisation to the public and are responsible for creating the public's first impression of the organisation. They are one of the branch's most valuable marketing tools for communicating messages to new/potential customers. As well as attracting new business they can be used as a method of building and strengthening the organisation's brand. Because of this, a great deal of attention, resource and capital is spent on the design of this particular aspect of the branch.

3.7 An example of the evolution of branch design can be seen in Figure 14.1.

Fig 14.1 Branch layout

(a) Traditional branch layout

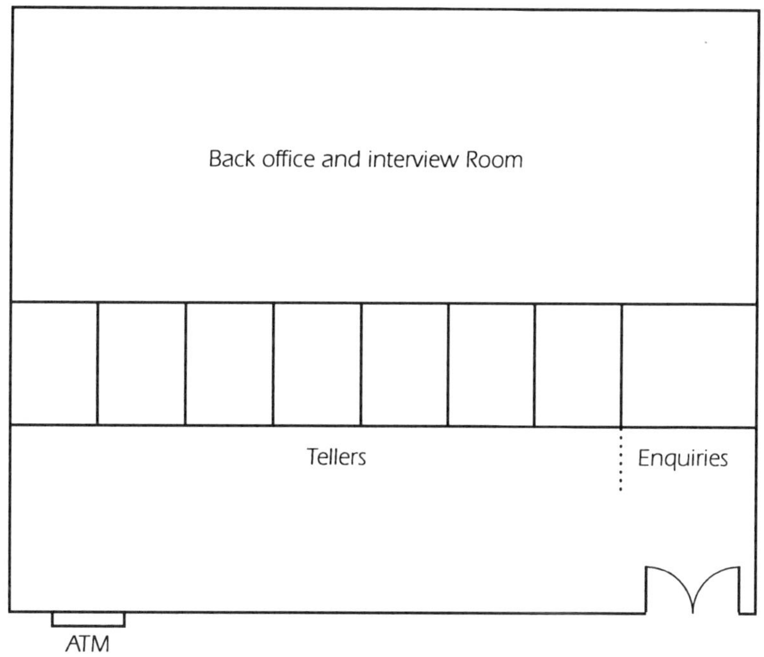

(b) Open plan branch design

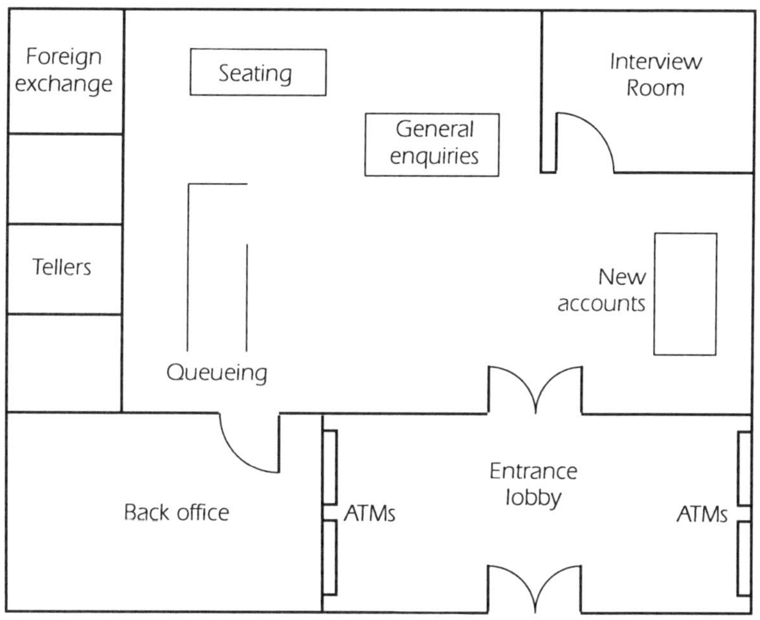

Student Activity

1 What role does the branch play in the retailing of financial services?

2 How has this role changed over the years?

3 How has the branch design changed in order to reflect the new role of the branch?

4 Key considerations in branch design

4.1 Having selected a site for a branch and decided what part the branch will play in the overall branch network, the retailer needs to decide what the branch will actually look like, both inside and out. When designing a branch many things need to be considered, as described below.

Customer base

4.2 A financial services retailer needs to understand the market segments they are trying to appeal to, and to tailor their branch design to those segments. As many retailers are trying to appeal to a wide variety of market segments, they must endeavour to find an image that is attractive to the majority of their prospective customers and that is not offensive or objectionable to any of them.

Footfall

4.3 The number of customers a branch expects to deal with is also an important consideration. If a branch expects a large amount of traffic it may require separate entrances and exits, or need to consider the flow of that traffic and possible queueing systems. None of these issues would require consideration in a smaller, quieter branch.

Costs

4.4 With most retailers now operating very large branch networks, and with the need for organisations to remain competitive in an increasingly 'price aware' industry, the cost of refurbishment must be a major consideration. For example, the retailer might think that larger premises with additional seating and a coffee area would attract many more customers. However, such a scheme is unlikely to be implemented because the cost of introducing and maintaining it across the network would be prohibitive when compared to the return it would be likely to bring.

Corporate image

4.5 Every retailer must decide what corporate image it wishes to portray, and this will have an impact on the way in which it designs its branches. Everything, from the very building in which it is situated right through to the furnishings, décor, staff uniforms, and stationery, must be designed in a way that reflects the brand of the provider (for example, one of high quality or one of simple value for money).

Uniformity

4.6 An organisation should aim to have a level of uniformity across its branch network. Branches will vary in size and shape, particularly if the retailer has adopted either a 'hub and spoke' approach or the introduction of specialist branches. However, there should be a look and 'feel' that is similar across every outlet. The main advantages of this are as follows.

- It provides comfort and reassurance to customers who use a branch other than their own.
- It provides both regional and national advertising for the retailer as it creates an image that the customer will immediately recognise.

Layout

4.7 A great deal of thought needs to be given to the layout of the branch to ensure that it creates the desired atmosphere. The branch should appear welcoming while having a layout that enables it to meet its customers' needs. The layout must also be constrained by the need to ensure the outlet is secure, as security must always be a key consideration when retailing financial services.

Services offered

4.8 The branch must be designed to best suit the services it offers. For example, a branch in a busy out of town shopping centre that expects to deal mainly with requests for cash, many of which will be best served by ATMs, needs more space dedicated to ATMs and less space for use by tellers. There is likely to be little demand for private consultation and therefore there is unlikely to be a need for private offices. On the other hand, in a branch that is focused on retailing, arranging mortgages and personal loans, there will be a much greater need for offices for confidential discussions and also for seated waiting areas. The principal function of the branch also dictates whether there is a need for large merchandising displays, or for such things as leaflet dispensers and large marketing displays.

Staff

4.9 The number of staff who work at the branch must also be considered, as must the tasks that those staff perform. If the staff are employed only to deal with the customers who visit the branch (that is, where a policy of centralised support is in operation), this will limit the back office support required.

Student Activity

1 List three major considerations when undertaking the design of a new branch.

2 Explain why each of these factors is important.

5 Branch design and reconfiguration programmes

5.1 Traditionally the design of the branch and the need for any refurbishment was a decision taken on a local level: it involved the branch manager and the needs of his or her staff. More recently the market in which these branches operate and their changing role, have led many organisations to move these decisions to a central support function. The argument for these decisions to be made centrally is further strengthened by the need to portray a strong corporate image that is uniform across the entire network. Also, the number of mergers and takeovers that have been seen in the industry in recent years have left organisations with a mix of styles that need to addressed; this can only be done effectively by a dedicated function.

5.2 With a shift in focus to the needs of the customer rather than the needs of the branch staff, and with consideration being given to the changing role of the branch, complete reviews of the branch network are being undertaken by many banks and building societies. This type of review is conducted by a team of people at the company's head office and naturally includes a review of branch design.

5.3 The team of people involved in the decision-making must contain representatives from many different functions of the organisation to ensure that the design meets all the business needs. It has been suggested that the most effective team should consist of team members from the following areas.

- **Premises.** They will need to input information about the number of branches, size, location, amount of window space, security, etc. All these are essential in any decision making process.
- **Marketing.** They will be required to ensure that the design created properly conveys the brand of the organisation and to ensure that the design is capable of carrying out all the promotional activity they have planned in order to meet sales targets.
- **Research.** The research department will be able to provide valuable information for the planning stage of any reconfiguration programme. They will be able to provide facts on such things as: the type of customer they expect to use the branch, the frequency and purpose of customer visits, what will attract those customers to use a certain facility, and what such customers expect from their branch. Research staff are also likely to be able to supply useful information about competitor branch design.
- **Network/branch.** There will need to be at least one representative from the network who will input into the process on behalf of the staff members who are expected to work in the newly reconfigured branches. Although the main focus of discussions is, quite correctly, on suitability for the customers' needs, consideration also needs to be given to the staff and their requirements.
- **External design agency.** The majority of organisations also employ an external design agency to input ideas as to how the branch can be designed to best suit the needs of the company and its customers, and to bring design expertise and experience to the team.

- **Operational/project management.** Such a huge undertaking as a reconfiguration process is likely to need the services of a project manager. The project manager will act as a co-ordinator between the various functions that are either involved or that will be affected. They will also take overall responsibility for delivering the new design.

Student Activity

1 Describe the purpose of a reconfiguration programme.

2 Who would be involved in such a project and what role would they play?

Areas for consideration

5.4 The team of people who are charged with the network reconfiguration programme first of all need to establish exactly what they can and cannot change; that is, exactly what the scope of the project is. Generally, anything that is a component of the branch environment needs to be considered as a part of the programme; this will include the following.

- **The external look of the branch.** The team need to consider what image they wish to portray to the many people who pass the branch without entering. They must ensure that this image is in line with the company brand. Should the branch look grand and imposing, giving an impression of security? Or should it appear open and modern like other retailing outlets?
- **External ATMs.** The team need to consider the number of external ATMs. This may well be influenced by the decision on branch opening hours and on whether to allow entry to a lobby area out of hours.
- **Window space and usage.** If the branch is in a retailing area of the city centre there is likely to be a great deal of window space. The team need to consider how this will be used. It is likely that the marketing team will have plans to use the space for advertising and so special equipment such as boards may need to be installed.
- **Number and position of internal ATMs.** The team may decide to install internal ATMs, and the number will depend largely on research carried out as to the type of customers the branch will service and how they are likely to use it. The positioning of the internal ATMs will also be important because, if there is likely to be a queue, this should not block the entrance. However, internal ATMs need to be situated in an entrance lobby if there is to be 24-hour access to them.
- **Look and feel of the banking hall.** One of the most important aspects for consideration is the overall look and 'feel' once the customer enters the main banking hall. It must appear welcoming while being extremely functional; again, it must carry an image in line with the company brand.
- **Heating and lighting.** These are important as they go a long way to creating the comfortable atmosphere the organisation wishes to achieve. The decision over what the correct temperature should be needs to be taken with consideration to both the customers and the purposes of their visits, and the staff.

- **Floor covering and wall covering** must both be practical, cost effective and in line with the general look and 'feel' of the hall. It is likely that the walls will also be used for advertising and therefore merchandising stands should be considered.
- **Seating** should be included for the comfort of the customers, particularly if the branch is to be involved in the retailing of such things as mortgages and insurance where customers may need to wait for an appointment.
- **Number and position of tellers** and the queueing system. This will depend largely on the expected customer base and predictions as to their behaviour.
- **Position of enquiry desk.** A decision must be made as to where to site the enquiry desk and any other specialist counters (e.g. for new accounts). The siting of such desks must be designed to lower queueing times and increase customer service.
- **Number of private interview rooms** or desks will depend on the nature of the business conducted within the branch. While the open plan design may be favoured to give an impression of friendliness, the need for private discussion cannot be ignored.
- **Staff space** (desks, staff room, storage space, etc.). While we have already discussed the desire to dedicate as much space as possible to the customer, we cannot ignore the needs of the staff and therefore there must be consultation with the branch staff to ensure that they have the necessary facilities.
- **Staff uniforms.** There will need to be a decision on whether the staff are required to wear uniforms. If they are, the reconfiguration team will need to ensure that this uniform complements the image of the branch.
- **Security arrangements.** Whatever design is selected, there will also be a requirement to ensure that the staff and the premises are secure. While the branch design should be geared to creating a feeling of openness and ease of use, personal safety should never be compromised. It will be necessary to consider the safety arrangements all the way through the reconfiguration programme.

5.5 Before consideration can be given to each of these aspects, the team need to put together a list of objectives, that is, things they want to achieve from the new design. They should then ensure that when a decision is made about any of the items above it contributes to achieving the stated objective.

Student Activity

1 List five examples of factors that need to be considered within a reconfiguration programme.

2 Explain why these factors are important to the overall branch design.

The reconfiguration process

5.6 It is extremely important that for an undertaking of the magnitude of a reconfiguration programme there is a detailed plan showing exactly how the requirements will be moved forward by the team. Progress must be monitored regularly. The size of the reconfiguration process will vary between organisations, as will the number of people involved and the process that they go through in order to complete the task they have undertaken. This said, there is a natural order of events that most companies follow, and this is shown in Figure 14.2.

Figure 14.2 The reconfiguration process

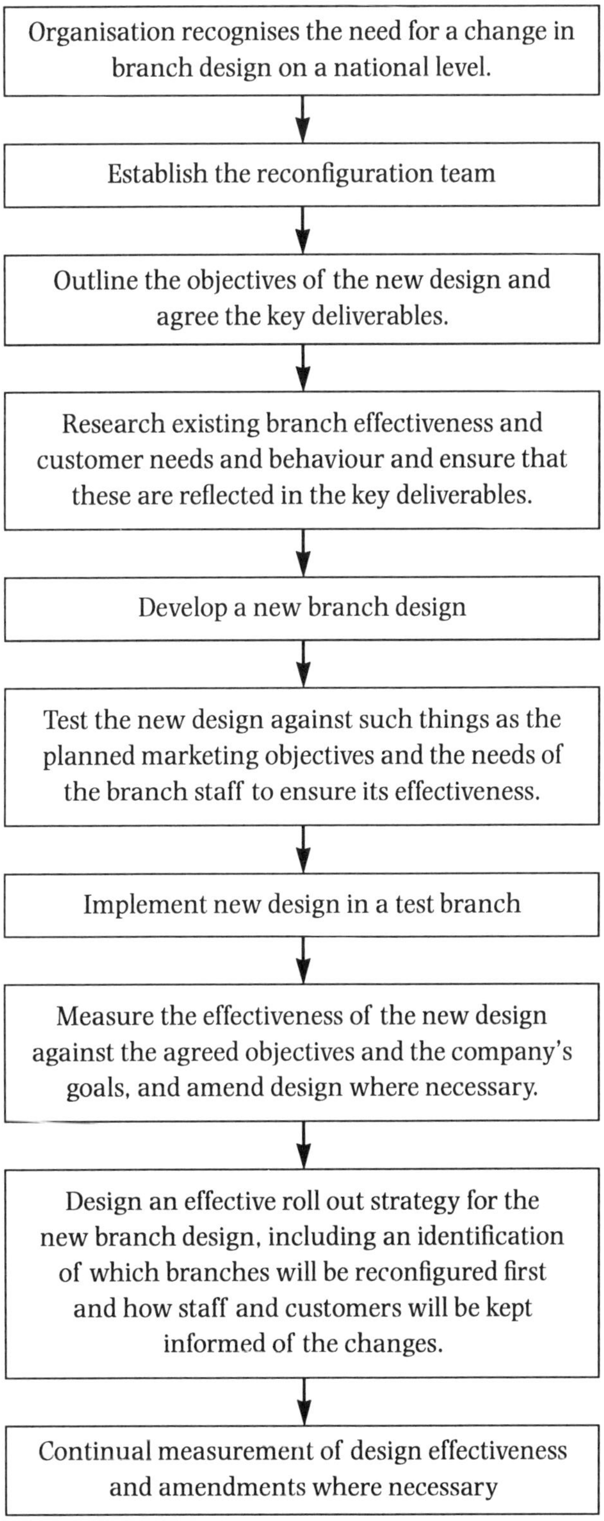

5.7 All the stages shown in Figure 11.2 are vitally important, but none more so than the initial research that must be completed before anything further can be done. The research conducted for a project as large as a national reconfiguration programme needs to be extremely thorough and to involve a great deal of customer input. The aim is to gain a greater understanding of the customers and their behaviour in order to tailor the design to suit them. This can be done by studying the customers' current behaviour when they use a branch, and by questioning them about their preferences. Some institutions may even go as far as building a 'mock' branch and asking customers to try it and comment on what they found useful and what they disliked. Another source for the research stage is the branch staff, who will have valuable ideas as to how the current design can be improved and what they feel the customers would like to see.

5.8 Once the objectives of the programme have been outlined, it is possible to identify some key deliverables. Here are a few examples.

- A branch design that reduces the queueing time for customers by 50%.
- A design that allows access to an ATM lobby 24 hours a day
- Window space that will allow the display of two sets of marketing material on poster size boards.
- An overall look and 'feel' that is rated as either 'welcoming' or 'very welcoming' by at least 80% of customers who use it.

5.9 With these objectives and deliverables in mind, the team can go about selecting a branch design. It is likely that they will involve an external design agency, and therefore this part of the process will involve briefing the agency as to what the design needs to achieve and then selecting what is and is not appropriate from the ideas the agency puts forward.

5.10 The selected design must be agreed by all areas of the business. For example, a design may be ideal for the purposes of the marketing department and branch staff, but unless it is appropriate from a security viewpoint it cannot be developed. The most successful designs are those that can be adapted to suit both large and small branches, and those with different functions. In addition, some flexibility is needed to suit individual branches. For example, if a branch is situated in an area of historical importance the exterior may to need to be maintained rather than changed to the new style. Similarly, if a particular branch has suffered an unusually high number of raids, then the desire to remove the screens in favour of an open plan design may not be appropriate.

5.11 Once all areas of the business have agreed a design there must be some level of testing before a national roll out is undertaken. This is usually done by means of a test branch: one branch is selected to be reconfigured and the work is carried out. There is then a period of reflection during which branch performance is measured against the design objectives. If there is a shortfall in any area, this is taken back to the reconfiguration team in order that the design can be amended. Only when everybody is happy that the design meets the objectives is a national roll out planned. The test branch then becomes a blueprint for other branches, who must adhere strictly to the new branch design (although there will always be some restraints imposed by individual sites as described above).

5.12 Owing to the size of the networks of many of the country's financial services organisations, a national roll out is likely to be undertaken on a piecemeal approach taking anything up to three or four years to complete. During this national roll out there will be continual testing and amending of the key design.

Student Activity

1 Outline, briefly, the stages that make up a reconfiguration programme.

2 Explain why it is important to have sufficient research before a branch design is selected.

6 Measuring design performance and evaluating the branch environment

6.1 Following the opening of a new branch, or the redesign of a branch within a reconfiguration programme, the retailer must evaluate the design performance in order to identify and rectify any deficiencies. This is essential to ensure that the best possible design is implemented in future branch designs.

6.2 We have already seen some of the components that make up a branch design, and we have looked briefly at the role they play in creating the desired branch environment. Initially it would seem sensible to evaluate the design by simply asking the customers to give their opinion of each of these components and to tell us which they believe encourage a positive response to the branch and which do not. Unfortunately, this simplistic approach does not give true results, as many environmental aspects have a positive or negative effect on the customer at a subconscious level. For example, customers may not immediately think that they have any positive feeling toward the lighting used in the branch, but it may well contribute significantly to their experience of an overall feeling of warmth and friendliness. This needs to be considered when looking at any analysis of the effectiveness of a branch design, otherwise the results can be misinterpreted.

6.3 To measure design performance it is essential to start with very clear design objectives: there must be something to measure performance against. Different organisations have different ways of measuring the performance of a design; we now look at a selection of these.

Branch productivity

6.4 The ultimate objective of any branch redesign must be to increase productivity. It should be fairly easy to measure the productivity before and after the reconfiguration and so to see if this has been achieved. Of course it is not always this simple, as other factors may affect the result. If the branch has moved locations, or if, following merger or take-over within the organisation, two branches have been combined, then a simple before and after comparison is difficult. Newly refurbished branches usually re-open with some kind of promotional activity, and the extent to which any increase in sales is due to marketing activity is difficult to ascertain.

6.5 While being able to measure sales is relatively straightforward, the measuring of productivity in a service related area is a more difficult task, especially as the desired increase may have been in quality rather than in quantity.

Surveys and questionnaires

6.6 Questioning the customers who use the branch is a particularly useful way of gaining feedback on the new design (bearing in mind the caveats in 6.2 above). The questions asked can be structured to gain specific information on customers' feelings and therefore to measure the achievement of the design objectives. This method is useful for testing such things as

- the emotional impact of the design on the branch user
- any change in the perceived quality of products and services of the provider following the refurbishment
- any change in customers' behaviour following the introduction of the new design.

6.7 The customers can be questioned individually or in a group discussion environment; there are pros and cons to each approach. While the group environment may encourage the customers to speak more and to be more open about their feelings, there is always the danger that people's feelings and opinions will be swayed by the rest of the group. The venue for the questionnaire or group discussion can also affect the results. Probably the best results will be gained from those who are questioned while they are in the branch, and who therefore do not have to rely on memory in order to answer. If people are not being questioned while actually inside the branch, then consideration must be given to the time lag between the questions and the last visit to the branch. The longer the gap, the more likely it is that the outcome will be distorted by memory.

Key design performance indicators

6.8 The reconfiguration team will have a list of key factors that they wish to measure the performance of. They will tailor the questions to ensure that they receive feedback on the appropriate areas. It is easy to see what the key design performance indicators are if the project has clearly defined and measurable objectives and deliverables.

6.9 The type of questions asked are likely to include the following.

- How friendly and helpful is the service you receive from the branch?
- How often do you visit the branch?
- Do you spend time reading the promotional literature available?
- Do you like the exterior/interior of the branch?
- Do you feel you need to queue for too long before being served?
- What impression do you gain about the organisation from the look of the branch?

- Would you recommend the organisation to a friend?

6.10 The customer may be asked to provide text answers in their own words or to rate the branch on a given scale for each of these areas.

Emotional impact

6.11 The organisation will be interested in the emotional impact of the branch on the customer. As well as wanting to know factual information such as how often the customer now visits the branch, they will be particularly interested in the way the customer feels about the new branch and what impression they gain of the organisation from the new design. The reason for their interest lies largely with the fact that branches are now required to provide both the service and sales functions and are an important marketing tool. While the environment in which people are sold things is always significant, it has a much greater role to play when the product being sold is intangible, as is the case for financial services products. Because the products cannot be seen or touched, the customer is more likely to judge their quality by the environment in which they are being sold.

Student Activity

1 Why is it important to evaluate the branch design following implementation?

2 What are the advantages and disadvantages of asking customers to comment on the design?

3 Why might branch productivity levels following a reconfiguration not give an accurate assessment of the new design?

4 Why is the emotional impact of the new design an important factor?

7 Case study and analysis

7.1 The Norfolk Building Society has just agreed to a merger with the North of Britain Society, which will happen at the start of next year. The new company will be called the North and Norfolk. It will have branches throughout the country. From day one of the new company, all branches will have their frontage changed to carry the new name, and all stationery will be amended.

7.2 Once the merger has actually taken place, the new society will take the opportunity to carry out a reconfiguration programme. Although the two societies had their roots in different parts of the country, there are some towns where the merger will result in more branches than are required. It is likely that there will be a number of branch closures.

7.3 It is expected that the project will also result in increased efficiency and an increase in the retailing ability of the branches. The branches of both societies are very traditional in appearance, being situated in large impressive buildings and having a high number of staff. A typical branch layout is shown below.

Figure 14.3 Typical branch layout at time of merger

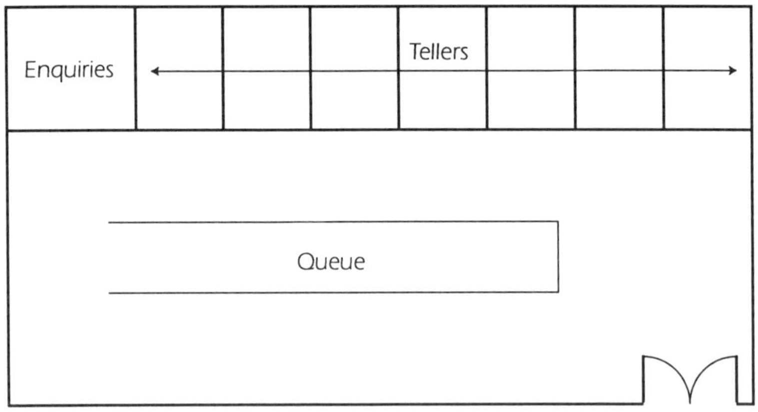

7.4 Imagine that you have been given the task of carrying out the reconfiguration project and keeping the management team updated as to what you recommend they should do.

- Set objectives for the reconfiguration programme to achieve.
- Outline who you would appoint as members of the project team.
- Write a project plan, and explain briefly what activities would take place during each stage of the process.
- Show a plan of how a new branch layout might look.
- Explain how you would evaluate the success of the new branch environment.

7.5 A real study like this would be more detailed, but would need to include the following points.

- *Objectives* for the reconfiguration programme could include the following.
  - To ensure that all branches are of uniform design and layout.
  - To ensure that the new branch design reflects the brand of the new North and Norfolk Building Society.
  - To ensure a branch design is achieved that is suited to the main business activities of the society and its outlets, namely retail and servicing.
  - To design branches where customers can more easily access the services they require.
  - To design branches where a reduced number of staff are required, but where customers will still feel they have received the level of attention they seek.
  - To create an atmosphere which customers feel is warm and welcoming, and which appeals to all segments of the market with which the North and Norfolk expects to do business.
  - To allow marketing material to have a prominent position within the outlet.

- The manager responsible for the reconfiguration process would appoint a team of people, and this team should include representatives from the following areas.
  - An external design agency; they will have fresh ideas and experience of branch design.
  - The society's research department, who will be able to explain who the North and Norfolk's customers are, and what they are looking for.
  - Marketing, to ensure that the marketing activity they have planned can be achieved through the new design.
  - Premises, who will assess whether the new design is suitable for the types of outlet that the North and Norfolk have, and give some guidance on the cost of the proposed refurbishment.
  - Members of the branch team must also be included, to ensure the branch meets the needs of the staff as well as those of the customers.
- A *project plan* should look something like the plan below.

Appoint reconfiguration team

↓

Set objectives for the programme and decide on time scales

↓

Brief external design agency as to requirements and available budget

↓

Agency presents ideas; team selects preferred design

↓

Design checked by all team members and business areas, to ensure suitability. Design checked against objectives and brand requirements

↓

One branch selected and reconfigured

↓

Reconfigured branch is evaluated to ensure it meets objectives

↓

Design is amended as necessary following the evaluation process

↓

Roll out planned and carried out

- A new branch design for the North and Norfolk might look something like Figure 14.4.

Figure 14.4 Post-merger branch layout

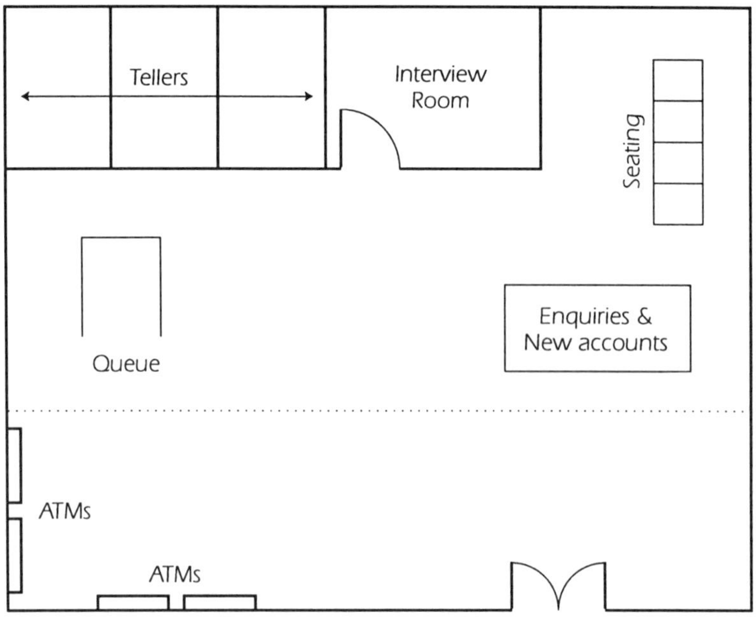

- The new design would need to be evaluated, both following the reconfiguration of the test branch and also following the national roll out.
- This could be done by measuring branch productivity. This may not be the most effective method, however. Because the North and Norfolk has just undergone a merger, the activity within each branch is likely to change. It will be difficult to know how much of this change can be attributed to the branch design.
- The best way to test the design against its objectives may be by questioning the customers. This can be done either in the branches, or in focus groups away from the branch environment.

Summary

The need for greater efficiency in a now highly competitive market has led many organisations to re-assess the role of the branch. Branches now play a crucial role in the marketing of the company's products and the attracting of new customers. Many organisations have also undergone mergers or take-overs and this, along with the desire to increase productivity, has led to a rationalisation of the branch network and a new focus on the potential benefits to be gained from an effective branch environment.

It is known that the branch design can have a significant impact on the customer satisfaction and the job satisfaction of the staff. The layout of the branch can also be designed in such a way as to significantly improve the marketing performance.

The new branch designs are aimed at creating a retail outlet type appearance that is welcoming to the customer and convenient for them to use. The objective of any new design must be to increase productivity and customer satisfaction.

Given the need for a nationwide corporate identity, many organisations have undergone reconfiguration programmes whereby a new, effective design is selected and all branches across the network are refurbished. This is a task usually undertaken by a centrally organised specialist team made up of representatives from across many interested areas of the business.

Now that you have completed this unit you should be able to

- ❑ **describe the changing role of UK branch design**
- ❑ **explain the purpose and process of reconfiguration programmes**
- ❑ **describe the key considerations in branch design**
- ❑ **explain how to measure design performance and evaluate the branch environment.**

Self-assessment exercises

1 Write a few paragraphs to describe the way that the role of branch design has changed in the UK over recent years.

2 (a) Why might an organisation decide to implement a reconfiguration programme?

(b) Describe the reconfiguration process, including diagrams if appropriate. Your answer should explain who should be involved in the process and what they should contribute.

3 List eight key considerations for branch design and briefly describe each.

4 Describe four methods for measuring design performance and evaluating the branch environment. Give any advantages or disadvantages associated with each of these.

Index

A

Above-the-line activity 186
ACORN 147
Advertising 185
Advocate channels 183
Affordable budget setting 184
Ageing of the population 14
Allocation of units 176
Analysis of market research 147
Ansoff matrix 69, 88
APACS (Automated Payments and Clearing Systems) 27
Appropriateness of use 31
Attitudes 57
Authorisation, enforcement and consumer relations 18
Automatic Teller Machines (ATMs) 22, 113, 232
  external 237
  internal 237
Awareness, Interest, Desire, Action (AIDA) 54

B

Backward integration 34
Bancassurance 25
Bank of England 18
Banking Act 1987 18
Banking hall 237
Benefits 75
Best-case scenario 92
Bid/offer spread 176
Boston Consulting Group (BCG) matrix 154
Branch
  external look of 237
  relocation of 119
  role of in pricing 178
  the role of in product management 164
  the role of in sales management 224
Branch audit 84
Branch design 236
  emotional impact of 243
  evolution of 231
  key considerations 234
Branch environment 230
  evaluating 241
Branch layout 235
Branch location 112
Branch marketing plan 92
Branch network 112
Branch numbers 113
Branch performance 103
Branch productivity 241
Branch strategy 113
Branch valuation procedures 114
Branches
  closing 118
  continuing with underperforming 118
  opening 117
Brand loyalty 189
Branding 187
Brokers 136, 137
Budgets 70, 98, 183
Building Societies Act 1962 16
Building Societies Act 1986 17
Building Societies Acts 16
Buyer behaviour 52
Buyer behaviour for financial services 54

C

Cash cows 155
Category A advertising 186
Censuses 146
Characteristics of successful salespeople 211
Checklists 115
  branch activity 115
  centre details 116
  geodemographics 115
  premises 116
Choice of distribution channel 138
Coaching skills 216
Commission only sales force 223
Commitment 72
Community programmes 189
Company factors 151
Company–bank relationships 56
Comparative analysis 80
Compensation 20
Competition 77, 95
Competitive analysis 29
Competitive environment 29
Competitive parity 184
Competitive situation 181
Competitive strategies 45
Competitive strategy 89
Competitive strength grid 43

Competitor information 45
Competitors 149
  assessing strengths and weaknesses of 39
  cost structure of 38
  current 29
  current and past strategies of 37
  exit barriers for 38
  identifying 29
  image and positioning of 36
  objectives and commitment of 37
  organisationa dn culture of 38
  potential 34
  size, growth and profitability of 36
  skills and assets of 39
  success of 40
  understanding 35
Competitors' prices 170
Complexity 97
Compliance 20
Concreteness 185
Conglomerates 25
Connect 26
Consumer buying behaviour 52-53, 55, 57, 59, 61, 63
Consumer interest 9
Consumer surveys 92
Contingency plans 110
Control 99
Core conduct of business rules 21
Corporate identity 188
Corporate image 188, 196, 234
Corporate manifestation 188
Corporate objectives 67, 99
Cost components 40
Cost focus strategy 49
Cost leadership 90
Cost leadership strategy 46
Cost-to-income ratio 24
Costs 94
  of a service 170
  of the branch network 234
Credence products 90
Credit and debt
  attitudes towards 58
Credit cards
  pricing of 174
Criteria evaluation 202
Customer base 234
Customer care 200
Customer data 146
Customer knowledge 9
Customer motivations 40
Customer needs 149
Customer perspective 30
Customer responses 75
Customer selection 30
Customers 8
  identifying potential 213
  needs 214
  willingness to pay of 170

D

Data collection techniques 147
Decline of a product 154
Defensive strategies 35
Demographic trends 14
Demographics 75
Deposits and savings
  pricing of 171
Deregulation 25
Design agency 236
Design performance
  indicators 242
  measuring 241
Development of a product 152, 161
Differential advantage (DA) 80
Differentiation focus strategy 49
Differentiation strategy 48, 90
Direct Line 129
Direct mail 132-134
Direct marketing 190
Directional policy matrix 156
Disposable income 13
Distribution 112
  channels 126, 138
  strategy 139-40
  systems 79
Divergence 97
Diversification 8
Documentation 185
Dogs 156

E

Elasticity of demand 94
Electronic Funds Transfer at Point Of Sales (EFTPOS) 22, 134
Electronic fund transfers at place of living (EFTPOL) 134
Electronic fund transfers at place of banking (EFTPOB) 135
Electronic purse 135
Emotional messages 182
Enquiry desk 238
Environment 181, 230
  changing, for financial services 7
Evaluation 184
Experience products 90
Expert channels 183
Export of assets or skills 35
Extrapolation 92

F

Fast moving consumer goods (FMCGs) 8
Financial advisers 128, 136, 137, 141
Financial environment 12

Financial projections 103, 108
Financial responsibility 53
Financial results 92
Financial Services 7
Financial Services Act 1986 16, 19
Financial Services Authority (FSA) 18, 20
Financial services industry
 characteristics of 9
Financial services
 pricing 171
 providers 7
Financial supervision 18
First Direct 26, 129
Floor covering 238
Focus strategy 49, 90
Footfall 234
Forecasting 92, 158
Forward integration 35

G

G mapping 193
Gap analysis 88, 104
General insurance
 pricing of 177
Geodemographics 123, 147
Geography 75
Global cash management 22
Global targeting 63
Gravity models 116
Growth of a product 153

H

Halifax Building Society 63
Heating 237
Heterogeneity 53, 185
Hierarchy of effects model 181
Home and office banking 22, 134
Home ownership 13
Housing market 58
Humour
 using it in promotion 182

I

Implementation 99
IMRO 20
Indirect competition 30
Inflation 59
Information sources 146
Information technology 21
Inherited wealth 13
Innovations 159
Inseparability 53, 185
Intangibility 9, 52, 185
Interaction Model 56
Interactive television 23
Internal marketing 208
Internationalisation 23
Internet 8, 22
Interpersonal skills 212, 216
Interview rooms 238
Introduction of a product 152

K

Key activity calendar 111
Key assumptions 68-69, 86

L

Legislation 151
Life assurance
 claims costs 175
 costs of 175
 pricing of 175
 profit 176
 simplicity of pricing 175
Life cycle curve 83
Life cycles 83
Lighting 237
Line management 72
Listening skills 216
Location evaluation techniques 114
Loyalty 76

M

Management
 fee 176
 information 225
 of sales 221
Margin of error 92
Market
 effectiveness 114
 expansion 34
 growth 78
 overview 105
 profitability 78
 research 77, 145
 segmentation 60
 size 78
 structures 24
 trends/developments 26, 79
Marketing audit 68, 73, 88, 103
Marketing Information Systems (MKISs) 21
Marketing mix 10, 92, 98
Marketing objectives 87, 107
Marketing strategies 107
Marketing planning 65
 process 102
Marketing programme 99
Maturity of a product 153
Merger 113
Micro-targeting 62
Mission 67
Mobility barriers 32, 40
Mondex 22
Moral messages 182
Mortgage and Banking Codes of Practice 197

Mortgages and loans
pricing of 174
MOSAIC 147
Motivation 213, 223
Multiple regression 117
Mutual funds
pricing of 173

N

New branches
planning permission for 118
New lines 159
New product development 158
Non-personal channels 183

O

Objective and task budget setting 184
Objectives 69, 87, 91
Official statistics 146
Oligopoly 24
On job training 218
One-off charges 177
One-year marketing plan 108, 111
Ongoing service 215
Operating results 111
Operational support
centralised 120
Operations 18
Organisational buying behaviour 56
Organisational skills 216
Outlet location 112
Overall strategies 109

P

Pension and illness cover 15
Pensions and endowments
pricing of 176
People 96
PEPs 24
Perishability 53, 185
Personal bankers 201
Personal channels 183
Personal Equity Plan 15, 141
Personal income 12
Personal selling 192
PEST 79
Physical evidence 97
PIA 20
Place 95
Plan fee 177
Planning calendar 73
Planning period 67
Point of sale debit cards 26
Political trends 15
Porter, Michael 41, 45, 89
Porter's model 78
Positioning 80
Post-purchase anxiety 187
Price 93
Pricing 170
method 95
of services 170
Primary activities 41
Problem child 154
Process 97
Product 93, 148
augmented 149
core of 148
development 160
elimination 164
expansion 34
expected 148
launch 162
life cycles 151
management 145
planning 158
Product modification 163
costs of 163
Product strategy
influences on 149
Project management 237
Promotion 96, 180
types of 185
Promotional activities 158
role of the branch in 193
Promotional mix 180
analysing the situation 181
choosing the mix 184
designing the message 182
developing objectives 181
evaluation 184
preparing budgets 183
selecting channels 183
Psychographics 75
Public relations (PR) 187

Q

Qualitative analysis 73
Qualitative research 147
Quality 72
Quantitative research 147
Quantity 72
Queries, dealing with 215
Questioning skills 215
Questionnaires 242

R

Ratio of financial assets to personal income 13
Rational messages 182
Recession 59
Reconfiguration
objectives for 240
Reconfiguration process 238
Reconfiguration programmes 236
Recruitment 222
Regional area offices 71
Regression analysis 92

Regulation 9, 16
Regulator's objectives 19
Relationship pricing 95
Remuneration 222
Reputation 185
Residual budget setting 184
Resource assessment 98
Resources 98
Retailing 8
Retailing mix 10
Retaliatory strategies 35
Retirement
  early 14
Reward 224
Risk taking
  factors affecting 13

S

Sales force 222
  direct 127-9
Salary and commission 223
Sales management 211, 221
Sales promotion 189
Sales training 217
Savings and investment
  attitudes towards 59
Search products 90
Seasonal variations in demand 9
Seating 238
Securities and Investment Board (SIB) 20
Security 238
Segmentation 52, 76
Segmentation pricing 53, 55, 57, 59, 61, 63
Selection criteria 97
Self-employed people 14
Selling process 213
Selling skills 215
Senior management 71
Sequence of events 185
Service 76, 93, 196
Service audit 79
Service encounters 198
Service plan 197
Services offered
  by a branch 235
Service quality gap 199
SERVQUAL 196, 204
Seven Ps 92
Short-termism 67
Single purchases 10
Single-person and single-parent households 14
Skills analysis 97
Smart card 22
SMART criteria 88
Social channels 183
Socio-economic trends 14
Socio-economics 75
Spatial techniques 117
Sponsorship 188
SRO/RPB rules 21
Staff 235
Staff space 238
Standard Industrial Classification type (SIC) 75
Stars 155
State retirement age for women 15
Statements of Principle 20
Strategic grouping 31
Strategic plan 102-103
Strategies 45, 67, 69, 87
  selecting 50
Strengths and weaknesses
  checklist of 42
Structured career progression 97
Sub-objectives 109
Substitute products 30
Support activities 42
Surveys 242
Switch 27
SWOT analysis 68-69, 73, 84, 88, 105
Syndicated market research 146

T

Tactical plan 102
Tactics 67
Takeover 113
Target audience 181
Targeting 62
Technology 8
Telemarketing 131, 191
Telephone banking 26, 113
Telephone-based sales 129-130
Telephone skills 216
Tellers 238
Ten-step plan 70
Terminology 72
TESSAs 24
Test marketing 92
Testing of a product 161
Three-year strategic plan 111
TOWS analysis 84
Training 72, 217-218
  programmes 97
Two-way information 54

U

UK branch design 231
Unemployment levels 59
Uniformity
  of the branch network 235
Uniforms 238
Unique selling propositions (USPs) 11, 22
Usage 75

V

Value chain 41

W

Wall covering 238
Wealth 12
  regional differences in 13
Window space 237
Worst-case scenario 92

£30-00